Managing a Network Vulnerability Assessment

Managing a Network Vulnerability Assessment

**THOMAS R. PELTIER,
JUSTIN PELTIER,
and JOHN A. BLACKLEY**

AUERBACH PUBLICATIONS

A CRC Press Company
Boca Raton London New York Washington, D.C.

Library of Congress Cataloging-in-Publication Data

Peltier, Thomas R.
    Managing network vulnerability assessment / Thomas R. Peltier, Justin Peltier, John A. Blackley,
        p. cm.
    Includes bibliographical references and index.
    ISBN 0-8493-1270-1 (alk. paper)
        1. Computer networks--Security measures. 2. Risk assessment. 3. Computer
crimes--Prevention. I. Peltier, Justin. II. Blackley, John A. III. Title.

    TK5105.59.P453 2003
    005.8--dc21

                                                                                2003041801

Visit the CRC Press Web site at www.crcpress.com

© 2003 by CRC Press LLC
Auerbach is an imprint of CRC Press LLC

No claim to original U.S. Government works
International Standard Book Number 0-8493-1270-1
Library of Congress Card Number 2003041801
Printed in the United States of America 1 2 3 4 5 6 7 8 9 0
Printed on acid-free paper

Dedication

To Lisa, Julie, and Amanda, our teammates and better halves.

Contents

Acknowledgments

People who take sole credit for any task completed or process "developed" have forgotten where they came from and who helped them get to where they are now. When discussing network vulnerability assessment, many people do not want to have their names associated in any way with the process. However, this is one of those tasks that needs to be done, and the best way to do it is to make the task as simple as possible. Over the years we have been able to learn the process of network vulnerability assessment from the best teachers around, our peers.

First on our list of acknowledgments is our mentor and friend, John O'Leary, the Director of the Computer Security Institute's Education Resource Center. One of the first training sessions I attended as a neophyte security professional was John's "Computer and Network Security" class. This class laid the foundation for my understanding that a network is a scary place, but that with proper review and attention it can serve us well.

The next two people who need to be acknowledged are Dr. Dan Webb and Dr. Peter Stephenson. Dr. Dan showed me the fundamentals of vulnerability assessment, and Dr. Stephenson helped me fine-tune the process we worked on together for just over two years. Dr. Stephenson's books on computer forensics are used as industry benchmarks for all security professionals. His willingness to share ideas and his findings has helped move our profession forward.

Michael Cannon, Larry Degg, Gene Traylor, and John Riske helped me begin the process of assessing network vulnerabilities. We worked together for seven years and drew up the prototype for a business-based information security program.

Justin would like to acknowledge his dad, for all his loving support and the opportunity to be part of this industry; Dr. Peter Stephenson, for patiently teaching him how to correctly perform a vulnerability assessment; Paul Immo and Marc Harwin for their friendship and support; and Julie, for being the love of his life and taking care of him so well.

Who can leave out their publisher? Certainly not us! Rich O'Hanley has taken the time to discuss security issues with numerous organizations to understand what their needs are and then presented these findings to us. A great deal of our work here is a direct result of what Rich discovered that the industry wanted. Rich O'Hanley, not only the world's best editor and task master, but a good friend and source of knowledge. Thanks Rich!

About the Authors

John A. Blackley, a native of Scotland, completed his bachelors' degree in electrical engineering at Glasgow University in 1974. Since moving to the United States in 1982, his career has included 19 years in information security.

John's first information security position was with a financial services company in Louisville, Kentucky. Starting in security administration, he gained experience and breadth of knowledge and went on to become the Director of Information Security and Business Contingency Planning. During that time, John also became a member of the faculty at Eastern Kentucky University, advising on the university's loss prevention program.

Moving to Texas in 1992, John was Manager of Information Security and Business Contingency Planning for one of the nation's Fortune 100 corporations. He developed that organization's Business Contingency Planning program, and organized and developed every aspect of its comprehensive information security program.

In 1995, John became a senior consultant for Europe's largest dedicated information security consultancy and carried out engagements for national and multi-national organizations in such locations as Seoul, Mauritius, Brussels, London, Lisbon, and Dublin.

Returning to Texas, John joined Netigy (now Thrupoint) as Regional Information Security Practice Manager and went on to become Principal Security Architect in Netigy's Global Security Practice. John is now a member of Peltier & Associates and manages operations in the U.S. southern states.

John has published a number of articles in the business press and has been a speaker at conferences and seminars around the world. He teaches on subjects such as privacy management, policy creation and implementation, risk management, and information security awareness. In addition, John's classes and seminars address organization and management issues relating to the practice of information security.

Justin Peltier, CISSP, MCNE, MCP, CCSE, RHCE, CCNA, is a Senior Security Consultant with Peltier & Associates, with more than eight years of experience in planning, designing, and implementing technical security solutions in a wide range of operating environments. As a consultant, Justin has been involved in implementing, supporting, and developing security solutions, and has taught courses on many facets including vulnerability assessment and CISSP preparation. Formerly with Suntel Services, Justin directed the security practice development. Prior to that, he was with Netigy where he was involved with the corporate training effort, serving as the company's primary technical instructor in the areas of vulnerability assessment, risk analysis, virtual private networking, policies and procedures, and penetration testing. Mr. Peltier has lead classes for MIS, Netigy, Computer Security Institute, Suntel Services, and Sherwood Associates. He has expert-level experience with projects related to Novell, NT, Sun Solaris, Linux, and Netscape systems, as well as with Ethernet, Token Ring, TCP/IP, and IPX/SPX topologies and protocols. Mr. Peltier's CBK specialty domains include Telecommunications and Network Security; Cryptography; Access Control Systems and Methodologies; and Security Architecture and Models.

Tom Peltier is in his fifth decade of computer technology. During this time he has shared his experiences with fellow professionals and, because of his work, was given the 1993 Computer Security Institute's (CSI) Lifetime Achievement Award. In 1999, the Information Systems Security Association (ISSA) bestowed its Individual Contribution to the Profession Award and in 2001 he was inducted into the ISSA Hall of Fame. Tom was also awarded the CSI Lifetime Emeritus Membership Award. He began his career five decades ago as an operator, moving on to become an applications programmer and systems programmer, systems analyst, and information systems security officer. Currently, he is the president of Peltier & Associates, an information security training firm. Prior to this he was Director of Policies and Administration for Netigy's Global Security Practice. Tom was the National Director for Consulting Services for CyberSafe Corporation, and the Corporate Information Protection Coordinator for Detroit Edison. This program has been recognized for excellence in the field of computer and information security by winning the Computer Security Institute's Information Security Program of the Year for 1996. Tom previously was the Information Security Specialist for General Motors Corporation, responsible for implementing an information security program for GM's worldwide activities.

Over the past decade, Tom has averaged four published articles a year on various computer and information security issues, including developing policies and procedures, disaster recovery planning, copyright compliance, virus management, and security controls. He has had four books published: *Policies, Standards, Guidelines and Procedures: Information Security Risk Analysis; Information System Security Policies and Procedures: A Practitioners' Reference; The Complete Manual of Policies and Procedures for Data Security* and is the co-editor and contributing author for the *CISSP Prep for Success Handbook*; and a contributing author for the *Computer Security Handbook, 3rd* and *5th editions,* and *Data Security Management.*

Tom has been the technical advisor on a number of security films from Commonwealth Films. He is the past chairman of the Computer Security Institute (CSI) advisory council, the chairman of the 18th Annual CSI Conference, founder and past-president of the Southeast Michigan Computer Security Special Interest Group, and a former member of the board of directors for (ISC)², the security professional certification organization. He conducts numerous seminars and workshops on various security topics and has led seminars for CSI, Crisis Management, American Institute of Banking, the American Institute of Certified Public Accountants, Institute of Internal Auditors, ISACA, and Sungard Planning Solutions. Tom was also an instructor at the graduate level for Eastern Michigan University.

Chapter 1

Introduction

The growth of distributed computing has been one of the major drivers of network security. With the exponential growth of networks, the ease with which information can be shared between and among computers makes security more important but more difficult to implement and manage. Also, computers are no longer connected to one trusted network; they are potentially connected to every other network and its computers in the world, with or without security implementations of their own.

In the old mainframe environment, security meant keeping the computer in a locked room with limited access. As computing power and its physical presence are distributed, it becomes increasingly difficult to control access by physical means. With a distributed network architecture, it is impossible; even if it was possible to sequester your network within a secure building, it would still be possible for someone to eavesdrop remotely.

This book assists the security professional in understanding what must be done to conduct a network vulnerability assessment. Because no organization has unlimited resources to devote to security, this book will help determine the severity of the risks your networks face and the most effective counter-measures to mitigate those risks.

Information Security Life Cycle

When implementing a Network Vulnerability Assessment (NVA), it will be necessary to view this process as part of the ongoing information security life cycle (see Exhibit 1). As with any business process, the information security life cycle starts with a risk analysis. Management is charged with showing that "due diligence" is performed during decision-making processes for any enterprise. A formal risk analysis provides the documentation that due diligence is performed.

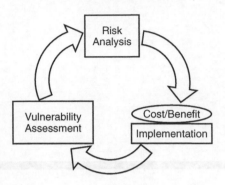

Exhibit 1.   Information Security Life Cycle

A risk analysis also lets an enterprise take control of its own destiny. With an effective risk analysis process in place, only those controls and safeguards that are actually needed will be implemented. An enterprise will never again face having to implement a mandated control to "be in compliance with audit requirements."

A risk analysis should be conducted whenever money or resources are to be spent. Before starting a task, project, or development cycle, an enterprise should conduct an analysis of the need for the project. Understanding the concepts of risk analysis and applying them to the business needs of the enterprise will ensure that only necessary spending is done.

Once a risk analysis has been conducted, it will be necessary to conduct a cost-benefit analysis to determine which controls will help mitigate the risk to an acceptable level at a cost the enterprise can afford. It is unwise to implement controls or safeguards just because they appear to be the right thing to do, or that other enterprises are doing so. Each organization is unique, and the levels of revenue and exposure are different. By conducting a proper risk analysis, the controls or safeguards will meet the enterprise's specific needs. (For more information on risk analysis, see *Information Security Risk Analysis* by Thomas Peltier (Auerbach Publications).)

Once the controls or safeguards have been implemented, it is appropriate to conduct an assessment to determine if the controls are working. In the information security profession, the term "vulnerability" has been defined as a condition of a missing or ineffectively administered safeguard or control that allows a threat to occur with a greater impact or frequency, or both. When conducting an NVA, the team will be assessing existing controls, safeguards, and processes that are part of the network. This process — the assessment — will ensure that controls are effective and that they will remain so.

Network Vulnerability Assessment (NVA)

This book was developed to assist the reader in managing all aspects of the network vulnerability assessment (NVA) process. We examine the development of a proper project plan, how to assess your biggest needs, what methodology to use, what tools to employ, and what a typical report should look like.

Along the way, we present real-world examples and give advice from those who have previously worked on NVAs.

Do I Need to Be a Technical Expert to Run an NVA?

The short answer is no. You do not need to be a technical expert to run a network vulnerability assessment. In most cases, you are working as part of a team, and while it is often beneficial to have a technical expert on the team, not everyone on the team has to be a technical expert. However, if you have no technical background, you may be overwhelmed by some of the more technical aspects of an NVA. Just remember to ask questions of those who have the right answers. *Note:* For more on team members, see Chapter 3.

What Skill Level Is Needed?

One of the most important skills inside the technical aspects of an NVA are basic networking skills. An understanding of how a network is put together is absolutely essential for at least one team member to have. This includes both sides of network architecture: logical and physical. This means that someone on the team should have the knowledge of switches, routers, hubs, workstations, and servers, and also the components of common network protocols.

Most of the networks that are being evaluated today are Internet Protocol (IP)-based networks. For knowledge of IP networks, one must be familiar with subnetting and common IP subnet ranges, the basics of routing and routing protocols, and an understanding of how to use a network sniffer.

While most networks are going to be IP based, not all networks are. There is still a pretty fair amount of networks that run the Internet Packet Exchange (IPX) protocol used by Novell servers and clients. While there are other networks types, the vast majority are IP-based networks, so this is where we focus most of our efforts in the book.

What Specific Skills Are Needed?

From a technical perspective, a number of different skills may be required, but the most essential role in the NVA will be project management. It is not uncommon to see a skilled security practitioner lose all track of dates and times, as he is off delving deeper and deeper into the security mysteries of the network. That same security engineer might also have a genetic predisposition to perform tasks of slightly less importance to the NVA, such as playing online fantasy football. Good project management can help fight all of this.

In addition to project management, it is necessary to at least understand the basics of operating systems, Web servers, and routing and switching security vulnerabilities.

Can One Person Perform an NVA?

Yes, but it depends on the depth of the NVA. While a good security practitioner can perform all the technical aspects of an NVA, it is very difficult to find one person who can perform the technical testing *and* functions such as policy and procedure review. And if this individual is capable of doing both, the next question becomes: can he or she perform both functions well? In essence, it really requires a team to run an NVA, unless it is restricted to a technical-only NVA or the organization is very small.

Introduction to Vulnerability Assessment

The technical aspects of an NVA are often downplayed or given very little thought. This component of an NVA is often left to the software to do, and little or no consideration is given to the operator or the testing methodology. The most enjoyable part of this component is the tools. Everyone wants to hear about the tools. No one wants to learn how the tools interact, or how a good methodology can save hours, if not days, of the time needed to complete a vulnerability assessment. Everyone wants to hear about the tools. Do not fret; we will spend plenty of time discussing tools and sites for tools, and our opinion of each. Before we get there, however, we will spend some time going over the process and methodology for the technical aspects of network vulnerability assessment.

Goals of Vulnerability Assessment

There are two major goals of a network vulnerability assessment. The first goal of a technical vulnerability assessment is to test everything possible. It is often useful to think in "new-age" terms and consider the NVA a holistic NVA. The reason that it is important to test the entire security domain is somewhat obvious. An intruder only needs one hole to break into the network; if that hole lies in the primary firewall or through a modem connected to an executive's desktop computer, it really does not matter. There are some factors that will limit how deep you can make the NVA. The two factors that most often get in the way of a complete NVA are time and cost. The time you spend running your NVA is generally time that you are not spending on your other job functions, and this can cost your company money or impact your company in other ways. Also, the cost of the NVA may limit the tools at your disposal for the testing period. If your organization has a somewhat meager budget for the technical areas of an NVA, do not worry too much. There are a number of great tools that are completely free, which will allow you to run a very respectable NVA without spending a fortune collecting tools. We further discuss tools in Chapter 6.

The second goal of a technical NVA is to generate a clear, concise report that will be read and used by your management or your customers. One of the most common rookie mistakes in running a NVA is to run a NVA tool with all the default options, have it generate a default report, and then print out thousands of pages with every vulnerability inside a client's domain — all the way from huge vulnerabilities such as a nonpassword-protected telnet session on the company's primary Internet router, down to very small vulnerabilities such as a workstation responding to a ping. This method delivers a significant number of pages for the customer to read, and a very thick binder that will look impressive sitting on a shelf of the CSO's office for years to come. The question lies in the value of this type of vulnerability assessment.

As a consultant, we sometimes get asked to perform this kind of NVA. Sometimes, the customer just wants someone to come into their network and run ISS Internet Scanner, and then go home. I try to discourage the customer from selecting this type of NVA; however, it often proves more difficult to dissuade the salesperson from selling this type of engagement than to change the customer's mind. However, NVAs are an important tool in the defense of computer systems and networks. Many information-seeking professionals rely solely on the latest available scanning tools to perform assessments; but scanners are only one part of a complete vulnerability assessment. Overreliance on them can leave holes in the assessment, thereby compromising information security.

In a perfect world the actual goal of an NVA is to produce useful results. A handy thing to remember is that useful to one type of individual is not necessarily as useful to other types of people. For example, a CEO is going to care little about the details of a potential security hole involving malformed ICMP packets, but this type of information is going to be very useful for the technician who may be charged with the task of fixing the problem. The CEO is more likely to be concerned with how the entire security system is doing compared to evaluation criteria or industry standards.

To help produce useful results, the amount of data given in a final report must be readable by the audience desired for each segment. Typically, an NVA report will begin with a one-page summary detailing how the security of the customer is doing in general. This is intended for senior management types to read. Following this section of the report is the general opinion section. This section is intended to be for line managers who will want more level of detail than senior management, but not as much as the company technicians who will be more interested in the next section.

The next section of the report has the specific vulnerability findings from the assessment. In this area, vulnerabilities are listed by name with a description of the vulnerability, why this vulnerability is important to fix, the areas of the enterprise that could be affected by this vulnerability, and finally the steps needed to fix the hole from a high level of detail.

After the three aforementioned sections, the next section details what you did as part of the NVA and what you would have liked to do. The first component describes how you would typically run an NVA and the steps involved. The second component shows what deviations from your normal testing policy you followed at the customer's wishes. This is where you can get even with the customer who just wanted to have you come in, run a single tool, and then leave. It also stops would-be vulnerability assessment runners

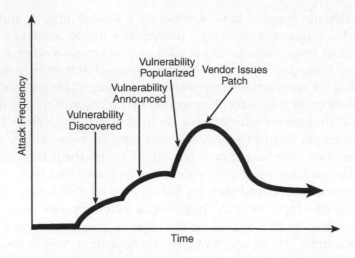

Exhibit 2. The Vulnerability Life Cycle

from coming in and stating that they run a much more complete vulnerability assessment and can provide more value than the vulnerability assessment that you had run.

How Many Trees Should Die to Generate This Type of Report?

It all depends. Yes, this is the typical consultant answer for everything but a good rule-of-thumb is that the report should be no more than 50 pages. Try to keep the report in the 20- to 30-page range, but sometimes this just cannot be done. This type of report may not look as impressive sitting on the shelf behind the CSO. However, it is more likely to be read and used.

What Are Vulnerabilities?

Vulnerabilities are documented problems or errors that can be used maliciously to make the system perform in a way unintended. There are undocumented vulnerabilities in all systems but trying to test for the unknown will be a very daunting task. We discuss in the application scanning tools section some tools that will help look for vulnerabilities in the custom-written portions of Web-enabled applications; but on the whole, a technical NVA will only look for the holes that have been published. However, this is where the largest amount of attacks will come from, as illustrated in Exhibit 2.

Vulnerability Discovered

In Exhibit 2, there are four different stages in the vulnerability life cycle. In the first phase, "Vulnerability Discovered," is where someone uncovers the vulnerability. This often happens through a Web site posting, where someone has an idea that might produce a hole and asks for comment on the potential feasibility. The next step in the discovery phase is where a "proof of concept" script is written. At this stage, the script is only created to answer the question posted to the newsgroup or Web site. Very few people are making use of the newfound vulnerability. The only people who would know of the new vulnerability's existence would be friends of the person who submitted the idea or regular readers of the Web site where it was initially posted. If the script that was written to answer the original question is successful, the next phase begins.

Vulnerability Announced

The second phase, "Vulnerability Announced," is where Web sites that specialize in announcing new vulnerabilities post a warning about the new hole discovered. In this phase, more attackers are checking for the exploit and testing many systems on the Internet. Because many people subscribe to e-mail announcements from these places, such as Security Focus, the general knowledge of the exploit has increased considerably.

Vulnerability Popularized

The next phase, "Vulnerability Popularized," occurs when a very easy-to-use script is written or a point-and-click tool is created. At this point, general knowledge of the vulnerability has spread to include almost anyone who would have an interest. This is where the group of Internet malcontents, generally referred to as "script kiddies," would be out running the script or tool against very large numbers of Internet hosts. If the vulnerability is big enough to reach popular news outlets, it will happen during this phase.

Patch Released

The final phase of the vulnerability life cycle occurs when the vendor affected by the vulnerability or security device vendors release a fix to protect against the automated attacks. An important note to consider is that once the vulnerability has a patch to protect against it, the attacks do not completely stop. Just think of the recent, well-publicized vulnerabilities such as Code Red. While most large companies patched their systems long ago, some systems on the Internet are still vulnerable. And as long as some systems are still vulnerable, attackers are going to continue to see if the target system is vulnerable.

Classes of Vulnerabilities

There are two primary classes of vulnerabilities; hard and soft. Hard vulnerabilities are mistakes made by the company that wrote the software and has left open a hole for potential exploit. These types of vulnerabilities are often

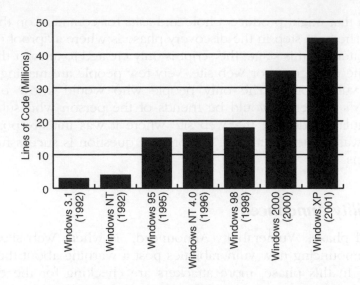

Exhibit 3. The Number of Lines of Code in Popular Operating Systems

referred to as "bugs" and are fixed with service packs and hotfixes. However, it is frequently getting more difficult to keep up-to-date with the nearly constant patching and hotfixing of all the systems in a complex enterprise. A major security vendor observed some time ago that on a Windows NT system, a new vulnerability was being discovered almost on a daily basis. This often leads to missed service patches and vulnerabilities being left open, even after the fix has been released. The reason for this large number of vulnerabilities lies in system complexity. While system complexity leads to an easier-to-use system, it increases both the number of lines of code necessary, and also the number of services running on a system. While most vendors do an exceptional job of checking for error in coding, the raw number of lines of code that needs to be checked is absolutely enormous. The numbers of lines of code in popular operating systems are listed in Exhibit 3.

The second type of vulnerability — a soft vulnerability — can in no way be blamed on the software manufacturer. Soft vulnerabilities are often misconfigurations by network and security administrators. In this tumultuous economic environment, capital resources may not be available to send administrators to training on the very products they must support. This can lead to mistakes in both the setup and maintenance of devices, as well as configurations that do not support the company's information security policies. When performing a technical network vulnerability assessment, you must look for both kinds of vulnerabilities. Also note that soft vulnerabilities may be the result of a network or security device being "hacked." Once a penetrator gets into a system, he may modify the operational parameters in any way he wishes. As a rule-of-thumb, if you ever see profanity in the configuration files of a system, it might be wise to look deeper for evidence of a penetration. The most notable exception seems to be in the title of the security configuration policy itself — where it is not uncommon to see titles such as "last <expletive deleted> try."

There are additional types of soft vulnerabilities, including:

- A lack of general security policies
- General security policies go against industry best practices
- A lack of security system procedures
- A lack of configuration or change management
- Logging not enabled
- Log files ignored or deleted frequently

Elements of a Good Vulnerability Assessment

To perform a good network vulnerability assessment, you should incorporate at least four elements:

1. Comprehensive
2. Experience
3. Results must be reproducible
4. Multi-Test Environment (MTE)

The comprehensiveness of network vulnerability assessment is generally affected or set by the scope statement we will discuss later. In addition, the comprehensiveness of your network vulnerability assessment will be affected by two major factors. The first of the two encountered will be the amount of time you can dedicate to the network vulnerability assessment; the second is the amount of capital resources you can devote to the network vulnerability assessment itself. In a very complete network vulnerability assessment, it may become necessary to acquire a large number of tools and some relatively current hardware. The hardware is not the largest expense by far — it is the software that's going to consume most of your capital resources. It is not uncommon for a vulnerability assessment toolkit to have over 40 tools, and this, of course, is dependent on the areas of the network you will be testing, the type of network to be tested, and the make up of the target network. We will discuss this more in the methodology section.

Experience

There is no substitute for experience. While reading this book, attending training classes, and practicing with the tools would give you a "leg up" towards actually running a good network vulnerability assessment, the only way to get better at doing vulnerability assessments is to do vulnerability assessments. The best way to gain this kind of experience is to practice on your own. One of the ways is to set up a target network on your own internal LAN. You can also run tests against Internet available resources that you have permission to test. However, you must resist the urge to test systems on the Internet you do not have permission to test. If you have any friends that are network administrators for smaller companies, they may be able to get you permission from their senior management to test their network. Resisting the urge to test systems without permission is a good way to avoid career-limiting moves and to also avoid getting phone calls and appearances by your local law enforcement.

The hardware requirements for conducting a network vulnerability assessment are not all that severe. As of this writing, we are currently using two laptops with 600 MHz processors and 288 MB of RAM in each. These are far from state-of-the-art machines, but they are still sufficiently powerful to do most all of what you would like to do. The reason we have to separate machines is to monitor for data leakage. Data leakage is a vulnerability the affected a number of manufacturers a few years ago. Some time ago, most of these affected companies released patches to repair the data leakage vulnerabilities. However, many people have not applied these patches because some of the manufacturers required a paid subscription service to receive these updates. So, it still remains a good idea to continue to test for these vulnerabilities.

The way we test for these vulnerabilities is to deploy a laptop with an intelligent network Sniffer and place it behind the corporate firewall or router. The other laptop will be in your vulnerability assessment toolkit, performing scans over the Internet, directed at the network behind the firewall or router. Certain types of firewalls and routers may be susceptible to data leakage. The vulnerability uses small, fragmented packets and directs them towards the inside network. For the sake of efficiency, the firewall or router may pass these packets on before they are reassembled and checked. If these devices have been sufficiently patched, none of the attack information should be bleeding through. However, if you are seeing attacks that make it through the perimeter security devices, the vulnerability still exists. If fragmentation attacks make it through the router and the firewall, you will see some of them in the packet captures on the laptop running the intelligent network Sniffer.

In terms of the operating systems that are running, the scanning laptop should dual boot between Windows NT and Red Hat Linux. The reason we use the two operating systems is to allow for the greatest access to the tools and latest vulnerability check we can get. New tools or scripts tend to come out first on the Linux operating system because the open source nature of Linux allows people to write custom scripts much more quickly than for the windows NT environment. However, we rarely go with a completely Linux vulnerability assessment because most of the paid products are built around the Windows NT platform. This provides support in case of ever running into a tool that is consistently crashing a laptop. With the paid products, there is a 1-800-number to call for support. Most scripts will have been ported over from the Linux operating system to Windows NT. You can make a very decent vulnerability assessment using just one of the two operating systems mentioned here. And, in fact, a large number of companies choose to do just that. This is primarily done so they do not need the expertise on both operating systems. However, for your needs, the two operating systems may be beneficial; this also depends on your requirements for the specific vulnerability assessment.

Summary

Network vulnerability assessments are often abused offerings from consulting companies. The major reasons for this include the depth and breadth of a NVA, which can be quite large and will generally require a team of people, and not just one employee, and the less technical aspects that can be completely overlooked. When this is combined with a NVA, which is not part of a larger informaiton security life cycle, it can quickly become a wasted expense.

The team required to run a NVA must be made up of folks with a variety of different skillsets. Some of the most commonly needed skills are project management, interview and interrogation skills, policy and procedure writing and reviewing skills, and technical network skills. This team will combine their efforts into a clear and concise report, not more than 50 pages, and generally in the 20 to 30-page range. While this report will not have the weight to get you into the world's strongest man contests, it will easily provide usable content for the customer.

Chapter 2

Project Scoping

If project content is allowed to change freely, the rate of change will eventually exceed the rate of progress.

— Unknown

Developing the scope of a project is the early work where we decide what boundaries we will set to limit the work of the project. Those boundaries (in a network vulnerability assessment project) are defined by:

- What physical limits will exist?
- What parts of the organization will be included?
- How much (if not all) of the network will be reviewed?
- How many people will be consulted?
- How many people will be working on the project?

Most failed projects come to grief because the scope of the project was poorly defined to begin with, or because the scope was not managed well and was allowed to "creep" until it was out of control. If we are going to manage the project well, then setting the scope for the project is key to its success.

Setting the scope for a network vulnerability assessment (NVA) project means that we will start with a Project Overview Statement and then develop the Project Scope Document. The Project Scope Document consists of elements of the Project Overview Statement, a Task List, and the documents that set limits on the Task List. The Task List and the documents that set limits on the tasks will form the basis of our project plan for the NVA.

This chapter presents a general overview of Project Overview Statements and the documents that go together to make up the Project Scope Document, and then discusses how to define the scope (using those two documents) for a network vulnerability analysis. (A blank Project Overview Statement is shown in Exhibit 9 and a blank Project Scope Document is shown in Exhibit 10.) This chapter also discusses what might well be the most important part of project scope: *how to manage scope change.*

A note here about project management style and specifically about the definition of what is "in scope" and "out of scope" in a project: some project managers take the time and trouble to define activities, organizations, and data that is "out of scope" (in addition to those that are "in scope"). As a matter of personal preference, we work on the assumption that anything not specifically defined as "in scope" is out of the scope of the project.

General Scoping Practices

Project Overview Statement

The first step in developing a Project Scope Document for any project is drafting the Project Overview Statement, a document that we use to convince management that our project is worthwhile and will bring benefit to the organization. The Project Overview Statement is also the equivalent of a charter for the project and will set out — in the broadest of terms — what the project is about.

We must be mindful of the audience for the Project Overview Statement. The document's readership will include management who are not IT management (i.e., internal audit, business unit management, compliance, human resources, facilities management, etc.). The writing in the Project Overview Statement must be clear, to the point, and, most importantly, free of acronyms and technology terms. We will use language that is easily understood by the nontechnologist.

The Project Overview Statement for an NVA should be one page, simple in its statements, and clear in its objectives. It should contain:

- *Project definition:* a short description of the purpose of the project and must contain a statement of the benefit that doing the project will bring
- *Project goal:* one or two sentences that state what problem or weakness the project will address
- *Objectives:* a short list of objectives that have to be met to reach the project goal
- *Success factors:* quantification of the benefits of doing the project. For an NVA, the success factor can be a detailed knowledge of the weaknesses in the organization's network (knowledge is a benefit). Note: this section is not intended for the "old favorite" project success factors such as on time, within budget, etc.
- *Assumptions:* details of the strengths, weaknesses, opportunities, and threats involved in the project, but simplicity is the key

Once completed, the Project Overview Statement will be sent to the members of management who have control over the budget for the project, plus others who have oversight responsibility or a vested interest. These others may be internal audit, compliance, human resources, facilities management, IT management, information security management, and the management of the business units that use the network. Each should be asked to signal their agreement to the content of the Project Overview Statement before any work begins.

Be prepared for the Project Overview Statement to "bounce" back and forth a few times. Each recipient of the document may have concerns about the wording or might be unclear about its meaning. It is our job to make sure that, at the Project Overview Statement stage, everyone with a vested interest understands what is going to happen, why it is going to happen, and what the benefit will be.

The Project Overview Statement serves as a check for subsequent documents produced in the planning stage of the project. As we develop the scope of a project, the details we put into subsequent documents must all reflect the Project Overview Statement. That is, if we find something to be done in the project that cannot be recognized as clearly fitting in the Project Overview Statement, then either that task or the Project Overview Statement needs to be changed. If we change the Project Overview Statement after all other parties have signed it, then the document must be "re-reviewed" by all those who reviewed the original. When the changed Project Overview Statement is sent out for review a second (or subsequent) time, each party who approved the original must approve the change(s).

Work Breakdown Structure or Task List

Once a Project Overview Statement has been issued for review, work can begin on a Work Breakdown Structure (which most people recognize as a Task List and so it is called a Task List here). The Task List is a part of our Project Scope Document and the basis of our project plan, so doing a good job of developing a Task List will help produce a good, manageable Project Scope Document.

In a perfect world it would be nice to wait on approval of the Project Overview Statement before starting the Task List but, because the Project Overview Document might "bounce" around for some time, it makes sense to start the Task List and amend it as changes are made to the Project Overview Document.

Developing a Task List means breaking down a piece of work into its component tasks. While this sounds easy enough, there are some other considerations when creating a Task List. These considerations include:

- Task status must be measurable.
- Each task must be a clearly defined event with a clear start and a clear end.
- Every task must have a deliverable.

For example, if we were to define a Task List for building a house, the actual construction part (once a foundation is established) might look similar to Exhibit 1. Notice what is not in our Task List at this point:

ⓘ	Task Name	Duration	p 22, '02	Sep 29, '02	Oct 6, '02
			M T W T F S	S M T W T F S	S M T W T F S
1	⊟ **Framing**	**1 day**			
2	⊟ **Floor Joists**	**1 day**			
3	Install first floor	1 day			
4	Install second floor	1 day			
5	⊟ **Subfloor**	**1 day**			
6	Install first floor	1 day			
7	Install second floor	1 day			
8	⊟ **Stud Walls**	**1 day**			
9	Erect first floor	1 day			
10	Erect second floor	1 day			
11	**Frame the roof**	**1 day**			

Exhibit 1. Sample Task List

- Where the tasks start and end
- Time estimates
- Resources assigned to each task
- Task dependencies

For our purpose (project scope), the most important of these is where the tasks start and end (physically and logically) because, with the Project Overview Statement and the Task List (complete with limits on the tasks), we can produce the Project Scope Document for an NVA. When we look at developing the Task List later in this chapter, we will have to go into more detail than we have here.

Developing the Project Overview Statement

We develop the Project Overview Statement by discussing the aims and benefits of the project with the project sponsor. This meeting might also involve other people, such as the manager of the budget that is going to pay for the project (if that is not the project sponsor) and some or all of the people with a vested interest in the project (described earlier in this chapter).

It is important to keep this meeting brief and "on track" because there will be a tendency for some of the attendees to want to develop many of the project documents in one sitting. Remember that this discussion is meant to define the project at a high level only. Remember also that each of the attendees will have a chance to comment on the Project Overview Statement after it has been drafted. Remind everybody present that they will be consulted at many points during development of the project document development. Trying to do more than develop the draft Project Overview Statement at this early stage will result in confusion and trying to address too many issues and agendas at one time.

The definition of the project, using the guidance provided earlier in the Project Overview Statement section will already have been thought of by the project sponsor, and he or she will be able to provide the project overview statement fairly concisely. An NVA project definition might read like this:

> This network vulnerability assessment is being carried out to measure the risk associated with operating [company name's] network in its current state. The result of this project will include detailed knowledge of vulnerabilities present in the network and the actions needed to reduce the risk posed by those vulnerabilities.

This project definition fulfills the requirements stated earlier, in that it is a short description and it contains a statement of the benefit of carrying out the project ("knowledge of vulnerabilities present in the network and the actions needed to reduce the risk posed by those vulnerabilities").

The goal of an NVA is fairly standard, and not much time needs to be spent working on this part. The goal of a NVA is:

> As network configurations, organizations, and the outside world change regularly, the risks associated with operating [company name] network change. The goal of this project is for [company name] management to be presented with a clear and concise view of the risks associated with operating the network in the current control environment.

Many times, when the objectives part of the Project Overview Statement is being developed, the meeting can "run away" from the meeting coordinator. There is often a temptation to put detailed objectives in a Project Overview Statement. Remember that a Project Overview Statement should ideally fill no more than one page, and the list of objectives contained in it should be short. A list of objectives for an NVA should resemble the following:

- Obtain or compile a book of [company name] business objectives, strategic business directions, mission statements, etc.
- Compile a book of [company name] Information Security Policies, Procedures, and Standards. Include applicable regulations, laws, guidelines, circulars, etc.
- Compile a book of network topography information that includes drawings, notes, updates, operating system information, release numbers, patches, etc.
- Create an analysis report that comments on the effectiveness of [company name] Information Security Policies, Procedures, Standards, etc.
- Create an analysis report that comments on the current network configuration.
- Produce a management report, based on the analyses, that states the risk associated with operating [company name] network in its current state, along with detailed information on the actions needed and costs associated with reducing that risk.

You can see from the above that the list of objectives looks like a very broad Task List, the basis of a project plan, and it is meant to. While the objectives listed here are necessarily broad, remember that the Project Overview Statement serves as a check for subsequent documents produced in the planning stage of the project. As we develop the scope of a project, the details put into subsequent documents must all reflect the Project Overview Statement.

Success factors are the benefits of doing the project. At this stage, it will not be possible to quantify, in dollar terms, the benefits of doing the project but there are clear benefits to be had. Some examples include:

- Documented details of [company name] Information Security Policies, Standards, and Procedures in one authoritative book.
- Details of [company name] network topography, to include drawings, notes, updates, operating system information, release numbers, patches, etc. in one authoritative book.
- [Company name] management knowledge of the risks associated with operating [company name] network in its current state — which will allow [company name] management to make informed decisions on how to or whether to reduce that risk.

Assumptions about the project comprise the final section of the Project Overview Statement and can be the most difficult to complete. It is here that we list the strengths, weaknesses, opportunities, and threats that might help or hinder us in completing the project. As with the Objectives section, there will be a strong tendency to let this list get too long. It is important that we manage the meeting so that only the most vital assumptions are added here. Some common assumptions about an NVA project include:

- Strengths:
  - Experience level of network management staff
  - Management's commitment to the project
  - Information security staff level of knowledge about network controls
- Weaknesses:
  - Network topography documentation
  - Location and currency of information security policies, standards, etc.
- Opportunities:
  - Willingness of network users to communicate
- Threats:
  - Availability of staff to interview

Exhibit 2 provides a completed Project Overview Statement.

Once the Project Overview Statement has been drafted, we must send it out to be reviewed and approved by the people who are likely to have a vested interest in the process of the network vulnerability assessment. In most organizations, the following are likely to be part of that group:

- Information security management
- Internal audit
- Compliance
- Legal

- Facilities management
- IT management
- Management of the business units that use the network

The Project Overview Statement will be accompanied by a cover letter asking the recipients to review the document and indicate their agreement to and understanding of the contents. In general, it is prudent to allow five business days for a response; and in some organizations, the cover letter can include words to the effect that a lack of response indicates agreement. While the aim here is not to deny anyone the opportunity to respond, we cannot allow the project to be held up because of a simple failure to respond.

If responses are received that indicate a lack of agreement or understanding of the contents of the Project Overview Statement, we should meet with the respondent one-on-one to correct the situation.

Although it would be nice to hold any further activity until all responses are in and everyone has agreed to the contents of the Project Overview Statement, we rarely have the luxury to waste that time. While the Project Overview Statement is out for review, we can go ahead and develop the Task List (changes to the Task List made necessary by changes to the Project Overview Statement can be incorporated as we develop the Task List).

Developing the Project Scope

Much of the information needed to determine the scope of the project can be gathered from the same audience that was needed to develop the Project Overview Statement but it should be done at a different time to avoid clouding the concentration when developing the Project Overview Statement.

Task List

In addition to administrative details and information drawn from the Project Overview Statement, the Project Scope Document includes a Task List — which will eventually be used in the project plan.

The Task List for an NVA is unusual in that it is fairly constant — changing only to accommodate the small variables within the environment being assessed. Otherwise, the tasks involved — and their sequence — remain constant. Later in the book we list the tasks required to carry out an NVA and so there is no need to list them here. However, a sample part of the Task List is shown here in Exhibit 3.

What must be done here is to show how to determine the scope of each task so that we can determine the overall scope of the project. The scope of each task defines where the task will start and end — both physically and logically. The NVA is a project with two distinct elements: top down and bottom up. Therefore, the scope of the project can be broken into two parts (and the tasks in each part scoped) before being put together again to form the entire scope of the project.

Exhibit 2. Project Overview Statement

Company Name:	Another Company	
Project Title:	Network Vulnerability Assessment	
Date:	11/01/03	Sponsor: A. N. Other
Project Manager:	T. R. Peltier	

Project Definition: This network vulnerability assessment is being carried out to measure the risk associated with operating Another Company's network in its current state. The result of this project will include detailed knowledge of vulnerabilities present in the network and the actions needed to reduce the risk posed by those vulnerabilities.

Project Goal: As network configurations, organizations, and the outside world change regularly, the risks associated with operating Another Company's network change. The goal of this project is for Another Company's management to be presented with a clear and concise view of the risks associated with operating the network in the current control environment.

Objectives:

Obtain or compile a book of [company name] business objectives, strategic business directions, mission statements, etc.

Compile a book of [company name] Information Security Policies, Procedures, and Standards. Include applicable regulations, laws, guidelines, circulars, etc.

Compile a book of network topography information that includes drawings, notes, updates, operating system information, release numbers, patches, etc.

Create an analysis report that comments on the effectiveness of [company name] Information Security Policies, Procedures, Standards, etc.

Create an analysis report that comments on the current network configuration.

Produce a management report, based on the analyses, which states the risk associated with operating [company name] network in its current state, along with detailed information on the actions needed and costs associated with reducing that risk.

Success Factors:
Documented details of [company name] Information Security Policies, Standards, and Procedures in one authoritative book.

Details of [company name] network topography, to include drawings, notes, updates, operating system information, release numbers, patches, etc. in one authoritative book.

[Company name] management knowledge of the risks associated with operating [company name] network in its current state — which will allow [company name] management to make informed decisions on how to or whether to reduce that risk.

Strengths:
Experience level of network management staff

Commitment of management to the project

Information security staff level of knowledge about network controls

Weaknesses:
Network topography documentation

Location and currency of information security policy, standards, etc.

Opportunities:
Willingness of network users to communicate

Threats:
Availability of staff to interview

	ⓘ	Task Name	Duration	Nov 24, '02
				T | F | S | S | M | T | W | T | F | S
1		⊟ **Phase 1 Data Collection**	**1 day**	
2		Collect business objec	1 day	
3		Review business obje	1 day	
4		Collect policies, etc.	1 day	
5		Review policies, etc.	1 day	
6		⊟ **Phase 2 Interviews**	**1 day**	
7		Interview dept. repres	1 day	
8		Interview internal cust	1 day	
9		Collect missing docume	1 day	

Exhibit 3. Task List

Scope of the Top-Down Assessment Tasks

When developing the scope of a project where the tasks are fairly predictable, the critical things to take into account are those that will vary from company to company. In a network vulnerability top-down assessment, the things that are most likely to vary include:

- Number, existence, location, and currency of documents; for example, business objectives; strategic business directions; mission statements; information security policies, procedures, and standards; applicable regulations; laws, guidelines; circulars; etc.
- Number of staff to be interviewed
- Number of physical locations
- The distance between remote locations and the main office

To begin to develop the scope of the top-down assessment, we need to know what documents will be available for review. The available documents vary widely from organization to organization. For example, regulated organizations (such as banking, insurance, etc.) are required to have detailed current policies, disaster recovery plans, etc. but nonregulated organizations (such as waste management, oil industries, etc.) are not.

Once again, to determine the scope of the project, it is necessary to complete a table to show which documents will be reviewed in the project. Exhibit 4 shows a sample of this table.

When discussing the number of staff, we are looking for people who need to be interviewed so that we can determine the state of the information security program as it pertains to network vulnerability. Typically, we would want to interview the same categories of people as were present at the meeting to develop the Project Overview Statement; that is:

Exhibit 4. NVA Step-by-Step: Document Table

Document	Location	Custodian

Exhibit 5. Interview List: Interviewees

Title	Name	Department	Location

- Information security management
- Internal audit
- Compliance
- Legal
- Facilities management
- IT management
- Management of the business units that use the network

In addition to these people, we will also want to interview:

- Network managers
- Systems programmers
- Applications developers

Taken together, these two lists form a group of people from whom we can gather a representative picture of the information security program as it pertains to network vulnerability. Of course, we can document the potential interviewees in a table similar to those used for locations and documents. Such a table would look similar to the one in Exhibit 5.

When we have discussed the location of staff to be interviewed, we can complete a table that shows the locations to be visited. This can differ widely from organization to organization. For example, organizations in the petroleum

Exhibit 6.   Physical Location List

Location	Description	City/State	To Be Included in Interview Schedule?	
			Y	N

industry may have one or two office locations where staff must be interviewed but may also have a number of refinery and distribution plants where the company feels there is not a strong need to interview staff. (We make no comment here on whether that decision is right or wrong.) In another industry — perhaps healthcare — the organization's management may decide that staff at each location must be interviewed. The healthcare organization may have its headquarters in one city and hospitals and doctors' offices in many cities located many miles apart.

In each case, we will need to know how many offices are to be visited and their location. We will document that in a table such as the one shown in Exhibit 6.

If an organization — at the stage of the project when the scope is being developed — cannot fully answer the questions needed to complete the above tables (i.e., those in Exhibits 4 through 6), it is still necessary to enter some values for each of the three areas discussed above. It is acceptable, instead of entering specific values in each of the three tables above, to enter more vague descriptions such as "Interview five key personnel to be named" or "Spend ten hours collecting and reviewing documents" — as long as specific values are substituted for these vague descriptions before project kickoff. If the vague details turn out to be too small to accommodate the specific values (for example, if eight specific individuals need to be interviewed instead of just five), then a scope change must be initiated. Scope change is discussed at the end of this chapter.

When these three tables are complete (even temporarily, with vague descriptions), we have the scope of the top-down assessment and can move on to developing the scope of the bottom-up assessment.

Scope of the Bottom-Up Assessment Tasks

As we will see later in the book, the bottom-up examination concentrates on hardware and software implementations of network security by assessing the network as a discrete entity and by assessing the security of individual components.

To define the scope of the bottom-up assessment part of the overall network vulnerability assessment, we need to understand what network components will be involved in the test and what types of tests we are going to run. This information can be broken into seven elements for the purpose of developing the scope and, as with the tables in Exhibits 4, 5, and 6, combined to make an attachment to the Project Scope Document. The seven elements in the scope of a bottom-up assessment are:

1. Testing parameters
2. IP addresses
3. Configuration audit
4. Cryptographic analysis
5. Password cracking
6. Application examination
7. War dialing

For each of these seven elements, the information needed to define the scope of the project can be gathered in a questionnaire. Exhibit 7 shows an example of the questionnaire.

Exhibit 7. Bottom-Up Scope Questionnaire

Testing Parameters

The following are specific test parameters agreed upon by the assessment project manager and (project sponsor):

Systems being tested are [production/development/both production and development] systems.

The test team [has/has not] been granted permission to install ESM agents for configuration audits. *Note:* ESM is discussed in Chapter 6.

[The assessment project manager/client/both] will choose the devices for point scans.

[The assessment project manager/client/both] will choose the devices for configuration audits.

Client [has/has not] authorized the assessment project manager to perform denial-of-service testing.

A physical security assessment [was/was not] requested.

Social engineering [was/was not] requested.

The assessment project manager [has/has not] been requested to evaluate the following, if present:

The test team is restricted to after-hours testing as follows:

Light network scans	[Yes/No]	[Time range]
Heavy network scans	[Yes/No]	[Time range]
Point scan testing	[Yes/No]	[Time range]
Denial-of-service testing	[Yes/No]	[Time range]
Configuration audits	[Yes/No]	[Time range]
War dialing	[Yes/No]	[Time range]

The test team has been requested to follow additional guidelines while testing:
[Specify any additional guidelines]

Exhibit 7.   Bottom-Up Scope Questionnaire (continued)

IP Addresses

List of IP addresses to be tested:
  [List IP addresses and ranges to be tested]

Specific IP addresses targeted for point scans
  Chosen by client:
  [List IP addresses and ranges to be tested]

  Chosen by the test team:
  [List IP addresses and ranges to be tested]

Specific IP addresses to be used for the ESM (Enterprise Security Manager) configuration audit
  Chosen by client:
  [List IP addresses and ranges to be tested]

  Chosen by the test team:
  [List IP addresses and ranges to be tested]

Configuration Audit

Number of SysLog Servers:	[x]
Windows NT	
Number of servers:	[x]
Percentage of servers to be tested:	[x]
Number of workstations:	[x]
Percentage of workstations to be tested:	[x]
Number of domain controllers:	[x]
Sun Solaris	
Number of servers:	[x]
Percentage of servers to be tested:	[x]
Number of workstations:	[x]
Percentage of workstations to be tested:	[x]
Other UNIX	
Number of servers:	[x]
Percentage of servers to be tested:	[x]
Number of workstations:	[x]
Percentage of workstations to be tested:	[x]
VAX/VMS	
Number of servers:	[x]
Percentage of servers to be tested:	[x]
Number of workstations:	[x]
Percentage of workstations to be tested:	[x]
Linux	
Number of servers:	[x]
Percentage of servers to be tested:	[x]
Number of workstations:	[x]
Percentage of workstations to be tested:	[x]
Win2000	
Number of servers:	[x]
Percentage of servers to be tested:	[x]
Number of workstations:	[x]
Percentage of workstations to be tested:	[x]
Other Operating Systems	
Number of servers:	[x]
Percentage of servers to be tested:	[x]
Number of workstations:	[x]
Percentage of workstations to be tested:	[x]

Exhibit 7.   Bottom-Up Scope Questionnaire (continued)

Firewalls
    Boundary firewall(s) type: [list]
    Number of boundary firewall(s):   [x]
    Internal firewall(s) type: [list]
    Number of internal firewall(s):   [x]

Cryptographic Analysis
Client has requested that the test team examine the design of the following cryptosystems·
    [List cryptosystems, such as PKI system or IPSec, that have been requested]

Password Cracking
Windows NT
    SMB capture passwords: [Yes/No]
    Retrieve from domain controller: [Yes/No]
    Brute-force standard alphabet: [Yes/No]
    Brute-force all characters: [Yes/No]
    Time to run: [Hours, up to 24]
Novell NetWare
    Brute-force standard alphabet: [Yes/No]
    Brute-force all characters: [Yes/No]
    Time to run: [Hours, up to 24]
UNIX
    Brute-force standard alphabet: [Yes/No]
    Brute-force all characters: [Yes/No]
    Time to run: [Hours, up to 24]
Linux
    Brute-force standard alphabet: [Yes/No]
    Brute-force all characters: [Yes/No]
    Time to run: [Hours, up to 24]
Win2000
    Brute-force standard alphabet: [Yes/No]
    Brute-force all characters: [Yes/No]
    Time to run: [Hours, up to 24]

Application Examination
Client has requested that the test team examine the source code of the following applications
for vulnerabilities:
    [List applications requested]

War Dialing
    [List phone number ranges]

Project Scope Document

When the initial Task List and the two task scope documents (top down and
bottom up) have been developed, it is time to put them together with the
Project Scope Document and send them out for review and comment. A
completed Project Scope Document is shown in Exhibit 8.

Exhibit 8.   Project Scope Document

Project Title:	Network Vulnerability Assessment		
Date:	10/10/03	**Project Number:**	PA101003
Project Manager:	John A. Blackley		
Sponsor:			
Project Description:	This network vulnerability assessment is being carried out to measure the risk associated with operating Another Company's network in its current state. The result of this project will include detailed knowledge of vulnerabilities present in the network and the actions needed to reduce the risk posed by those vulnerabilities.		
Project Goals:	Obtain or compile a book of [company name] business objectives, strategic business directions, mission statements, etc.		
	Compile a book of [company name) Information Security Policies, procedures, and standards. Include applicable regulations, laws, guidelines, circulars, etc.		
	Compile a book of network topography information that includes drawings, notes, updates, operating system information, release numbers, patches, etc.		
	Create an analysis report that comments on the effectiveness of [company name] Information Security Policies, Procedures, Standards, etc.		
	Create an analysis report that comments on the current network configuration.		
	Produce a management report, based on the analyses, that states the risk associated with operating [company name] network in its current state, along with detailed information on the actions needed and costs associated with reducing that risk.		
Project Scope:	See attached document(s)		
Signed:	Project Manager: _____ _____ (Attach separate page for other signatures)		

Reviewing the Scope Documents

The audience for the NVA Project Scope Document will be the same as for the Project Definition Statement. Once again, as with the Project Definition Statement, we should allow reasonable time (e.g., five days) for review and comment; and where permissible, indicate that "no response" means agreement with the contents of the document. Once again, there is no need to

Exhibit 9. Blank Project Overview Statement		
Company Name:		
Project Title:		
Date:	**Sponsor:**	
Project Manager:		
Project Definition:		
Project Goal:		
Objectives:		
Success Factors:		
Strengths:		
Weaknesses:		
Opportunities:		
Threats:		

wait for those five days to elapse before starting the preparation work for the project itself.

Project Scope Change

It is inevitable that, after the Project Overview Statement (Exhibit 9) has been approved and the Project Scope Document (Exhibit 10) drafted, someone will require a change in the scope of the project. The key to a successful project is to effectively manage scope change.

Managing scope change begins with a formal process for requesting a change in scope. Exhibit 11 provides a sample Scope Change Request Form. The project manager should be the first to review requests for scope change and should be the "gatekeeper" (i.e., has authority to accept or refuse requests within certain parameters). For those requests that are outside the project manager's authority, the project manager should write an Impact Statement (what will happen if the request is granted), attach it to the Scope Change Request Form, and forward both to a review committee. The review committee should consist of those people who were invited to review the original Project Overview Statement and the Project Scope Document.

As with the other documents discussed in this chapter, the request for a change of scope in the project should be reviewed within a fixed time limit (to avoid unnecessary delay in the project) — with a caveat that a failure to respond to the review request indicates agreement with the request to change the scope of the project.

Exhibit 10. Blank Project Scope Document

Project Title:			
Date:		Project Number:	
Project Manager:			
Sponsor:			
Project Description:			
Project Goals:			
Project Scope:			
Signed:	**Project Manager:** _____ **(Attach separate page for other signatures)**		

Exhibit 11. Project Scope Change Request

Project Title:			
Project Number:			
Change Requested By:		Date:	
Change Description:			
Impact (if change not granted):			
(To Be Completed by Project Manager) Change Request Number:			
Request Granted?	Y		N	
If 'Y,' Change Request Resulted in Project Plan Version Number:			
Review Committee Signatures:	(Attach separate sheet if necessary)		

Summary

Most failed projects come to grief because the scope of the project was poorly defined to begin with, or because the scope was not managed well. This chapter discussed Project Overview Statements and the Project Scope Document for an NVA, the processes needed to gather the information for the Project Overview Document, and what may be the most important part of a project scope — how to manage scope change.

Chapter 3

Assessing Current Network Concerns

The number of reported incidents to the Computer Incident Advisory Capability (CIAC)1 and the CERT2 Coordination Center has seen an increase each year since its founding in 1988. This chapter examines current trends in network incidents. As an individual charged with conducting a network vulnerability assessment (NVA) within your own enterprise, you will quickly discover that there are more possible problems or risks than you will have time to assess. To improve your chances of being successful, it will be necessary to identify which risks concern your enterprise most and then concentrate on them.

This chapter examines some current network concerns and provides a brief discussion on how to minimize their impact on your organization. The chapter then reviews two checklists that can be used as examples to help ensure that important concerns are addressed. As with all checklists, I must caution you that they are only a starting point. All too often, individuals employing checklists complete the items identified and assume that they have completed the task. Checklists are only starting points in a complete review process. Use them as reminders of items to look for but keep an open mind for additional risk or threats.

Making a quantitative determination of the value of the information and resources you need to protect is a first step in developing a comprehensive information security plan. This determination can allow you to address areas of greatest concern first and then look to lesser concerns as time and budget permit. A balance between the budget available for protecting your network and the value of that which is to be protected is what we seek.

Specific aspects of a network vulnerability assessment (NVA) include:

- An analysis of the physical topology and architecture of the network
- A critique of UNIX, which versions and revisions are part of the network

---

1 http://www.CIAC.org
2 http://www.CERT.org

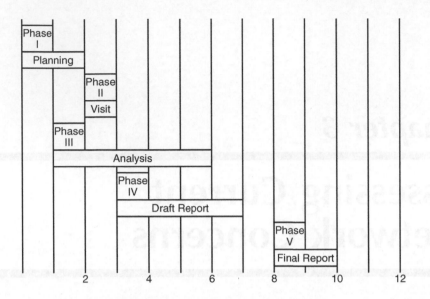

Exhibit 1. Network Vulnerability Assessment Timeline

- A survey of network protocols being used on the network and their current uses
- An investigation into WAN (Wide Area Network) connections; do you have one?
- An examination of data and information available over the WAN link
- An inspection of the authentication process used to access network resources
- An analysis of the nature and sensitivity of the data residing on systems connected to the main network backbone
- An examination of dial-up points-of-entry into the network
- A critique of policies in place to protect information from unauthorized access, modification, disclosure, and destruction
- An analysis of access granting authority and the process
- A critique of the system administration responsibilities

Network Vulnerability Assessment Timeline

A typical NVA might take as long as 12 weeks, especially if you are attempting to complete the task while maintaining your current responsibilities (see Exhibit 1). This process should result in an extensive report detailing points of weakness found in the network with respect to data and resource vulnerabilities.

Recommendations made should address:

- Policy and procedure modifications
- Architecture and topology changes
- Possible security hardware (firewalls, switches, physical separation of subnets) and software (encryption, remote access controls, single sign-on, authentication) implementation recommendations

Network Vulnerability Assessment Team (NVAT)

When assembling a team to assist in the tasks of an NVA, it is important to ensure that each of the various infrastructure support areas is either an active member of the team or a support member. NVA team members should include representatives from:

- Information protection
- Operations
- Telecommunications
- Systems support
- Network management
- Desktop deployment
- Account administration
- Auditing

The task of an NVA crosses departmental lines and therefore should not be viewed as an information-technology-only process. To be successful, the NVA team should include other departments and business units that can be used as support members. Support NVA team members should include representatives from the following areas:

- Physical security
- Facilities management
- Human resources
- Legal

It will be necessary to ensure that the team membership meets the needs of the assessment scope (see Chapter 2, Project Scoping). To be successful, it will be necessary to ensure that political as well as technical members are part of the team. There may be an employee or two at your work site who has the ear of management and takes offense if his or her input is not included in any task that appears to be as important as a vulnerability assessment. Make certain that any person who can torpedo the findings is part of the team. It will be more difficult for such people to attack the results if they are part of the assessment team.

Threats to Computer Systems

Computer systems are vulnerable to many threats that can inflict various types of damage and result in significant losses. Damage can range from minor errors that impact database integrity to fires that destroy entire computer centers. Losses can stem from the actions of supposedly trusted employees to defraud the system, to outside hackers roaming freely through the Internet. The exact extent of computer-related losses is unknowable; many losses are never discovered and others are covered up to avoid unfavorable publicity. The Computer Security Institute (CSI)[1] and the Federal Bureau of Investigation

(FBI) publish an annual report on computer crime. While not the complete picture, this report provides NVA teams with a starting point to begin their assessments. A sample of the recent 2002 report includes the following information:

> Based on responses from 503 computer security practitioners in U.S. corporations, government agencies, financial institutions, medical institutions, and universities, the findings of the "2002 Computer Crime and Security Survey" confirm that the threat from computer crime and other information security breaches continues unabated and that the financial toll is mounting.
>
> Highlights of the "2002 Computer Crime and Security Survey" include:
>
> Ninety percent of respondents (primarily large corporations and government agencies) detected computer security breaches within the past 12 months.
>
> Eighty percent acknowledged financial losses due to computer breaches.
>
> Forty-four percent (223 respondents) were willing and able to quantify their financial losses. These 223 respondents reported $455,848,000 in financial losses.
>
> As in previous years, the most serious financial losses occurred through theft of proprietary information (26 respondents reported $170,827,000) and financial fraud (25 respondents reported $115,753,000).
>
> For the fifth year in a row, more respondents (74 percent) cited their Internet connection as a frequent point of attack than cited their internal systems as a frequent point of attack (33 percent).
>
> Thirty-four percent reported the intrusions to law enforcement. (In 1996, only 16 percent acknowledged reporting intrusions to law enforcement.)
>
> Respondents detected a wide range of attacks and abuses. Some examples of attacks and abuses include:
>
> Forty percent detected system penetration from the outside.
>
> Forty percent detected denial-of-service attacks.
>
> Seventy-eight percent detected employee abuse of Internet access privileges (e.g., downloading pornography or pirated software, or inappropriate use of e-mail systems).
>
> Eighty-five percent detected computer viruses.
>
> For the fourth year, we asked some questions about electronic commerce over the Internet. The results revealed that:
>
> Ninety-eight percent of respondents have WWW sites.
>
> Fifty-two percent conduct electronic commerce on their sites.
>
> Thirty-eight percent suffered unauthorized access or misuse on their Web sites within the past 12 months; twenty-one percent said that they did not know if there had been unauthorized access or misuse.

Twenty-five percent of those acknowledging attacks reported from two to five incidents; thirty-nine percent reported ten or more incidents.

Seventy percent of those attacked reported vandalism (only 64 percent in 2000).

Fifty-five percent reported denial of service (only 60 percent in 2000).

Twelve percent reported theft of transaction information.

Six percent reported financial fraud (only 3 percent in 2000).[2]

Other Concerns

In addition to the published report discussed above, there are other sources we can examine to identify threats to computer systems. We will do this by giving a broad picture of the threat environment in which systems are currently operated. An overview of many of today's common threats is useful to organizations studying their own threat environments with a view toward developing solutions specific to their organization.

A wide variety of threats face today's computer systems and the information they process. To control the risks of operating an information system, managers and users must know the vulnerabilities of the system and the threats that might exploit them. Knowledge of the threat environment allows management to implement the most cost-effective security measures. In some cases, managers may find it most cost-effective to simply tolerate the expected losses.

Computer Viruses

Currently, the more common, more ambitious, and more sophisticated attacks are coming from a new crop of virus specialists who have been sending out new viruses at an alarming rate. Nimda, a mass-mailing worm with an attachment entitled "readme.exe." Anna Kournikova, written by a 20-year-old Dutchman who did it to prove that it was simple to make a virus and that companies would be vulnerable to it. The Code Red worm has caused $1.2 billion in damage to networks and the I Love You virus infected more than 15 million computers.

The number of corporations infected by viruses this year (2002) has risen by 20 percent (ICSA.net) and typical losses cost between $100K to $1 million annually. Nearly 40 percent of companies report having data loss due to viruses. A study released by the Omni Consulting Group of 3000 businesses worldwide reported that security invasions cost companies between 5 and 7 percent of their annual revenue.

Computer Hackers

According to "The Jargon File" (AKA, _The New Hacker's Dictionary) the hacker mind-set is not confined to this software-hacker culture. There are people who apply the hacker attitude to other things, such as electronics or music; actually, you can find it at the highest levels of any science or art. Software hackers recognize these kindred spirits elsewhere and may call them "hackers" too — and some claim that the hacker nature is really independent of the particular medium in which the hacker works.

There is another group of people who loudly call themselves hackers, but are not. These are people (mainly adolescent males) who get a kick out of breaking into computers and phreaking the phone system. Real hackers call these people "crackers" and want nothing to do with them. Real hackers mostly think crackers are lazy, irresponsible, and not very bright, and object that being able to break security does not make you a hacker any more than being able to hot-wire cars makes you an automotive engineer. Unfortunately, many journalists and writers have been fooled into using the word "hacker" to describe crackers; this irritates real hackers to no end.

> Two Russians were indicted on computer-crime charges stemming from a rash of intrusions into the networks of banks, Internet service providers, and other companies. Federal authorities say they also found evidence that the two intended to create a Web page made to resemble the site of online cash-transfer service PayPal to nab credit card numbers from more victims.

> Hackers force some banks to cancel VISA debit cards. The online merchant customer database had been hacked and one bank had over 3000 customers impacted.

> A well-known Web site that tracks defacements on other sites by hackers PoizonBox was itself defaced yesterday by a hacker going under the name of ThePike. Alldas.de is one of a shrinking number of sites that track a growing number of defacements. At the end of May a similar site, called Attrition.org, said it would stop tracking Web site defacements because the volunteer staff can no longer keep up with the volume.

Denial-of-Service Attacks

A denial-of-service attack (DoS attack) is characterized by an explicit attempt by attackers to prevent legitimate users of a service from using that service. Examples include attempts to:

- "Flood" a network, thereby preventing legitimate network traffic
- Disrupt connections between two machines, thereby preventing access to a service
- Prevent a particular individual from accessing a service
- Disrupt service to a specific system or person

Not all service outages — even those that result from malicious activity — are necessarily DoS attacks. Other types of attack include a denial-of-service as a component, but the denial-of-service may be part of a larger attack. Illegitimate use of resources may also result in a denial-of-service. For example, an intruder might use your anonymous FTP area as a place to store illegal copies of commercial software, consuming disk space and generating network traffic:

- Animal activists targeted the Web site of a U.S. investment bank that saved a controversial drug-testing company from liquidation. They used a hacking tool called Floodnet that sent download requests, making it too busy for other use.
- A former network administrator for a U.S. District Court launched a DoS attack against that Court's Web site to prove to officials how vulnerable it was.
- BidBay, a California-based online auction site, was put out of business for hours by hackers. The attack occurred when thousands of new registered users were being welcomed.

E-Mail Mistakes

E-mail is an easy and immediate way of communicating with almost anyone, from business associates to friends, to people we have not even met. And it is growing in use. Studies show that two thirds of U.S. workers have access to e-mail at work, and they use it more than any other form of communication. In general, about 110 million Americans have e-mail, and the average e-mail user has more than one mailbox, according to Eric Arnum, editor of *Messaging Online,* an electronic publication covering e-mail issues. By his best guess, between 100 and 700 billion e-mails are sent in this country each year. But as e-mails increase, so do e-mail errors. Among the gaffes that have made the news:

- Paul Chung, a recently hired associate at Carlyle Group in its office in Seoul, South Korea, was forced to resign after boasting about his sexual exploits and new lavish lifestyle in an e-mail message to his buddies in New York. Unfortunately for Chung, a 24-year-old Princeton graduate who had moved to Seoul only three days earlier to start his job, the message was forwarded and passed around to thousands on Wall Street and wound up being forwarded to his bosses at Carlyle Group, a private equity firm. Chung was given the option of resigning or being dismissed, a Carlyle executive said.
- District of Columbia police were caught sending racist, vulgar, and homophobic messages via patrol car computers.
- Dow Chemical Co. fired 50 employees and disciplined 200 others after an e-mail investigation turned up hard-core pornography and violent subject matter on company systems.

Disgruntled Employees

Rich Brewer of International Data Corp. (IDC) commented during Directions '99 that "the perception is that most hack attacks come from political activities and professional industrial thieves, but the reality is that approximately 70 percent of attacks come from within a company. Most security breaches are committed through a bunch of holes, enabling hackers to steal assets and, more important, ideas."

"Hackers are benefiting from a company's silence," Brewer said, adding that "according to the FBI, fewer than 3 percent of hack attacks were detected last year, and out of those, fewer than 1 percent were reported to the FBI." To defend against hack attacks, "products alone can't save" companies. Companies will have to look at all options: security consulting and implementation; managed firewalls; an intrusion, detection, and response operation; and hacker insurance.

- In 1998, a disgruntled programmer at defense contractor Omega Engineering Corp. set off a digital bomb, destroying $10 million in data.
- A temporary employee working as a computer technician at *Forbes Magazine* was charged with crashing the company's network and causing more than $100,000 in damage.

Industrial Spying

The gathering of competitive business intelligence is now considerably easier and more effective because of the Internet. Clues to competitors' intellectual property development and strategic plans have grown so accessible that management might fear repercussions from shareholders for not gathering such material. It is very easy to gather such information from private-sector and government Web sites, news groups, chat rooms, and other quite public gathering spots of the information age. It is so easy that it is almost criminal.

- Recently, the European Union warned that the Russian secret service is committed to stealing technology.
- According to the Futures Group, some 60 percent of companies have organized systems for collecting information on rivals.

Additional Threats

To successfully identify possible threats, there are a number of services that can provide current threat information and possible solutions. The contacts most commonly used include:

- Vendors
- CERT Coordination Center (www.cert.org/advisories)
- Computer Incident Advisory Capability (CIAC)
- Federal Information Processing Standards Publications (FIPS Pub) (www.itl.nist.gov/fipspub)

- National Institute of Standards and Technology (NIST) publications
- Generally Accepted System Security Principles (GASSP)
- British Standard (BS) 7799
- International Standard for Information Security (ISO 17799)
- Global Information Assurance Certification (GIAC) (www.giac.org) by the SANS Institute

Some additional threats identified by these organizations include:

- *Firewall and system probing.* Hackers are using sophisticated, automated tools to scan for the vulnerabilities of a company's corporate firewall and systems behind the firewall. These hacker tools have proved quite effective, with the average computer scan taking less than three minutes to identify and compromise security.
  - *Safeguard/control.* Companies can prevent this by ensuring that their systems sit behind a network firewall, and any services available through this firewall are carefully monitored for potential security exposures.
- *Network file systems (NFS) application attacks.* Hackers attempt to exploit well-known vulnerabilities in the NFS application that is used to share files between systems. These attacks, usually through network firewalls, can result in compromised administrator access.
  - *Safeguard/control.* To combat this, ensure that systems do not allow NFS through the firewall, and enable NFS protections to restrict access to files.
- *Vendor default password attacks.* Systems of all types come with vendor-installed user names and passwords. Hackers are well educated on these default user names and passwords, and use these accounts to gain unauthorized administrative access to systems.
  - *Safeguard/control.* Protect systems by ensuring that all vendor passwords have been changed.
- *Spoofing, sniffing, fragmentation, and splicing attacks.* Recently, computer hackers have been using sophisticated techniques and tools at their disposal to identify and expose vulnerabilities on Internet networks. These tools and techniques can be used to capture user names and passwords, as well as compromise trusted systems through the firewall.
  - *Safeguard/control.* To protect systems from this type of attack, check with computer and firewall vendors to identify possible security precautions.
- *Social engineering attacks.* Hackers will attempt to gain sensitive or confidential information from companies by placing calls to employees and pretending to be another employee. These types of attacks can be effective in gaining user names and passwords as well as other sensitive information.
  - *Safeguard/control.* Train employees to use a "call-back" procedure to verify the distribution of any sensitive information over the phone.
- *Prefix scanning.* Computer hackers will be scanning company telephone numbers, looking for modem lines that they can use to gain access to internal systems. These modem lines bypass network firewalls and usually bypass most security policies. These "backdoors" can easily be used to compromise internal systems.

- *Safeguard/control.* Protect against this intrusion by ensuring that modems are protected from brute-force attacks. Place these modems behind firewalls, make use of one-time passwords, or have these modems disabled.
■ *Trojan horses.* Hackers will install "backdoor" or "Trojan horse" programs on business computer systems, allowing for unrestricted access to internal systems, which will bypass security monitoring and auditing policies.
  - *Safeguard/control.* Conduct regular security analysis audits to identify potential security vulnerabilities and security exposures.
■ *Threats to personal privacy.* The accumulation of vast amounts of electronic information about individuals by the government, credit bureaus, and private companies, combined with the ability of computers to monitor, process, aggregate, and record information about individuals, have created a very real threat to individual privacy. The possibility that all this information and technology could be linked together has loomed as a specter of the modern information age. This phenomenon is known as "big brother."

Prioritizing Risks and Threats

Once the possible threats have been identified, it is necessary to prioritize those risks so that the NVA can focus on those of highest concern. To accomplish this task as quickly as possible, it is necessary to assemble a team of interested employees. This team will determine the probability that the identified risk might occur and what its impact would be if it did occur.

It is necessary to define what probability and impact mean so that the team can use common criteria for assessment. Over the past ten years, the following definitions have become a mainstay in the risk analysis process that we use. These terms have been adopted and modified to meet each organization's specific needs. You will have to do the same. Use the nine-box square shown in Exhibit 2 to help establish the priority.

The definitions of probability and impact are as follows:

■ *Impact:* a measure of the magnitude of loss or harm on the value of an asset
  - *Low impact:* when the business objective or mission of enterprise is not significantly affected
  - *Medium impact:* when the event is limited to a business objective or a business unit is affected
  - *High impact:* when the entire business or mission of the enterprise is affected
■ *Probability:* the chance that an event will occur or that a specific loss value will be incurred should the event occur
  - *Low probability:* highly unlikely that the risk will occur during the next year
  - *Medium probability:* possible that the risk will occur during the next year
  - *High probability:* very likely that the risk will occur within the next year

		Impact to the Organization/Network		
		Low	Medium	High
Probability	Low	1	4	7
	Medium	2	5	8
	High	3	6	9

Exhibit 2. Network Security Concerns Priority Matrix

The NVA will concentrate on those items prioritized as a level 6 or higher. If there is time and additional resources available after the high-priority items have been addressed, then the team can look at priority items 4 and 5.

Other Considerations

The primary objective of human resource management is to make the most effective use of the people involved with the project. Activities included are planning the organizational structure of the project, acquiring staff, and developing team members. The resources necessary to carry out the project and to ensure its success should be clearly defined and documented in terms of their roles and responsibilities. Reporting relationships can also be documented, if necessary. Each person in the project should understand his or her responsibilities and should have the time available to carry out those responsibilities.

Today's computer systems, linked by national and global networks, face a variety of threats that can result in significant financial and information losses. Threats vary considerably, from threats to data integrity resulting from unintentional errors and omissions, to threats to system availability from malicious hackers attempting to crash a system. An understanding of the types of threats in today's computing environment can assist a security manager in selecting appropriate cost-effective controls to protect valuable information resources.

Assessment of the network involves systematic consideration of:

- The business harm likely to result from a significant breach of network security (taking into account the consequences of failures of information confidentiality, integrity, and availability)
- The realistic likelihood of such a breach occurring in light of prevailing threats and existing controls

Assessment of these two aspects of risk depends on the following factors:

- The nature of the business information and systems
- The business purpose for which the information is used
- The environment in which the system is used and operated
- The protection provided by the controls

The NVA might identify exceptional business security risks requiring stronger controls that are additional to the recommendations given in enterprise standards. Additional controls will need to be justified on the basis of the conclusions of the security assessment.

Checklists

To a large extent, the need for concern regarding information security is independent of the size of the organization's network. The object of an NVA is not to find the 100-percent security solution; that is not a viable option. We must look to find ways to level risks to network usage to an acceptable range. For years, organizations have worked to secure access to the technology centers that process the organization's information. To that end, there has been a decidedly positive outcome. However, once the information is transmitted out of the technology center to where the employees are, then the controls and safeguards begin to become suspect.

Public telecommunication networks, which handle a tremendous amount of traffic, are not secure. The Internet was not designed to be a secure mechanism for the transmission of confidential information. The confidentiality and integrity of the information carried over this medium is not assured. Microwave communications and other technological advances, such as satellites, fax machines, videoconferencing, and cellular communications, are also susceptible to control breaches.

Current thinking about protection suggests that all communication controls are subsets of information protection. Effective control measures are a balance of technology and personnel management. Network control is the protection resulting from application of specific technical controls, as well as physical security measures to protect all elements of the transmission and connection process.

These measures are taken to deny unauthorized persons information of value that might be derived from the possession and study of portions of information available from numerous sources throughout the enterprise. Therefore, network controls must extend beyond the user of unique userids and confidential passwords.

As previously discussed, control needs differ for each organization. Sooner or later, most organizations will have to identify control issues for their environment. By establishing a standard set of control elements and using them as a starting-point checklist, the NVA can assess the level of readiness for a network review.

To establish your unique checklist, use the ones included in this book, but also set aside a two-hour meeting of the infrastructure support departments, audit, and some user representatives; brainstorm additional items; and review and edit the ones provided in this book.

Three checklists are provided in Appendix A:

1. ISO 17799 Self-Assessment Questionnaire
2. Network Vulnerability Assessment Checklist
3. Window NT Server 4.0[3]

When developing your checklist, it might be helpful to establish categories to review. In ISO 17799, the Communications and Operations Management section 8.5, Network Management, identifies "network controls" and a topic to be covered. Section 9, Access Controls, is subdivided into 9.4, Network Access Controls; 9.7, Event Monitoring; and 9.8, Mobile Computing and Teleworking (Telecommuting). Use these as a starting point for categories or use the following:

- Environmental hazards
- Power supplies
- Cabling security
- Equipment maintenance
- Off-premises equipment security
- Disposal of equipment

Summary

To be successful, the NVA team must identify what network security concerns have the highest priority. This allows the team to focus on those threats and risks that can cause the enterprise the most damage. Understanding that the security concerns include personnel and physical as well as technical issues will ensure the most comprehensive assessment prospect.

Establishing a team that represents the enterprise also adds to the creditability of the assessment results. Using enterprise personnel will ensure that those individuals with the most intimate knowledge of how the network works and how it is supposed to work will have input into the report. Be sure to include representatives from the user community. Some of the best and most knowledgeable network users come from the business units.

Use all of the resources available to plot what threats will be addressed. Do your research to gather significant issues and then prioritize these risks based on probability of occurrence and impact to the enterprise or network. Concentrate on those issues that will bring the biggest impact to your organization. Use your team to identify additional items and measure their specific impact.

Developing a checklist will assist the NVA team in ensuring that basic security controls are examined. Do not just use the checklist. Listen and ask questions, and be ready to include additional information into the examination process.

An NVA can take a considerable amount of time to complete. Divide the total mission into manageable chunks and then begin the process. Complete one phase before moving on to the next. Be sure to get support from the infrastructure groups; this will make the task easier. Remember that it is not your NVA; it is the NVA of the organization.

Notes

1. The Computer Security Institute (CSI) is the world's leading membership organization specifically dedicated to serving and training the information, computer, and network security professional. Since 1974, the CSI has been providing education and aggressively advocating the critical importance of protecting information assets. The CSI sponsors two conference and exhibitions each year (NetSec in June and the CSI Annual in November), as well as seminars on encryption, intrusion management, the Internet, firewalls, awareness, Windows, and more. CSI membership benefits include the *ALERT* newsletter, the quarterly *Journal,* and the *Buyers Guide.*
2. The Computer Crime and Security Survey is available for no charge from the CSI by accessing its Web site at www.gocsi.com.
3. Window NT Server 4.0 was developed by Bob Cartwright, CISSP, of ESAAG, Concord, Calfornia, and is presented here with his permission.

Chapter 4

Network Vulnerability Assessment Methodology

The growth of distributed computing has been one of the major drivers for network security. With the exponential growth of networks, the ease with which information can be shared between and among computer networks makes security more important but more difficult to implement and manage. Computers are no longer connected to one trusted network; they are potentially connected to every other network and its computers in the world, with or without security implementations of their own.

In the old mainframe environment, security meant keeping the computer in a locked room with limited access. As computing power and its physical presence are distributed, it becomes increasingly difficult to control access by physical means. With remote-access architecture, it is impossible; even if one could sequester the network within a secure building, it would still be possible for someone to eavesdrop remotely.

An effective network vulnerability assessment (NVA) will help an organization develop a security architecture that will provide the best protection for the least investment in staff, hardware, software, and time. Because no organization has unlimited resources to devote to security, it will be necessary to determine the severity of the risks that the network faces and the most effective countermeasures to mitigate those risks.

Methodology Purpose

This book is intended to help you perform a sanctioned NVA, the key term being "sanctioned." It could be a "carrier limiting decision" to conduct a NVA, even for your own company, without prior management approval. The NVA book provides an outline and supplementary materials to assist you in providing excellent assessment services to your management and user community. This chapter provides the following resources to assist you in performing a comprehensive, accurate, and useful assessment of an organization's network security, controls, and safeguards:

- Sample schedule and agenda
- Requirements document
- Documentation checklist
- Key personnel checklist
- Interview questions
- Recommended tools
- Sample network vulnerability assessment

Definitions

The NVA is the process by which organizations can evaluate their policies, business practices, network(s) and network devices, hardware, software, staffing, and training to determine the vulnerabilities that threaten the integrity of their networks and supporting infrastructure. Once the vulnerabilities have been identified, the NVA will be necessary to determine appropriate and cost-effective mitigation for securing the enterprise's data and network infrastructure.

Key terms used in the NVA include the following:

- *Risk:* the probability that a threat will exploit a vulnerability to adversely affect an information asset
- *Threat:* an event, the occurrence of which could have an undesired impart
- *Threat impact:* a measure of the magnitude of loss or harm on the value of an asset
- *Threat probability:* the chance that an event will occur or that a specific loss value may be attained should the event occur
- *Safeguard:* a risk-reducing measure that acts to detect, prevent, or minimize loss associated with the occurrence of a specified threat or category of threats
- *Vulnerability:* the absence or weakness of a risk-reducing safeguard

Justification

Originally, the utility of computers lay in their ability to accelerate business processes. If the system went down, it was inconvenient but it was not catastrophic. Today, we use computers and the networks they are attached to for so much more than just automating our business processes. If the network is down, the enterprise is not working. If the data in the customer database is not available, we are either losing business or not providing service. If a safety-critical system is down, lives might be endangered. We depend on our computers and networks; they are integral to the success of the enterprise.

Business decisions are based on information stored, generated, transmitted, and presented electronically. How sure is management that the data on which it is making business decisions is accurate? How much trust can be placed in that information? Management is required to perform due diligence, which means that management needs availability to accurate information. The networks must be available, the information contained in them must have integrity, and all sensitive information must be kept confidential. The ISO 17799 defines these three terms in the following manner:

1. *Integrity.* The information is as intended without inappropriate modification or corruption.
2. *Confidentiality.* The information is protected from unauthorized or accidental disclosure.
3. *Availability.* Authorized users can access applications and systems when required to do their jobs.

The NVA ensures that these three key information security concepts are met within the network infrastructure. The NVA provides management with the information it needs to determine the risks, threats, safeguards, and vulnerabilities of the information and processes stored on its network(s). The NVA outlines the existing vulnerabilities in the system and identifies strategies for mitigating those vulnerabilities.

Philosophy

Because every organization has different security requirements, an NVA must be implemented to meet specific security needs. The NVA is used to evaluate the systems and the data in the context of one's operating environment, business practices, and strategic goals. The goal is always to reach the right balance among security and effective system utilization.

The NVA examines the network systems from both a policy and a practice point of view — this is identified as top-down and bottom-up assessments (see Exhibit 1). The advantage of this dual approach is that it is thorough. The top-down assessment uses existing security-related policies and procedures, and the bottom-up assessment uses commonly accepted security practices, known problems, and vulnerabilities.

Top-Down Examination

The top-down examination concentrates on the extent to which policies and procedures promote a secure computing environment. The NVA team examines the procedural framework that corporate security rests on and also the depth to which these policies and procedures are understood and implemented in the organization. The top-down examination evaluates the areas listed in Exhibit 2.

Using this information, you will be able to identify vulnerabilities resulting from missing or inadequate policies and procedures, and how these affect the

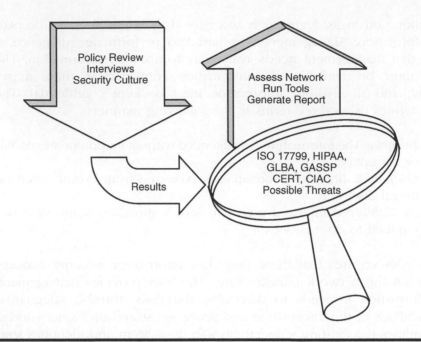

Policy Review
Interviews
Security Culture

Assess Network
Run Tools
Generate Report

ISO 17799, HIPAA,
GLBA, GASSP
CERT, CIAC
Possible Threats

Results

Exhibit 1.   Network Vulnerability Assessment Top-Down, Bottom-Up Methodology

organization's ability to manage the security of its network. The results of the top-down examination are used in the bottom-up examination. The NVA report must make specific recommendations for solving identified problems and suggests implementation strategies.

Bottom-Up Examination

The bottom-up examination concentrates on the hardware and software implementations of network security by assessing the network as a discrete entity and by assessing the security of individual components. The NVA uses two standards for the adequacy of the network's security: (1) the results of the top-down examination and (2) commonly accepted security practices, as applied to the network environment and the current professional understanding of network threats, vulnerabilities, and countermeasures.

Because most networks are quite extensive and the NVA team alone cannot provide a comprehensive evaluation of the entire network and its devices, it will be necessary to have the supporting infrastructure groups assist in running diagnostic tests to determine the security of each class of network (e.g., routers, bridges, gateways, hosts, servers, and cabling). This assessment identifies concerns regarding the management, operation, and maintenance of the network, including a security analysis of the areas listed in Exhibit 3.

The actual processes for the bottom-up examination are discussed in detail in Chapter 6. This gives the NVA technical team an idea of the items that ISO

17799[1] addresses as a minimum of concern for the area of technical network security. The Generally Accepted System Security Principles (GASSP), NIST Special Publication 800-14, do not specifically address network security. Additional information and guidelines can be obtained by accessing the NIST Web site (csrc.nist.gov/publications/nistpubs/) and reviewing the 800 Series (refer to Appendix D for a list of NIST 800 Series publications).

Network Vulnerability Assessment Methodology

The NVA methodology outlines the steps that security professionals should follow when performing an NVA. This methodology demonstrates a commitment to the requirements of the International Standards for Information Security (ISO 17799) and the CISSP (Certified Information Systems Security Professional) common body of knowledge as criteria for security assessments.

After assignment of the project, the NVA Team Lead meets with the sponsor to review goals and objectives and to ensure that both parties understand the defined scope of the assessment. With this as a starting point, the team then can map out how to approach all the major business units of the organization. It will be necessary to arrange appointments with key people in the network community. Examine what their needs and concerns are, and then draft a report of all the comments that derive from top management and the information technology (IT) department or the service provider.

The review of the enterprise network includes the following basic steps:

- *Phase I:* Data Collection (Pre-NVA Checklist, see Appendix B)
  - Collect and begin review of business objectives, strategic business directions, mission statements, etc.
  - Collect and begin review of existing policies, procedures, standards, applicable regulations, laws, guidelines, circulars, letters, memos, audit comments, etc. Use ISO 17799 Self-Assessment Checklist to determine deficiencies.
- *Phase II:* Interviews, Information Review, and Hands-on Investigation
  - Interview key department representatives and business units.
  - Interview internal customers of the network environment.
  - Collect any documentation (policy, procedures, etc.) that was discovered missing from Phase I.
  - Evaluate the security performance of key hardware, network, and software implementations.
- *Phase III:* Analysis
  - Identify existing concerns and critical security success factors, and analyze possible mitigating circumstances.
  - Identify critical and sensitive data issues and practices.
  - Identify security risks and formulate recommendations for mitigating those risks.
  - Formulate actions to facilitate a successful implementation of the client's security program.

- *Phase IV:* Draft Report
  - Assess the existing security policies and procedures, and make recommendations where appropriate.
  - Evaluate risks implicit in the existing network implementation and make recommendations for improved security practices, where appropriate.
  - Assess the effectiveness of safeguards currently implemented (including firewalls) and make recommendations for improvement, where appropriate.
  - Present the Draft Report to the sponsor and the NVA team for their comments, which will be included in the Final Report.
- *Phase V:* Final Report
  - Provide the Final Report and make a presentation as requested by the sponsor; the Network Vulnerability Assessment Team should be available to answer questions and clarify issues, as needed.

Example Schedule

The NVA cycle starts when the sponsor assigns the project. The five NVA phases generally follow each other sequentially, except for the Analysis phase, which begins soon after the first documents have been received. Note that some phases may overlap each other. Some phases will occur simultaneously and perhaps even repeatedly (e.g., additional interviews or investigation between the Draft Report and Final Report phases, if needed). A tentative schedule is produced by the NVA Lead (and approved by the sponsor). An example of such a schedule is depicted in Exhibit 4.

Team Members

Your investigative team will consist of several people, each of whom understands the overall scope of the NVA and who has specialized skills to perform the following job functions. Some of the team members may serve multiple team functions or share team functions with other team members. All of this depends on the particulars of the client's environment and scope of the assessment. The major job roles in a NVA team include:

- *NVA Lead:* manages the project and serves as liaison to the client
- *Policy Examiner(s):* analyzes security policies and management practices
- *Technical Examiner(s):* analyzes technical aspects of the client's network; there may be several Technical Examiners, each with specialized knowledge, such as UNIX, MVS, NetWare, Win NT server configurations, routers and network architecture, and other technical knowledge specific to the client's environment

You must be sure that the following essential skill and knowledge sets are represented among the NVA team members:

Exhibit 2. ISO 17799 NVA Evaluation Areas

ISO 17799 Section	Description	Group Responsible
3.1.1 Information Security Policy	Develop an Information Security Policy.	Information Security
4.1.1 Management IS Forum	Establish a corporate committee to oversee information security.	IS Steering Committee
4.1.2 Information Security Coordination	Develop and implement an Information Security Organization mission statement.	Information Security
4.2.1 Identification of Risks from Third-Party Access	Implement a process to analyze third party connection risks.	Information Security
4.3.1 Security Requirements in Outsourcing Contracts	Implement standards to address security requirements of the information owners been in a contract between the owners and any outsource organization.	Procurement
5.1.1 Inventory of Assets	Establish an inventory of major assets associated with each information system.	Operations
7.2.1 Equipment Location and Protection	Implement standards to ensure that equipment is located properly to reduce risks of environmental hazards and unauthorized access.	Operations
7.2.2 Power Supplies	Implement procedures for electronic equipment to protect them from power failures and other electrical anomalies.	Operations
7.2.3 Cabling Security	Implement standards to protect power and telecommunications cabling from interception or damage.	Operations/Facilities
7.2.4 Equipment Maintenance	Implement procedures to establish to correctly maintain IT equipment to ensure its continued availability and integrity.	Operations
8.1.2 Operational Change Control	Implement procedures for controlling changes to IT facilities and systems to ensure satisfactory control of all changes to equipment, software, or procedures.	Systems/Information Security
8.2.2 System Acceptance	Implement procedures to establish acceptance criteria for new systems, and that adequate tests have been performed prior to acceptance.	Systems
8.5.1 Network Controls	Implement appropriate standards to ensure the security of data in networks and the protection of connected services from unauthorized access.	Network Administration

Exhibit 2. ISO 17799 NVA Evaluation Areas (Continued)

ISO 17799 Section	Description	Group Responsible
8.7.4 Security of Electronic Mail	Implement standards and user training to reduce the business and security risks associated with electronic mail, to include interception, modification, and errors.	Operations & Network
8.7.5 Security of Electronic Office Systems	Implement a risk analysis process and resultant standards to control business and security risks associated with electronic office systems.	Information Security
8.7.6 Publicly Available Systems	Implement a formal policy to establish an authorization process for information that is to be made publicly available.	Corporate Communications
9.4.1 Policy on Use of Network Services	Implement procedures to ensure that network and computer services that can be accessed by an individual user or from a particular terminal are consistent with business access control policy.	Network
9.4.2 Enforced Path	Implement standards that restrict the route between a user terminal and the computer services that its user is authorized to access.	Network
9.4.3 User Authentication for External Connections	Implement standards to ensure that connections by remote users via public or nonorganization networks are authenticated to prevent unauthorized access to business applications.	Network
9.4.4 Node Authentication	Implement standards to ensure that connections by remote computer systems are authenticated to prevent unauthorized access to a business application.	Network
9.4.5 Remote Diagnostic Port Protection	Implement procedures to control access to diagnostic ports designed for remote use by maintenance engineers.	Network
9.4.6 Network Segregation	Implement standards to have large networks divided into separate domains to mitigate the risk of unauthorized access to existing computer systems that use the network.	Network
9.4.7 Network Connection Control	Implement standards to restrict the connection capability of users, in support of access policy requirements of business applications that extend across organizational boundaries.	Network
9.4.8 Network Routing Control	Implement standards that identify routing controls over shared networks across organizational boundaries to ensure those computer connections and information flows conform to the access policy of business units.	Network

9.4.9 Security in Network Services	Implement standards to capture network providers clearly security attributes of all services used, and use this information to establish the security controls to protect the confidentiality, integrity, and availability of business applications.	Network
9.5.1 Automatic Terminal Identification	Implement standards for automatic terminal identification to authenticate connections to specific locations.	Operations
9.5.2 Terminal Log-on Procedures	Implement procedures for logging into a computer system to minimize the opportunity for unauthorized access.	Operations

Exhibit 3. Areas of Concern and Supporting Departments

ISO 17799 Section	Description	Group Responsible
6.3.1 Reporting of Security Incidents	Implement procedures and standards for formal reporting and incident response action to be taken on receipt of an incident report.	Emergency Response Team (ERT)
6.3.2 Reporting of Security Weaknesses	Implement standards and procedures to ensure that users are aware of the requirement to note and report all observed or suspected security weaknesses in or threats to systems or services.	ERT
6.3.3 Reporting of Software Malfunctions	Implement standards and user training to ensure that users note and report to the proper location any software that does not function correctly.	ERT
8.1.3 Incident Management Procedures	Implement standards and procedures to identify incident management responsibilities and to ensure a quick, effective, orderly response to security incidents.	ERT
8.2.1 Capacity Planning	Implement standards to ensure that capacity requirements are monitored, and future requirements projected, to reduce the risk of system overload.	Systems & Operations
8.3.1 Controls against Malicious Software	Implement standards and user training to ensure that virus detection and prevention measures are adequate.	Operations
8.4.3 Fault Logging	Implement procedures for logging faults reported by users regarding problems with computer or communications systems.	Operations
8.5.1 Network Controls	Implement appropriate standards to ensure the security of data in networks and the protection of connected services from unauthorized access.	Network
9.7.1 Event Logging	Implement standards to have audit trails record exceptions and other security-relevant and that they are maintained to assist in future investigations and in access control monitoring.	Operations
9.7.2 Monitoring System Use	Implement procedures for monitoring system use to ensure that users are only performing processes that have been explicitly authorized.	Operations
9.7.3 Clock Synchronization	Implement standards to ensure computer or communications device clocks are correct and in synchronization.	Operations
9.5.1 Automatic Terminal Identification	Implement standards for automatic terminal identification to authenticate connections to specific locations.	Operations

9.5.5 Use of System Utilities	Implement standards to restrict access to system utility programs that could be used to override system and application controls.	Operations
9.5.8 Limitation of Connection Time	Implement standards to identify the period during which terminals can be connected to sensitive application systems.	Access Control
9.6.2 Isolation of Sensitive Systems	Implement standards to isolate sensitive application systems processing environment.	Operations
10.2.3 Message Authentication	Implement standards to ensure that message authentication is considered for applications that involve the transmission of sensitive data.	Applications
10.3.1 Policy on the Use of Cryptographic Controls	Implement policies and standards on the use of cryptographic controls, including management of encryption keys, and effective implementation.	Asset Classification
10.4.1 Control of Operational Software	Implement standards. Is strict control exercised over the implementation of software on operational systems?	Systems
10.5.1 Change Control Procedures	Implement standards and procedures for formal change control procedures.	Systems
10.5.2 Technical Review of Operating System Changes	Implement procedures to review application systems when changes to the operating systems occur.	Systems
10.5.3 Restrictions on Changes to Software Packages	Implement standards to restrict modifications to vendor-supplied software.	Systems & Applications
10.5.4 Covert Channels and Trojan Code	Implement standards and procedures to avoid covert channels or Trojan codes. These standards and procedures should address, at a minimum, that the organization: buy programs only from a reputable source; buy programs in source code that is verifiable; use only evaluated products; inspect all source code before operational use; control access to, and modification of, installed code; and use trusted staff to work on key systems.	Systems
11.1.1 Business Continuity Management Process	Implement procedures for the development and maintenance of business continuity plans (BCPs) across the organization.	BCP
11.1.5 Testing, Maintaining, and Reassessing Business Continuity Plans	Implement standards to ensure regular testing of the BCPs.	BCP

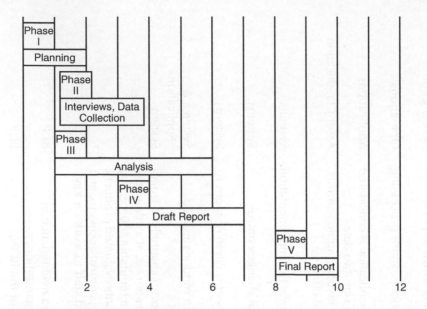

Exhibit 4. NVA Sample Schedule

- ■ Project management skills and knowledge:
  - – Client presentations
  - – Project planning and administration
  - – Effective communication (oral and written)
  - – Leadership
- ■ Policy examiner skills and knowledge:
  - – Research and analysis
  - – Security industry standards (ISO 17799, GASSP)
  - – Threat analysis
  - – Principles of security management
  - – Business continuity and disaster recovery standards
- ■ Technical examiner skills and knowledge:
  - – Client and server OS, NOS, UNIX, Linux hardware devices
  - – Software and hardware configuration management
  - – Reported bugs and security flaws
  - – Network and system testing protocols and devices
  - – Physical plant security
- ■ Other necessary skills and knowledge:
  - – Curiosity and willingness to investigate
  - – People skills: ability to nonthreateningly ask questions and provide suggestions
  - – Strong knowledge of communications technologies, both hardware and software

The NVA Process, Step-by-Step

This section provides details on the phases and sub-tasks involved in performing an NVA, and discusses the essential tasks in each phase and how to do each of the tasks and sub-tasks. Many of the documents referenced in this section can be found in the Appendices section of this book.

Project Initiation

Once the project has been assigned, the project or team lead will have to initiate the steps that follow. Each project requires a project plan as discussed in Chapter 2. At a minimum, the project lead and NVA team will have to ensure that these tasks are conducted.

- The NVA Team is assembled; team roles are tentatively assigned.
- The NVA Team Lead develops detailed project plan.
- Hold a kick-off meeting with the sponsor and the Pre-NVA Checklist (found in Appendix B).
- Project process, client expectations, project calendar established.
- A detailed project plan is approved by the sponsor.

Phase I: Data Collection

The NVA team draws up list of required documents and submits to client liaison (point-of-contact, POC) (see Appendix B for sample documentation list). Once this checklist is completed, the team will do the following:

- Review applicable state and federal laws affecting this particular client.
- Review available documentation; note areas of concern.
- Draw up a list of known bugs and security vulnerabilities to test for in the client environment.

Phase II: Interviews, Information Reviews, and Hands-On Investigation

The steps that the NVA team should perform during this phase of the process inlcude:

- The NVA team defines roles or functions about which it wants to gather information.
- The Team Lead and POC develop an interview schedule.
- The client POC arranges interviews with appropriate client staff members and provides office space for the NVA team
- Appropriate members of the NVA team interview identified appropriate staff members and other identified personnel. *Note:* sufficient and legible notes should be taken to document the information received from the interviews.
- The NVA team (usually) requests additional documents (that were not provided in Phase I).
- The NVA team requests additional interviews, as needed.

- The Team Lead requests facility and network clearance and passwords for team members from the client POC, as required.
- The NVA team tours computing facilities and conducts tests of operating systems, hardware, network devices, and software.
- The NVA team tours facilities and performs physical plant inspection.

Interviews

Interviews are conducted with key infrastructure support personnel and key business units. Interviews are also conducted with other third-party customers of the network environment. These interviews may continue after Phase IV (Draft Report) as issues arise or clarifications are needed.

The people who should be interviewed include those employees who are in charge of:

- System design and architecture
- Support services (customer support, technical support, help desk support)
- System management and administration
- Security policy design
- System installation

The NVA team should try to make the interview as nonthreatening as possible to the employee being interviewed. The interviewee should be informed that an assessment — not an audit — is being conducted. Additionally, the interviewee is not the specific focus of an investigation. It is the objective of the interview to get the interviewee to view this process as an opportunity to share comments regarding security and to make recommendations as to what needs to be changed without fearing any repercussions.

The key subject areas that need to be discussed during the interview process include:

- Who the employee is and his or her relationship to the network
- What data the employee accesses, how this is done, and what applications are made available to the employee, and for what purposes
- What the employee perceives to be critical or sensitive data and resources[2]
- What the employee's understanding is of company security policies and procedures
- What security vulnerabilities the employee is aware of
- What changes or solutions the employee would recommend to improve corporate security practices

Hands-On Investigation

This technical information is gathered from probing the network, evaluating central servers, investigating system and network configurations, and observing network usage. Critical systems and high-risk elements are emphasized in the report, although you should document other findings (i.e., less critical) as thoroughly as is feasible. If you discover any highly critical breaches of security, you should inform the appropriate persons immediately, and suggest appropriate countermeasures. Your hands-on investigation will, at a minimum, cover the following areas:

- Computer operations and telecommunications
- System and network configuration
- Network access and practices

Collect Additional Documents

During this phase you might come across areas not covered in the checklist of documents above. Collect documents for these areas (e.g., company-specific security implementations or policies) from the appropriate business units.

> **Note:** A too rigid adherence to the questions and processes in this manual may lead you to miss essential information. Be ready to pursue an interesting avenue that may provide useful insights into the security policies and practices at the client company. The questions are meant to provide you with guidelines, not to restrict your judgment in pursuing other investigative activities in support of the goals of the NVA.

Phase III: Analysis

The process of analysis actually begins with the acquisition of the first document and only ends in the generation of the Draft Report during Phase IV. Analysis spans most of the NVA process and generates the majority of content in the report. The initial and ongoing analysis shapes and directs further data collection and interviews. In the analysis phase, the objective is to identify threats and vulnerabilities, and make recommendations to mitigate the risks by implementing countermeasures. The ideal result of any analysis is a workable and cost-effective balance among the parts of the risk equation. During this phase, the NVA team will:

- Review, interview, and inspect results and analyze data for security vulnerabilities; identify risks to client's computing assets.
- Evaluate vulnerabilities for possible controls or safeguards that can be applied.

High risk levels may result from threats or vulnerabilities that are severe, or from countermeasures that are weak. The key is to balance the threats and vulnerabilities with affordable countermeasures. It is not possible to achieve an environment in which there are zero threats and zero vulnerabilities, and it is not possible for an organization to achieve low risk without some investment in countermeasures.

Analysis of the previously collected data (from Phase II) can focus on several different areas, both technical and policy related (see Exhibit 5). This

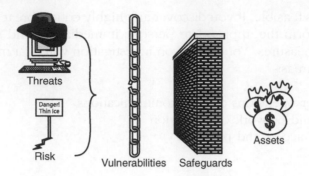

Threats

Danger!
Thin Ice

Risk   Vulnerabilities   Safeguards

Assets

Exhibit 5.   The Risk Equation

section presents explanations of the analysis process in general, analysis within various focal areas, and vulnerability hot-spot checklists for each area under investigation.

Risk Analysis

Practically speaking, evaluating threats and vulnerabilities is best done by trying to ascertain what types of damage can result from the failure of countermeasures. Once these basic investigations are performed, risk analysis looks at ways of dealing with these threats in a cost-effective manner. In fact, the primary goal of risk analysis is to provide data for making informed decisions about cost-effective safeguards. The NVA is not, properly speaking, a risk analysis study, but we do use some of the same assumptions and follow similar protocols in the course of the NVA. A true risk analysis would attempt to assign a risk priority to each threat (as previously discussed) by determining the probability of occurrence and the possible impact. (Note: *Information Security Risk Analysis* is available through CRC Press.)

Determining the damage that can result from the failure of countermeasures is difficult. That is, it is difficult to quantify the potential or probable monetary loss when a company loses intangibles, such as the following:

- *System configurations.* An accurate, up-to-date network map or system configuration list could be a critical resource in the hands of an attacker.
- *Passwords.* What does it mean to have a privileged password compromised? How does an organization value it — at the level of the damage caused?
- *Information loss.* What does it mean to have the Coca-Cola Company lose its secret formula? How does the organization value the damage — at the net worth of the company?
- *Errors.* How could a particular database error affect an organization's business?
- *Integrity.* What does it mean to lack the ability to detect unauthorized deletion, modification, duplication, or forgery of data?
- *CPU cycles and bandwidth.* What does it mean to lose the ability to do some activity because an unauthorized activity is taking place (denial-of-service)?

Determining the actual risk in terms of real potential loss to a particular asset requires a clear understanding of what is sensitive and critical to the enterprise. This is why careful interviewing of staff in Phase II and close collaboration with top management and network administrators throughout the NVA process are so important.

Bear in mind that the analysis needs to meet the business objectives or mission of the enterprise. The more you communicate with the business units and users during the NVA process, the more they will understand the context in which the final recommendations are communicated. In the end, what the sponsor wants to know is how to protect the business and what needs to be done to ensure that the company can recover and continue operations in the event of a critical service interruption.

Threat Analysis

Listed below are the critical areas related to threats and vulnerabilities that you should be sure to cover in your analysis. When you begin, you should use these to guide the inspection and analysis processes. Be sure and familiarize yourself with these issues before you begin Phase II; knowledge of these areas will assist you in gathering the information you need to perform a thorough analysis. Areas of investigation include:

- Application development
- Auditing
- Firewalls
- Organizational suitability
- Personnel
- Physical plant and facilities
- Standards and practices
- Technical safeguards
- Training

Security Policy

A security policy is the basis of any coordinated security effort and provides a framework from which to assess the security practices of the organization. Therefore, it is the starting point for an NVA. If the organization does not currently have a security policy, you will need to assess what is currently being done to provide security and make recommendations about writing a security policy. (Note: *Information Security Policies, Procedures and Standards* is available through Auerbach Publications.)

When analyzing security issues involving the company's security policies, the NVA team should consider the following:

- Does it explicitly state what is and is not permissible (e.g., employees can hold outside jobs, but employees cannot work for a competitor)?
- Does it cover all security-related factors in the company, from network security to physical security to noncompete agreements?

- Is the policy distributed to and understood by the company's workforce?
- Have actions ever been taken as a result of violations of the policy?

Security Handbook

ISO 17799 and industry practice recommend that every organization have a *security handbook* targeted to all employees. This handbook translates the company's security policy into specific practices for its employees, demonstrating how the security policy applies to them.

If the company has a security handbook, the NVA team should consider the following:

- Does it ensure that users can implement the security policy correctly?
- How specific is the security handbook? Does it address issues in generalities, or does it give specific examples?
- Does it show users how the company security policy affects the business objectives or mission?
- Does it make clear the consequences to the employee of not following the security policy?
- Does it give users an understanding of their responsibilities and stress the degree of personal accountability?
- Does it show users how to apply the security policy and procedures in their specific working environment?
- Does it cover security policies for remote users and "on-the-road" staff?
- Does it provide a method for reporting suspected security violations and explicitly support "whistle-blowers"?

It is imperative that employees receive these messages from their security handbook and their managers. The risk of ignorance is employees who are unsure about security and their role in upholding the organization's security practices. Experience shows that employees will assume they can do something rather than that they cannot do something (e.g., download public-domain software).

Standards and Practices

Standards and practices are the means by which a security policy is implemented throughout an organization. They help translate the high-level concepts of the policy into the day-to-day practice.

When assessing the security issues involving standards and procedures, the NVA team should consider the following:

- Does the company have the procedures in place to implement its security policy?
- Do the practices clearly reflect the goals of the security policy and how that policy supports the business objectives or mission of the enterprise?

- Does the company have a procedure for continually evaluating its current systems, security, and practices against new computing implementations and processes?
- Do project managers and senior management support security practices?
- Are the company's practices and standards intrusive? Do they hinder productivity?

Document Handling

Standards and practices should include document handling. Procedures for document creation, storage, backup, archival, retrieval, use, protection, tracking, and disposal need to be specified.

When assessing the security issues involving the document handling process, the NVA team should consider the following:

- Does the company have a reasonable and usable asset classification scheme for enterprise information, both hard copy and online documentation? Asset classification is the process by which an organization categorizes information and implements controls based on its level of sensitivity. Note that it is particularly important that proprietary information is classified as such, and personnel information is classified as confidential with appropriate controls.
- Is confidential material stored in a secure location (locked cabinets for hard copies; directories with limited access for online documents)? U.S. courts have determined that proprietary information (trade secrets) may not be considered proprietary if it can be demonstrated that the information was freely available to all employees.
- Is the classification scheme followed? You should have a copy of the asset classification standards; check to see if you can find sensitive documents left in insecure locations in violation of the stated standards.
- Is confidential material printed in an insecure area? Are printouts left overnight on the printer or in the photocopy machine?
- Are confidential materials disposed of in a wastebasket, rather than a shredder?
- Are confidential materials destroyed properly? Is the removal and destruction of confidential materials monitored by a trusted employee?
- Are backup media in a secure location with monitored access?
- How is the information record inventory managed and controlled?
- How accessible are sensitive documents? Are they easily accessible to those who have the authority to view them?
- Are practices in place that allow detection of unauthorized changes to documents?

Incident Handling

A security incident is commonly defined as any unwanted change in the security status quo of an infrastructure. Examples include a key resource that crashed due to an operating system bug, virus problems in office PCs, or an attack on the infrastructure by a malicious person (an insider or outsider) (*Note: Critical Incident Management* is available through Auerbach Publications.)

When assessing the company's incident handling procedures, the NVA team should consider the following:

- Has the company defined what constitutes a security incident?
- Are procedures in place to follow during a security incident?
- Are standards established on when to pursue an incident?
- Is there a process to determine when to prosecute an incident?
- Has the organization formed a computer incident response team (e.g., CIRT)?
- Are procedures in place to handle public relations during a security event?
- Is the organization actively monitoring the network infrastructure for security violations?

If the enterprise is not prepared for a security event, it is much less likely to recognize when an incident has occurred. For example, if system events are not logged, it may be impossible to recognize a system anomaly that indicates someone is trying to obtain illegitimate access to the system.

Furthermore, if someone has once gained undetected access to the system, the attacker is likely to try again, guessing that because the security hole he or she used to gain access is still available, the original hack went undetected. The probability that the company network will be attacked again while it is still vulnerable is correspondingly higher. Understanding the probability of a security incident and being prepared to deal with one gives the company the opportunity to detect security incidents expeditiously. With incident handling guidelines in place, the organization can control the situation and limit the damage.

Asset Protection Management and Awareness

When assessing the level of protection management and awareness in the network environment, the NVA team should consider the following:

- Have levels of trust been established within and outside the organization? In this case, "trust" can be defined as the ability of the system to perform data actions with integrity, to keep confidential information private, and to perform without interruption. The amount of trust you have in the system is partly a function of the quality of the protection of corporate assets.
- Are there business continuity and technology disaster recovery procedures in place? Have the plans been tested? It is always a good idea to test the procedures; just like fire drills, the results provide useful data about flaws in the disaster recovery process.
- Has the backup media been tested to ensure that they contain retrievable data?
- How is access determined and monitored?

- Is access revoked in a timely manner?
- What incidents have occurred recently? How were they handled?
- What were the employees' reactions to the incident handling?
- Could the incidents reoccur?

Organizational Suitability

When there is a mismatch between an organization's security policy and procedures and its corporate goals and environment, inevitably the security policy will not be honored in practice. If they do not work in that particular environment, they will not be implemented consistently or accurately. Security policy and procedures are only as strong as management's commitment to their practice. When assessing the organizational suitability of a security policy and procedures, the NVA team should consider the following:

- Is senior management openly supportive of the information security program?
- Do managers observe the security policy in their business practices? Employees will value that which their managers and senior management value.
- Are the employees able to perform their duties efficiently and effectively while following security procedures? Highly intrusive security procedures can stifle employee productivity. Either employees will spend more time worrying about following procedures than actually getting the job done, or they will use "short-cuts" to limit the irritation of doing the procedures properly.
- Does the company have the resources to adequately fund and staff its security efforts? For example, if the organization has a policy that states that no public-domain software can be run before a system administrator clears it, does the organization have the employees to support this? If the resources do not exist, then the result is that employees will run unapproved software, in contravention of the established policy.
- Does the enterprise enforce security policy throughout the organization? This goes along with clearly visible management support. If employees perceive that management support for security enforcement is weak, they will not be motivated to observe security practices.

Personnel Issues

An organization's security policy and procedures should be followed by all categories of staff (e.g., full- and part-time employees, contractors, temps, and interns). To work effectively, employees need to know what is expected of them and have the management and resource support they need to do their jobs.

When assessing the security issues involving employees, the NVA team should consider the following:

- Are there enough employees to support current business goals? Security errors and "short-cuts" are more likely to occur in highly stressed environments. If people are under pressure to produce under tight deadlines, careful observance of security practices is likely to be the first casualty.
- Do employees and project managers know their roles and responsibilities? Are current employees performing necessary and sufficient tasks, or could any of their tasks be considered wasteful? Ensuring that only necessary jobs are being done helps employees focus on keeping the essentials well organized. Ensuring that a sufficient job is being done ensures that time is not wasted in correcting problems caused by incomplete solutions. Efforts past sufficiency in a resource-poor environment are wasteful.
- Are employees performing their tasks efficiently and effectively? Ensuring that work is efficiently and effectively performed saves time and energy, allowing employees to complete tasks to a sufficient performance level.
- Are employees properly trained? Do they have the necessary expertise to implement security practices identified by the assessment process? Employees cannot implement that which they do not understand. Also, the organization needs to be sure that technology expertise is not concentrated in any single employee. What happens if key employees are disabled or unavailable? It is a good idea to spread critical knowledge around so that the loss of one critical employee does not precipitate a security incident.
- Does the organization need to acquire additional security expertise? Can current employees acquire additional expertise from training? From an employee skill assessment, the organization can determine where its employees lack qualifications and experience. Increased security may require additional, specialized expertise, which may be obtained by training employees.
- Does the organization need to hire outside expertise (consultant)? What are the security issues associated with outsourcing? Before adding outside expertise, the organization should evaluate the risks associated with outsourcing such activities.
- Does the organization handle employee terminations in such a way that data and physical security are maintained? Human resources procedures for employee termination need to be documented. For example, system administrators need to be formally notified by HR in a timely manner when someone leaves the company. System administrators need to know that employees and contractors are legitimate and what level of access they should have to company information.

Physical Plant and Facilities

The security of company equipment and facilities is just as important as the security of the network infrastructure. Inadequate physical security may allow theft or sabotage of information, and compromise the network. Once the network is compromised, the expectation of trust has been violated.

When assessing physical and facility security, the NVA team should consider the following:

- How is access to the buildings and computing facilities controlled?
- Who and how many have access to computing facilities? Computing facilities should be accessible to only staff members who have a demonstrated need for access. Automatic doors can be a security risk because they often close slowly, allowing "tailgaters" to gain access. Movement sensors that unlock doors also represent a risk.
- How is after-hours access controlled? Who has access to the building after hours?
- Are systems and other hardware adequately protected from theft?
- Are systems and hardware adequately protected from physical tampering? For example, are critical systems or communications links adequately protected? All the security employed across a network will be useless if an intruder can get at the network cabling or connections and sabotage them.
- How is trash disposed of? Are the members of the cleaning crew bonded?
- Are packages checked when carried into or out of the facilities?
- Does the security policy conflict with the corporate culture? If the organization reposes complete confidence in its employees, then certain security practices may not be acceptable. For example, it may not be "culturally" possible to monitor building access after hours, although it is certainly technically feasible.

After-Hours Review

Part of assessing physical security includes an after-hours review. The purpose of this review is to see how well security is implemented during off-hours. Even if security is enforced during working hours, the organization is at risk if sensitive or critical information and systems are accessible after hours.

The NVA team should consider the following:

- Is confidential information found in publicly accessible dumpsters? Yes, you will need to do some "dumpster-diving" to determine the answer to this question. You can also check wastebaskets after people have left but before the cleaning crew has arrived.
- Is confidential information left visible in unlocked offices and work areas?
- Does the cleaning crew have access to locked offices?
- Are workstations and servers left unlocked? Does the cleaning crew have access?
- Are keys left in accessible areas? Are passwords posted visibly?
- Is the building completely locked?
- What procedures does the cleaning crew follow (e.g., do they prop doors open)?

Training

The risk of not providing appropriate training for all employees is employees believing they have all the skills and knowledge necessary to perform their jobs. Employees may have the necessary job skills but they can be ignorant of the security procedures they are expected to follow. Training translates the policy and procedures given in the corporate security handbook and makes them applicable to each employee's job functions.

When assessing the security training at an organization, the NVA team should consider the following:

- Do employees know the business direction and goals?
- Do employees receive security-related training specific to their responsibilities?
- Are employees receiving both positive and negative feedback related to security on their performance evaluations?
- Are employees aware of the security-related risks of their jobs?
- Are system administrators given additional security training specific to their jobs? Security-specific training will make system administrators aware of new developments in security, new threats that emerge, and the technical advances that give hackers new methods for breaching an organization's security.

Auditing and Oversight

Security controls must be managed, tested, and enforced once they are in place. When assessing the oversight of the company's security policy and procedures, the NVA team should consider the following:

- Who is responsible for performing security audits? This could be a political "hot potato." Most organizations have an internal audit role or department. It makes sense that security auditing should be a responsibility of this group, but it does not always happen that way. Regardless of who is doing the auditing, be sure to evaluate whether that person(s) has the training to perform an adequate security audit. The process and responsibilities of the security audit function should be documented. Approach this issue with caution. Auditors know their job and perform it very well. Make sure that this topic is handled correctly.
- Are the security policy and procedures routinely tested? Are audits performed on a regular basis?
- Are exceptions to the security policy justified and documented?
- Are reporting mechanisms in place on the systems (e.g., system logging, monitoring, and assessment tools)?
- Who controls these and the data reported by them?
- Is the data stored in a secure location? How often are the logs reviewed?
- Are appropriate system, machine, and user parameters checked (configuration, management, file system, version numbers, traffic, etc.)?
- Are errors and failures tracked? Are anomalies defined and flagged?
- Are recurrences of these errors and failures prevented?
- When operator or user error or oversight is detected, is appropriate training or disciplinary action taken?

- Is a security incident response capability alerted when a security incident occurs?
- Who reviews the audit results?

Application Design, Development, Deployment, and Management

It is recommended that all organizations formalize their application development process, which includes architecture, design, implementation, testing, deployment, and security issues.

When assessing the security issues involving the application development process, the NVA team should consider the following:

- Is testing performed in an isolated environment?
- Is there a documented promotion-to-production procedure in place?
- How is the deployment of new applications approached? Is it phased into the production environment?
- How is data management handled? Is the data master stored securely?
- How is labeled data processed, transported, stored, and disposed of? The risk of not examining and securing separate steps of the application development process leaves the organization vulnerable to attack from within by disgruntled employees.

Technical Safeguards

Technical safeguards enforce security policy and procedures throughout the network infrastructure. The NVA team should assess the organization's technical safeguards by network type (e.g., LANs and WANs), network connections (e.g., bridges, routers, and gateways), and platform (e.g., desktop systems, file servers, and application servers). The assessment of technical safeguards makes up the greater part of the NVA.

When assessing the technical safeguards of the network infrastructure, the NVA team should consider the following:

- How is the network partitioned?
- How are desktop platforms secured?
- How are host systems and servers, as well as application servers, secured? Is the security commensurate with the trust level and risk?
- Are passwords and accounts shared? Are passwords managed securely?
- Are there unsecured user accounts in use (e.g., guest)?
- Is network management robust? Do network and system administrators have adequate experience and training to implement security correctly?
- What reporting mechanisms are used? Who reviews the reports?
- Are permissions set securely? How are permissions determined?
- Are administrators using the appropriate tools to perform their jobs?
- Is there a complete network diagram available? How current is it?
- How is access controlled?

- What network controls are being used?
- How is connectivity controlled?
- How is remote access controlled?
- Are critical systems protected with appropriate access controls?
- What vulnerabilities are inherent (known bugs) in the systems and applications in use?
- Have all systems and applications been brought up-to-date with appropriate patches and fixes (against known bugs and vulnerabilities)?
- Are critical systems adequately protected (e.g., are they backed up or replicated)? Are the backup media securely stored?
- What security auditing and assessing is being performed?
- How are backups scheduled and implemented?
- Is the data stored on laptops subject to more stringent security controls?

Firewalls

Assessing the security of a firewall begins with the organization's network security policy, which defines exactly what protocols are allowed to penetrate a security perimeter and under what conditions those penetrations are allowed. If such a policy does not exist, the NVA team should examine the internal infrastructure and its requirements and then report its determination of what this policy might be like and what it would need to contain.

When assessing the security of an organization's firewall, the NVA team should consider the following:

- What protocols are allowed to go across the firewall, and under what conditions? Typically, a common rule is used, such as: everything not explicitly disallowed is allowed. However, industry experts and NIST Special Publication 800-41 "Guidelines on Firewalls and Firewall Policy" recommend using the opposite of this rule by explicitly identifying connectivity: everything not explicitly allowed is disallowed.
- Is the approach used appropriate, given the economics of the organization, administration requirements, security control requirements, and any other factors the company has specified?
- Are the firewall and its role sufficient for the task of securing the organization from outside penetration?
- What products are used to implement the firewall? Are the firewalls the most effective for this operating environment? Have the products been rigorously tested in this environment?
- How is the firewall administered? Are audit logs maintained and reviewed?
- What services are offered across the firewall? How can existing services be operated better? Are there other services that can be offered to meet corporate goals?
- What is the internal structure of the network? What is the network construction of the firewall? Where is it located in the network? How is the connection made and administered?
- What practices exist to apply patches as soon as they become available?

Risk Aversion

Network vulnerability assessment and the formation of security-related plans do not result in risk-free systems. Perfect security and integrity are unattainable. People build and operate the technology used in systems; the inevitable result is errors and oversights. An organization cannot even approach zero risk; rather, it needs to find the balance between acceptable cost and acceptable risk that has been defined as practical and appropriate for this organization to meet its business needs.

Business Impact Analysis (BIA)

The principal objective of the business impact analysis (BIA) is to determine the effect of mission-critical information system failures on the viability and operations of enterprise core business processes. Using a standard assessment methodology, the enterprise should have a process in place to determine the relative criticality of all applications, systems, or other assets. This process should be employed as part of the normal business process and its results should be reviewed as part of the NVA. Once the critical resources are scored, the organization can then identify appropriate controls to ensure that the business continues to meet its business objectives or mission.

Direct Costs

Direct costs are out-of-pocket expenses. Monetary cost is the outright replacement cost of the asset. Insurance is used to balance such potential asset losses.

Legal liability is a value assigned by the actual mechanisms of insurance carriers or assessments made by the legal department of an organization. Injuries are accounted for with measurements that are similar to those of legal liability, for example, workers compensation. Loss of life and limb are handled in the same way as legal liability and injuries.

Indirect Costs

Indirect costs are difficult to quantify because evaluating the basis for these losses is a subjective effort. One of the most devastating losses of this type is loss of trust. The importance of being able to trust the infrastructure should not be underestimated. Loss of the ability to trust an infrastructure is disruptive. Even more disturbing is having to trust an infrastructure that an organization suspects has been compromised.

Loss of trust is related to the loss of system, network, or data integrity. Technical report MTR-8201 (Trusted Computer Systems Glossary, The Mitre Corporation, March 1987) defines integrity as "the assurance, under all conditions, that a system will reflect the logical correctness and reliability of the operating system; the logical completeness of the hardware and software that implement the protection mechanisms; and the consistency of data structures and the accuracy of the stored data." People generally trust their systems, networks, and data unthinkingly and assume that they are producing correct results. Proving that integrity has been maintained is difficult because you are trying to prove a negative.

Loss of personal privacy is a subset of trust — if an organization cannot trust the infrastructure, it does not know who is looking at its data.[3] In an employer–employee relationship, privacy is usually not an issue because most organizations claim rights to employee data and communications. However, issues of privacy and loss of privacy can arise. Supervisors who abuse their authority to look at users' electronic mail may be violating their employees' privacy, depending on the organization and the rules that have been established for the use of its communications. This underscores the importance of clearly articulate personnel policies and procedures.

Opportunity Costs

Opportunity cost is the most difficult to quantify and the least understood result of risk management. One of the organization's most important assets is its infrastructure. It is the combined actions of the people, computing capability, networks, and data of an organization's infrastructure that enables it to take advantage of opportunities that arise. Reducing the opportunity costs associated with an infrastructure means that the infrastructure should be protected, so that its resources are available when needed.

Phase IV: Draft Report

The results of your investigations and analysis should be documented in a Draft Report. The sponsor will review this report; and if any major changes or further investigations are required, a second draft can be generated and reviewed again. Management must understand and agree to all of the analysis before the Final Report and presentation (if required) are generated. Nothing in the Final Report should come as a surprise to the sponsor.

The Draft Report template is available in the PSO directory on the admin-server, and a sample Draft Report (for the Bogus Corporation) is included in Chapter 7 and Appendix C of this book. Rather than duplicate the entire report here, you can review the report attached in Chapter 7 and Appendix C. Below are descriptions, comments, and guidelines for each of the main report sections.

Title Page

Using the sample title page found in Appendix C, ensure that the company name and sponsor are correctly entered.

Information Classification

The information contained in a vulnerability assessment is normally classified as Confidential, and the sponsor is normally identified as the Owner.

Table of Contents

Refer to the sample report for a Table of Contents.

Executive Summary

This section should be no longer than two pages. It introduces the assessment methodology, overviews the critical findings, and summarizes the recommendations. This section should be generated last, after all the following sections have been completed (or at least clearly outlined). Bear in mind that busy executives will unlikely read much beyond these two pages, so they must be clear and concise, and convey the recommendations accurately and completely.

Methodology Overview

The Overview introduces the tour philosophy and approach to the NVA. It defines terms and outlines methodology, both in general and specifically, for the client. While some of the material will be "boiler-plate" as noted in the example, you need to read it carefully to make sure that all the information is appropriate for this particular NVA. The sources for making specific comments are company documentation, Statement of Work for the NVA, and results of the initial planning meetings with client management.

Security Profile

This section contains a basic profile of the client company's security environment. This information is based on documents and data collected during Phase I and Phase II of the assessment process. This includes background information on the network and its environment, a list of company documents (policy, procedures, and network topology), summaries of interview results, and reports from the actual hands-on investigation of the company's environment. Relevant company documents are collected together in the Appendices. The determination of which company documents should be included is somewhat difficult, especially because you will be reviewing, in some cases, a mass of information. Security-related documents should be included but other documents, unless they specifically cite an area of concern, should not.

The goal of this section is to summarize the client's network environment and existing security infrastructure, in preparation for the detailed identification of vulnerabilities.

Analysis

This section details vulnerabilities and risks discovered in the organization's environment (Phase III: Analysis). This analysis is divided into functional areas of policy, management, architecture, and safeguards. Emphasis is placed on the impact that these problems, vulnerabilities, and unmitigated risks have (or could have) on the organization's ability to do business. In addition to vulnerability identification and risk evaluation, the NVA team also provides recommendations to mitigate the risks. These recommendations (software, hardware, policy, and practice) should be nonjudgmental. Suggested products are usually included in the Appendices.

Example subsections are provided in the Draft Report template, and completed examples are available in the Sample report for the Bogus Corporation (see the Appendices). You may find that other subsections need to be included for the particular client.

Resources for completing your Analysis section will include all of the profile reports (documents, interviews, and hands-on investigation) known vulnerabilities reports and bulletins (see Appendices), online bug tracking information and known threats (see Appendices), follow-up interviews, and additional site visits, if they occur.

Because this is the largest section of the report, and requires the most amount of work, it is best divided among the appropriate NVA team members. For example, those NVA team members with strong skill sets in UNIX controls and NT security should generate the Analysis sections pertaining to those systems, NVA team members with a strong skill set in security policy analysis should be responsible for generating that subsection of Analysis, and so on.

It is important to remember that an NVA is *not* a security audit. The level of detail in technical analysis (i.e., system configuration, account permissions) should remain fairly high level and point out only the most critical issues. It should be made clear to the sponsor that this is *not* an audit, but it does provide a foundation of and justification for performing an audit.

Conclusions

This section reviews the nonjudgmental recommendations for minimizing vulnerabilities and mitigating risks detailed in the previous section (Analysis). These recommendations are ranked in order of their critical importance. This section concludes with a summary table listing all recommendations in order of importance (risk levels).

This section is essentially a summary of the previous section with emphasis placed on recommended mitigation and countermeasures. The subsections are limited to the areas of security that most critically need attention. The recommendations offered in the Executive Summary should map to the recommendations in this summary.

Summary Table of Risks

This table presents brief summaries of all the reported vulnerabilities, associated risk, and your recommendations in a conveniently organized table. These items are organized into the three main sections of risk: high, medium, and low. Within each risk section, the items are roughly organized in order of criticality, with the item at the top of each category being the most important.

Appendices

Each appendix is a freestanding document with its own page numbering. The Appendices should be prefaced with a complete list of the attached Appendices. The contents of the Appendices should be reflected in the Draft Report Table of Contents. Each appendix should be referenced in the text of the Draft Report, cited as follows:

The Appendices should contain, at a minimum, the following documents:

- Bogus Corporation Documentation Checklist
- Bogus Corporation Security Policy and Procedures
- Bogus Corporation Personnel Policies and Procedures
- Bogus Corporation Employee Security Training Materials
- Bogus Corporation Network Architecture/Network Topology
- Firewall Survey
- Information Classification
- Network Security Controls
- Known Vulnerabilities for Customer Systems
- Recommended Products
- Incident Handling Guidelines
- Information Security Reference Guide (ISRG)

To limit the size of this report, the appendix items should only contain document sections that are directly relevant to the NVA. For example, if the company offers a security class as part of its employee education program, then only the relevant sections of the class catalog need be included (not the entire class-offering catalog).

Document Collation

The Team Lead should designate a central collection point for all of the documentation as it is produced or assembled. This collection point could be either a designated person or a designated location (such as a directory with limited access on the server). The Team Lead can take on the responsibility for putting the report together, or he can delegate that task to an assigned documentation person. In either case, all the information that has been gathered by the team needs to be reviewed for completeness, integrated into the report, checked for accuracy and contradictions, and edited for grammatical correctness and rhetorical suitability. At some point, all members of the team should proofread the Draft Report.

Sponsor Review of the Draft Report

Once completed, the Team Lead submits the Draft Report to the sponsor, usually to the group that has contracted for the NVA. This group reviews the Draft Report and usually meets with the Team Lead to discuss the findings. The Team Lead works with the sponsor to make sure that they understand the report, the results, and the recommendations.

This part of the NVA usually requires tact and patience. Inevitably, some of the sponsor reviewers will see parts of the Draft Report as a direct reflection of their competence or job performance. It may be difficult to protect the integrity of your findings without offending some of the reviewers. Negotiate as much as you can, because it is important that everyone understand that the findings are intended to provide guidelines for improved security for the company, not to review anyone's performance.

Phase V: Final Report and Presentation

The Team Lead gathers the sponsor's comments and integrates them into the Final Report. The Final Report is then generated; a limited number of copies should be made. The Final Report follows the same format as the Draft Report. Each copy should be clearly numbered; the Team Lead will assign each numbered copy to a particular person and maintain a list of who gets which copy.

The NVA team should keep a backup copy of the Final Report. All other copies of the report are to be given to the sponsor, who has been identified as the Owner. This individual is responsible for authorizing access to the report based on the business needs of the asset classification policy.

The Team Lead is responsible for ensuring that all other materials relating to this NVA are destroyed or deleted.

The Team Lead delivers the Final Report to the sponsor. The POC should set up a meeting between the Team Lead and senior management to review the findings of the Final Report. The Team Lead (or appropriate NVA team members) will put together a presentation (i.e., PowerPoint) summarizing the NVA methodology and goals, the findings, and the recommendations. The Team Lead should be prepared to discuss strategies for implementing the findings, but he should be careful not to exceed the scope of the NVA.

In summary, the presentation of the Final Report should cover the following:

- Reintroduce the NVA process
- Explain what the team did
- Present the findings
- Provide general recommendations
- Provide specific recommendations
- Wrap up with questions and answers

Post Project

As with all projects, a Lessons Learned meeting with the NVA team can provide valuable insight into the NVA process, the strengths and weaknesses of the methodology, and the areas where we need to gain more expertise. The Team Lead is responsible for convening this meeting, documenting the results, and ensuring that the results are incorporated into the methodology and NVA materials.

Summary

To be successful, the NVA team will have to identify what network security concerns have the highest priority. This will allow the team to focus on those threats and risks that can cause the enterprise the most damage. Understanding that the security concerns include personnel and physical, as well as technical issues, will ensure the most comprehensive assessment prospect.

Establishing a team that represents the enterprise will also add to the creditability of the assessment results. Using enterprise personnel will ensure that those individuals with the most intimate knowledge of how the network works and how it is supposed to work will have input into the report. Be sure to include representatives from the user community. Some of the best and most knowledgeable network users come from the business units.

Use all of the resources available to plot what threats will be addressed. Do your research to gather significant issues and then prioritize these risks based on the probability of occurrence and impact to the enterprise or network. Concentrate on those issues that will bring the biggest impact to your organization. Use your team to identify additional items and measure their specific impact.

Developing a checklist will assist the NVA team in ensuring that basic security controls are examined. Do not just use the checklist. Listen and ask questions and be ready to include additional information in the examination process.

An NVA can take a considerable amount of time to complete. Divide the total mission into manageable chunks and then begin the process. Complete one phase before moving on to the next. Be sure to get support from the infrastructure groups; this will make the task easier. Remember that it is not *your* NVA, it is the *organization's* NVA.

Notes

1. The International Organization for Standardization (ISO) and the International Electrotechnical Commission (IEC) form a specialized system on worldwide standardization. National bodies that are members of ISO and IEC participate in the development of international standards through technical committees. The United States through the American National Standards Institute (ANSI) is the secretariat. Twenty-four other nations have participant status and 40 other nations are observers. National bodies that are members of ISO and IEC, like ANSI, participate in the development of international standards through technical committees. The draft standards are circulated to the national bodies for voting. Publication as an international standard requires approval by at least 75 percent of the national bodies casting a vote. ISO 17799 was adopted through this process in December 2001. A copy of the ISO 17799 can be obtained by accessing the URL www.iso17799.net. The cost of the document is approximately $140.
2. Critical data is that data the absence or misuse of which will cause the organizational entity to fail or incur serious loss. Sensitive data is that which, if r eleased or destroyed, would cause serious problems or embarrassment to the organization.
3. Personal privacy, within the context of an organization's infrastructure, is a matter of policy and can have little to do with people's rights outside an organization.

Chapter 5

Policy Review (Top-Down) Methodology

The cornerstones of effective information security programs are well-written policy statements. This is the wellspring of all other directives, standards, procedures, guidelines, and other supporting documents. As with any assessment process, it is important to ensure that policies establish the direction management wants to go with regard to security. The top-down portion of the network vulnerability assessment (NVA) looks at the policies requested in the Pre-NVA Checklist (see Appendix B).

The top-down review will assess policies in two ways:

1. Do they exist?
2. If so, how good is the content?

This chapter briefly examines what makes a good policy statement. For an in-depth discussion on information security policies, refer to the *Information Security Policies, Procedures, and Standards* by T.R. Peltier (Auerbach Publications, 2001). We will use portions of that book here and will rely on ISO 17799 to identify what policies are necessary and what their content should cover.

Definitions

Policy

A policy is a high-level statement of enterprise beliefs, goals, and objectives and the general means for their attainment for a specified subject area. A policy should be brief (which is highly recommended) and set at a high level.

General Program Policy

A general program policy sets the strategic directions of the enterprise for global behavior and assigns resources for its implementation. This includes such topics as information management, conflict of interest, employee standards of conduct, and general security measures.

Topic-Specific Policy

Topic-specific policy addresses specific issues of concern to the organization. Topic-specific policies might include e-mail usage, Internet usage, phone usage, physical security, application development, system maintenance, and network security.

System- or Application-Specific Policy

System- or application-specific policies focus on decisions taken by management to protect a particular application or system. System- or application-specific policy might include controls established for the financial management system, accounts payable, business expense forms, employee appraisal, and order inventory.

Policy Contents

When reviewing policies, it will be necessary to remember that there are three general types of policies:

1. *General or global policies.* These are high-level policy statements that define the intent of a specific topic and its scope within the organization. It also assigns responsibilities for implementation and compliance with the policy. Typical information security general or global policies include:
   - Information security policy
   - Information classification policy
   - Business continuity planning
2. *Topic-specific policies.* Key component areas of the information technology and information security areas are addressed in topic-specific policies. Unlike the general or global policies, the topic-specific policies narrow the focus to one issue at a time. Typical subjects for topic-specific policies include:
   - Physical security
   - Equipment security
   - Network access controls
   - Media disposal
   - User access
   - Technology disaster recovery plan

3. *System- and application-specific policies.* These policies focus on one specific system or application. As the construction of security architecture for an organization takes shape, the final element will be the translation of program and topic-specific policies to the application and system level. Typical subjects for application-specific policies include:
   - E-mail usage
   - Internet usage
   - Anti-virus programs

The components of a program policy should include:

- *Topic.* The topic portion of the policy normally defines the goals of the program. When discussing information, most program policies concentrate on protecting the confidentiality, integrity, availability, and authenticity of the information resources. Additionally, it will attempt to establish that information is an item of value to the enterprise and, as such, must be protected from unauthorized access, modification, disclosure, and destruction, whether accidental or deliberate.
- *Scope.* The scope is a way to broaden or narrow the topic, such as "all information wherever stored and however generated." This could expand the topic on information security, whereas a statement such as "computer-generated data only" would sharply narrow the topic scope. The scope statement can also broaden or narrow the audience affected by the policy. For example, the statement "the policy is intended for all employees" pretty much takes in all the people working for the enterprise, whereas "personnel with access to top-secret information" would limit the audience.
- *Responsibilities.* Typically, this section of the policy identifies who is responsible for what actions. The identification is done using job titles, not actual names. For a policy on information classification, the roles can be described as owner, custodian, and user. To be correct, ensure that every policy states what individual or groups of people are responsible for what action.
  - *Compliance.* A better term might be *noncompliance.* The policy will generally discuss two issues regarding compliance: What actions occur when an individual is found to be in noncompliance with the policy
  - What actions the business unit must take when found in a noncompliant situation

When critiquing a policy, remember to look for the four key elements:

1. Topic
2. Scope
3. Responsibilities
4. Compliance

Contents

ISO 17799 has established a set of guidelines for policy content. The NVA top-down policy reviewer should be familiar with these guidelines, as well as those discussed in the NIST Special Publication 800-12, "An Introduction to Computer Security."

The Information Security Policy should be approved by management, published, and communicated, as appropriate, to all employees. It should state management commitment and set out the organization's approach to managing information security. As a minimum, the following material should be included:

- A definition of information security
- A statement of management intent, supporting the goals and principles of information security
- A definition of general and specific responsibilities
- References to documentation that may support the policy

The Asset Classification Policy is developed to maintain appropriate protection of organizational assets. All major information assets should be accounted for and have Owners identified. Accountability for assets (which include information records, transactions, applications, network segments, etc.) is the responsibility for implementing controls is assigned to the Owner, with a Custodian responsible for implementing those controls.

Business continuity planning (BCP) and technology disaster recovery planning (DRP) are the next policies that need to be reviewed. The NIST Special Publication 800-34, "Contingency Planning Guide for Information Technology Systems," is available at the NIST Web site (crcs.nist/gov/publications/nistpubs/) and can provide the policy reviewer with the basic requirements needed in a general policy regarding BCP and technology DRP

For topic-specific policies, the areas listed in Exhibit 1 should be addressed and critiqued.

Review Elements

The written policy should clear up confusion, not generate new problems. When preparing a document for a specific audience, remember that the writer will not have the luxury to sit down with each reader and explain what each item means and how it impacts the user's daily assignments. Know the audience for whom the policies are being developed. Remember the reading and comprehension level of the average employee. When writing the policy, remember the "5 Ws of Journalism 101":

1. *What:* what is to be protected (the topic)
2. *Who:* who is responsible (responsibilities)
3. *Where:* where within the organization does the policy reach (scope)
4. *How:* how compliance will be monitored (compliance)
5. *When:* when does the policy take effect
6. *Why:* why the policy was developed

Exhibit 1. Topic-Specific Policies

ISO 17799	Topic-Specific Policy	Description
8.1.3	Incident Management Procedures	Implement standards and procedures to identify incident management responsibilities and to ensure a quick, effective, orderly response to security incidents.
8.2.2	System Acceptance	Implement procedures to establish acceptance criteria for new systems, and that adequate tests have been performed prior to acceptance.
8.3	Protection from Malicious Software	Implement anti-virus software
8.4.2	Operator Logs	Implement standards and procedures so that computer operators are required to maintain a log of all work performed.
8.5.1	Network Controls	Implement appropriate standards to ensure the security of data in networks and the protection of connected services from unauthorized access.
8.7.4	Security of Electronic Mail	Implement standards and user training to reduce the business and security risks associated with electronic mail, to include interception, modification, and errors.
8.7.5	Security of Electronic Office Systems	Implement a risk analysis process and resultant standards to control business and security risks associated with electronic office systems.
8.7.6	Publicly Available Systems	Implement a formal policy to establish an authorization process for information that is to be made publicly available.
9.1.1	Access Control Policy	Implement a risk analysis process to gather business requirements to document access control levels.
9.4.1	Use of Network Services	Implement procedures to ensure that network and computer services that can be accessed by an individual user or from a particular terminal are consistent with business access control policy.
9.4.2	Enforced Path	Implement standards that restrict the route between a user terminal and the computer services that its user is authorized to access.
9.4.3	User Authentication for External Connections	Implement standards to ensure that connections by remote users via public or nonorganization networks are authenticated to prevent unauthorized access to business applications.
9.4.4	Node Authentication	Implement standards to ensure that connections by remote computer systems are authenticated to prevent unauthorized access to a business application.
9.4.5	Remote Diagnostic Port Protection	Implement procedures to control access to diagnostic ports designed for remote use by maintenance engineers.

Exhibit 1.   Topic-Specific Policies (Continued)

ISO 17799	Topic-Specific Policy	Description
9.4.6	Network Segregation	Implement standards to have large networks divided into separate domains to mitigate the risk of unauthorized access to existing computer systems that use the network.
9.4.7	Network Connection Control	Implement standards to restrict the connection capability of users, in support of access policy requirements of business applications that extend across organizational boundaries.
9.4.8	Network Routing Control	Implement standards that identify routing controls over shared networks across organizational boundaries to ensure those computer connections and information flows conform to the access policy of business units.
9.4.9	Security in Network Services	Implement standards to clearly capture network providers' security attributes of all services used, and use this information to establish the security controls to protect the confidentiality, integrity, and availability of business applications.
9.7.1	Event Logging	Implement standards to have audit trails record exceptions and other security-relevant events, and that they are maintained to assist in future investigations and in access control monitoring.
9.7.2	Monitoring System Use	Implement procedures for monitoring system use to ensure that users are only performing processes that have been explicitly authorized.
9.7.3	Clock Synchronization	Implement standards to ensure that computer or communications device clocks are correct and in synchronization.
10.2.3	Message Authentication	Implement standards to ensure that message authentication is considered for applications that involve the transmission of sensitive data.
10.3.1	Use of Cryptographic Controls	Implement policies and standards on the use of cryptographic controls, including management of encryption keys, and effective implementation.
10.4.1	Control of Operational Software	Implement standards. Strict control should be exercised over the implementation of software on operational systems.
10.5.1	Change Control Procedures	Implement standards and procedures for a formal change control procedure.
10.5.2	Technical Review of Operating System Changes	Implement procedures to review application systems when changes to the operating systems occur.
10.5.3	Restrictions on Changes to Software Packages	Implement standards to restrict modifications to vendor-supplied software.

Items 5 (when) and 6 (why) are not usually considered part of the policy text. *When* a policy is in effect it is normally addressed in the transmittal document. When the policy is published, there is a document that goes with the policy that explains *why* the policy was developed and *when* it takes effect. Policies should not contain explanations as to why they were developed or a compliance date.

When assessing the policies, procedures, and standards that support the network environment, it is most important that there be some written and published documentation. Look to see what is there. Read the documents and then, during your interviews, ask the interviewees how they interpret the policy. Use this information and the resources discussed in this chapter and the previous chapter.

Summary

The review of supporting documentation will allow the bottom-up team to set expectations on what it should see in the network. If policies, standards, or procedures are missing, it will be necessary to identify which ones they are. Additionally, if these documents exist but are outdated or poorly written, it will be necessary to report this fact along with a recommendation to correct the problem.

Chapter 6

Technical (Bottom-Up) Methodology

The goal of this six-step process is to maximize the time spent during the technical phases of a network vulnerability assessment (NVA). The hope for the process is that it will give anyone running an NVA the most "bang for the buck." Each of the steps in the model builds on the previous steps. While it is possible to skip steps, it will often result in a less efficient NVA.

One key point about the technical vulnerability assessment model is that once you have completed Step 3, you then build a "Chinese wall" and do not draw upon information collected in the three previous steps. In this regard, it allows you to operate much closer to how an actual intruder would operate than what might be thought of in a traditional technical network vulnerability assessment.

Here is the six-step process:

Step 1: Site survey
Step 2: Develop a test plan
Step 3: Build the toolkit
Step 4: Conduct the assessment
Step 5: Analysis
Step 6: Documentation

Exhibit 1. Pre-Vulnerability Assessment Questionnaire

Date: 10/30/02
Client: ACME Corp.
Client Address: Michigan
Consultant Name: Rosalie Merpi

1. Do you have any security-related policies and standards?
2. If so, do you want us to review them?
3. Do you want us to perform a review of the physical security of your servers and network infrastructure?
4. How many Internet domains do you have?
5. How many Internet hosts do you have?
6. Do you want us to map your Internet presence? Otherwise, can you provide us with a detailed diagram of your Internet presence, including addresses, host OS types, and software in use on the hosts? We will also need addresses in use on both sides of the hosts if they connect to both the Internet and the internal network.
7. Do you want us to review the security of your routers and hubs?
8. If so, how many routers and hubs exist on your network?
9. Do you want us to perform a security review of the workstations on the network?
10. If so, what operating systems are the workstations running?
11. If so, how many workstations would you like tested?
12. Our review will assess five or less servers of each type (NT, UNIX, and Novell); do you want us to review more than that?
13. If so, how many of each?
14. Do you want denial-of-service testing to be conducted? This testing can have adverse effects on the systems tested. We can arrange to do this test during non-production hours.
15. Do you want us to perform a modem scan of your analog phone lines?
16. What kind of RAS server are you using, and how many modems are used?
17. Do you want us to travel to other sites to perform assessments on systems?

Step 1: Site Survey

The first step of the six-step model, site survey, is sometimes difficult to complete. The easiest way to get the background information necessary to build the test plan is to have the questionnaire shown in Exhibit 1 answered. This also ties into setting the project scope for the technical aspects of the NVA. As it was once explained to us, this step is necessary so that we do not end up trying to boil the ocean for $15,000. The primary questions you need to answer are listed in Exhibit 1 (also in Appendix B).

There are a few major points that you need to uncover during the site survey. They include the determination of many environmental considerations, such as the media types that your target network may have. There must be special consideration given to most non-Ethernet media types. This has become an even more important point with the proliferation of wireless networking. Wireless network testing will require that special tools be added to your toolkit and additional time be spent in the NVA. If you have to limit your scope to meet time or cost concerns, it is not recommended to skip the wireless network review. This is due to the many potential security holes in current wireless network technology. Special consideration for network media types does not end with just wireless networking, but also includes technologies such as Token Ring, FDDI (Fiber Distributed Data Interface) or other fiber-optic technologies, and some of the much older technologies such as arcnet.

In addition to the media types run on the target network, it is important to find out the makeup of the concentrator devices on the client network. Depending on whether the target network has primarily switches or hubs can create a large time difference in performing the NVA. This is due to the fact that using a network sniffer in an environment that has switches will be limited to that one network segment. The technology of switches is such that each port on a switch is, in effect, a single network segment. This is good in terms of bandwidth and security, but more difficult in terms of security assessment. For example, a 100-megabit switch provides a full 100 megabits for each port on the switch. If only one device is plugged into that particular port, which is generally the case, that machine has 100 megabits all to itself. Conversely, a hub shares the total bandwidth between all of its ports. This means that a 100-megabit, eight-port hub actually divides the 100 megabits between all eight ports. If you happen to be the only machine currently accessing the network on the eight-port hub, than you would get the full 100 megabits. However, if there are eight machines accessing the network on your hub, your effective bandwidth is one eighth of the 100 possible megabits. The impact on the assessment process is due to the fact that you could plug a network sniffer into any one of the ports on the hub and see all of the network traffic on the eight ports. If you plugged the same network sniffer into a switch, you would only see the network traffic for the machine plugged into your same network segment, plus broadcast traffic, which is meant for every-one on the network to see. This entire switch-versus-hub debate can be taken a step further when you also have to consider the smart switch, or "layer 3" switch as it is often called. A smart switch adds one more wrinkle. It really is not much of a switch anymore — it is really a multi-port router. The potential issue in terms of the assessment lies in the fact that a layer 3 switch can also segment itself into logical switches. This process is known as using a virtual local area network (VLAN). So by plugging your network sniffer into a smart switch with multiple VLANs, you would only see the network traffic for your network port and only the broadcast traffic for your VLAN. However, the layer 3 switch does have a feature that can help in performing network sniffing. This feature, known as a "span port," (*Note:* also known as port mirroring) allows your network sniffer to see all of the network traffic across all of the network ports into the switch. Of course, how well this works, if at all, depends on both the configuration and the manufacturer of the network device.

If you thought the site survey was complete after a determination of media type and concentrator type, think again. Another area for consideration in the site survey is the number and type of operating systems run on the target network. While there are some tools that run equally well against an NT machine or a UNIX machine, not all tools pull dual duty. In addition, there may be configuration changes between multiple operating systems on the same tool. This can also be impacted by the difficulty in finding tools to help assess the less popular operating systems. It is generally pretty easy to find tools to help assess Microsoft operating systems (Win9x, NT, 2000, or XP), common distributions of UNIX, and most distributions of Linux operating systems. However, it is becoming increasingly difficult to find tools to help with the once very popular Novell network operating system. Tools still exist for Novell but not near the range of the previously mentioned operating systems.

So now you know the network media, network concentrator type, and the number and types of operating systems. You are finished with the site survey, right? Well, not exactly, but you are getting close. Another factor you must determine in the site survey is an actual determination of where the network starts and stops. This seems like it might be an easy question to answer; but when you take into account all of the possible network extenders, such as virtual private networks (VPNs) or wide area network (WAN) connections, it can become a little more difficult to decide. So this step in the site survey is the best place to get the actual determination of where the network begins and ends, as well as what you are responsible for testing. It is better to get this fixed now during the site survey than to try to get it corrected during the presentation of your final results.

Another key issue that you must determine in the site survey is the number and type of network protocols on the target network. Because the Internet Protocol (IP) is the most popular, the majority of the tools we will discuss are IP based. However, there are many different network protocols that may still be found on your target network. So, similar to the previous step, it is much better to find out here in the site survey that your target network runs exclusively the Internet Packet Exchange (IPX) protocol.

A most important key issue to determine during the site survey is the location of sensitive information. This allows you to focus your security assessment on the parts of the network that would have the greatest impact on the organization if compromised. Just imagine yourself giving the final results presentation on your vulnerability assessment, and only then realize that you had exhaustively tested each workstation for vulnerabilities but missed the crucial network segment that contained all the company's financial and customer data. This could become what is known as a "career-limiting move."

The above issue is closely tied to the following issue. The number and location of servers almost always coincides with where the sensitive information is located. However, that may not always be the case. It is also important to find out the number of servers because you are more likely to run host-based security tools on servers. So, the larger the number of servers, the more time you can spend on running host-based tools. Do not worry if you are not familiar with the phrase "host-based tools;" we will spend some time looking at them in Step 3: Building the Toolkit.

The final question requiring an answer in the site survey is whether the physical security of your target network will be assessed as well. Often, performing the physical security review is one of the most entertaining tests you will conduct. For the site survey, you really just need to know if it is going to be included. However, even if a formal physical security review is not necessary on your target network, keep your eyes open for potential physical gaps in security. This is more applicable if you are a consultant than if you are running the NVA from inside your target organization. This is due to the fact that if you are an employee of the organization for which you are performing the security review, you will already know where the physical security holes are.

Having determined the media types, the concentrator types, the number and type of operating systems, the start and stop point of the target network, the network protocols in use on the target network, where the sensitive information is located, the number of servers, and whether or not you need to look at the physical security of your network, then you are finally finished with the site survey. All of this information becomes very important for the next step — developing a test plan. However, oftentimes you cannot get answers to all the questions in the site survey. This may be due to a new network administrator, a very large network, or just a general lack of documentation on the target network. To overcome any of this difficulty, you may want to employ a network discovery tool. These tools are listed later in the chapter under the heading "Zero-Information-Based Tools" (see Step 3). These tools may also be worthwhile as a verification component to your site survey. Not that anyone would ever intentionally mislead you, but it may be best to check your answers personally.

Step 2: Develop a Test Plan

The next step in the six-step process is developing a good test plan for executing the NVA. A key area that your test plan will help with is in the testing for new and sometimes high-profile vulnerabilities. From time to time, some computer vulnerabilities get enough attention that they make their way to mainstream news outlets such as CNN or *USA Today*. Code Red, Nimda, and the recent series of vulnerabilities inside SNMP are great examples. With that being said, it is very difficult to constantly keep up-to-the-minute information on what the latest vulnerabilities are. Most people who run an NVA do not run NVAs as their only job function. If this is true for you as well, then you will need to get the latest information from Internet sources that maintain up-to-date vulnerability assessment information. The next subsection ("Internet Sources") discusses some of the Internet sites that keep information on hacking, vulnerabilities, and other components of the Internet's underground. The list is by no means an exhaustive list of sites that house this kind of information but it should provide a good starting point for your research.

It is also important to note that during this phase it might seem like an easy chance to come up with a checklist of vulnerabilities to look for. In fact, we have included many checklists in this book. However, you should never use a checklist as an exhaustive list of tests to run on your target network.

Again, it was once explained to us, running a vulnerability assessment using only a checklist is like building a car by looking only at a parts checklist. In the car analogy, you would check to see if the car has the following appropriate parts:

- Car seats
- Steering wheel
- Seat belts
- Engine
- Four tires
- Transmission

Even if your car had all of the parts listed above, you still would not have a car. All you would have is a pile of car parts. This is the same as running the NVA using only a checklist. You would check for the vulnerabilities that you have on the checklist, but you will miss vulnerabilities that way. Instead, the best mind-set to have when running a vulnerability assessment is similar to that of a crime investigator. In this mind-set, each set of tools that you run will provide clues for what the correct next step of investigation should be. You might be saying that even crime scene investigators have procedures to follow, and that is true; but starting with a checklist and looking for other tests to run is very different from running the list that you compiled at this phase to the exclusion of all others. The best advice to remember at this point is to keep your eyes open because, just when you think you have seen it all in a vulnerability assessment, something new will come up and surprise you. Now, let's take a look at those Internet sites that can help you get a better understanding of new vulnerabilities.

Internet Sources

You might be thinking, "How often should I check for new vulnerabilities on the Internet?" The best answer is: "Before you start any vulnerability assessment." The number of types of vulnerabilities just keeps growing and growing, and it can be almost impossible to keep up with. It may often feel that if you have been away from network vulnerability assessment for more than two weeks that you are completely out-of-date; we know that we do. This is where a few hours of research on the Internet may be a great help. Also, the tools used in vulnerability assessment change almost as fast as the vulnerabilities themselves. Most of the same sites we will look at for vulnerabilities are also the sites to check for tools.

Part of the reason to do the research is for the sake of efficiency. A good test plan will help you maximize the time spent gathering data on the target network. The best test plans are gentle reminders that you need to check for certain high-impact vulnerabilities, but not such a complete list that you ignore the testing methodology.

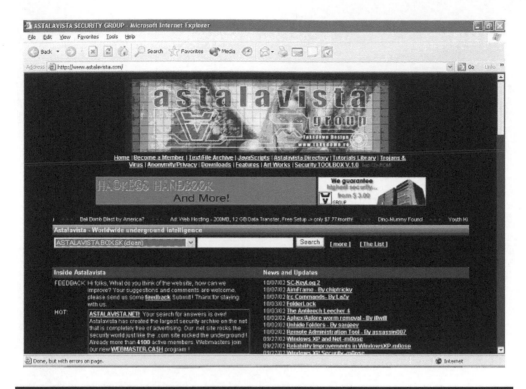

Exhibit 2. The Astalavista Web Site

Web Site: Astalavista

URL: http://astalavista.box.sk (Exhibit 2)

Description: Astalavista is a great site to begin any Internet search. It supports several sites internally and also has a search engine that looks at other sites as well. Lately, the site appears to be getting less support and maintenance than previously, but it is still a good starting point. The site has recently added an enormous number of pop-up ads whenever you perform a search. Hopefully, the pop-ups will be short-lived. On this site you can find information on security exploits, downloadable executables, and some articles on security in general. Due to the pop-up ads and the occasional adult content banners, this may *not* be the best site to search when at work.

Pop-Ups: Yes

Adult Content Banners: Yes

Website: Underground Systems Security Research

URL: http://www.ussrback.com (Exhibit 3)

Description: Underground Systems Security Research is a very good site specific to vulnerabilities. You can often find a posting about vulnerability, the code to execute the vulnerability, and a script or point-and-click

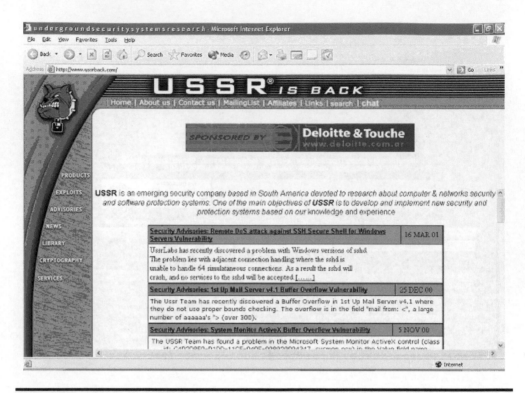

Exhibit 3.   The USSR Back Web Site

tool as well. It makes searching for vulnerabilities and tools that coincide much easier. Many of the links from this site are linked into the Astalavista search engine.
Pop-Ups: Yes
Adult Content Banners: Yes

Web Site: Attrition.org

URL: http://www.attrition.org/security (Exhibit 4)
Description: Attrition became famous for posting the high-profile defaced Web sites. It also has a very good list of vulnerabilities listed by product, a number of decent articles or postings, nice archives for older site posting, and a mailing list to which you can subscribe.
Pop-Ups: No
Adult Content Banners: No

Web Site: SecurityFocus

URL: http://www.securityfocus.com (Exhibit 5)
Description: SecurityFocus is as close to a definitive source of vulnerabilities as there is. You do have to register to get access to the vulnerability database, but registering is worthwhile. SecurityFocus also has several

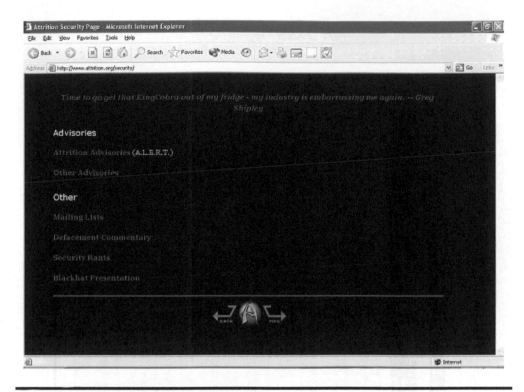

Exhibit 4. The attrition.org Web Site

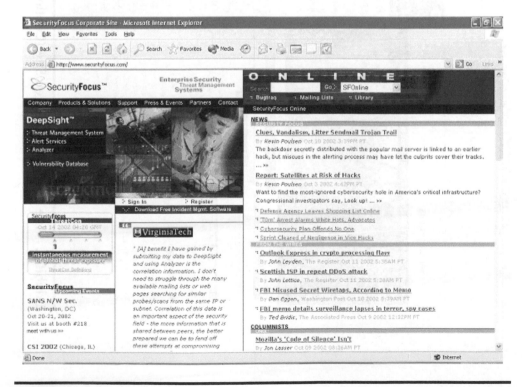

Exhibit 5. The SecurityFocus Web Site

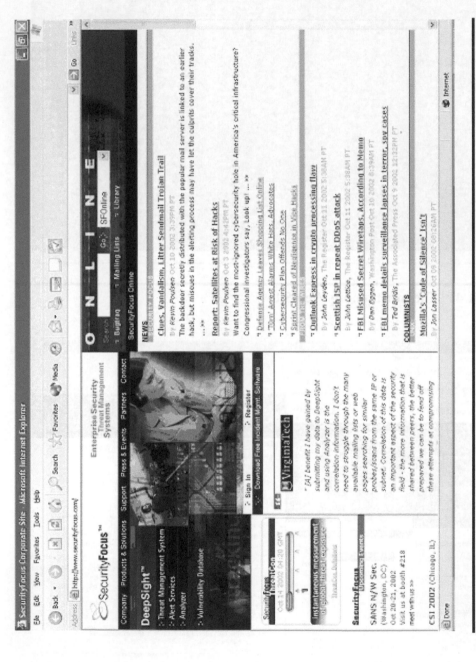

Exhibit 5.   The SecurityFocus Web Site (Continued)

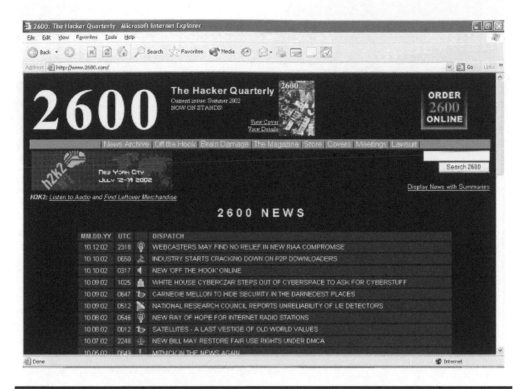

Exhibit 6. The 2600 Web Site

mailing lists that you can receive on a number of different subjects from Linux security to penetration testing. SecurityFocus is also home to bugtraq, the mailing list that alerts subscribed users to newly uncovered bugs. In addition to alerts, this site also contains news stories on the front page — all in all an amazing site.

Pop-Ups: No

Adult Content Banners: No

Web Site: 2600

URL: http://www.2600.com (Exhibit 6)

Description: The 2600 Web site can be reached at www.2600.<almost anything>. This is the Web site for the popular magazine that covers the hacker scene and hacker issues. There are articles, past issues of the magazine online, and mp3 talks from the large hacker conferences. While their charter is hacking, sometimes the site will digress into other issues.

Pop-Ups: No

Adult Content Banners: No

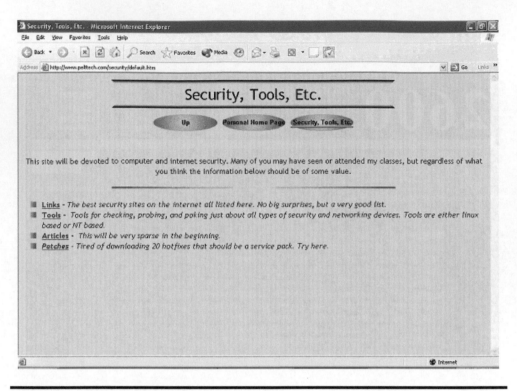

Exhibit 7. The Pelttech Web Site

Web Site: Pelttech

> *URL:* http://www.pelttech.com (Exhibit 7)
> *Description:* This is the companion Web site to the book you are currently
> reading. Most of the tools that we discuss later in this chapter are listed
> on the Web site for download. The site also contains links to other
> security sites, as well as articles and papers on security issues. The site
> is also a companion to the Computer Security Institute's "How to
> Conduct a Technical Network Vulnerability Assessment" course.
> *Pop-Ups:* No
> *Adult Content Banners:* No

Listing of Other Security Web Sites

Exhibit 8 provides a listing of other security Web sites.

Protecting Yourself from Internet Sources

You may be somewhat fearful going to the hacker sites listed above from
your home Internet service provider (ISP) account or your work Internet
connection. Here are a few, very basic steps that you can take to minimize
your exposure by going to these sites. [Note: We are not aware of any of the

Exhibit 8. Listing of Other Security Web Sites

Site Name	Description	URL
@Stake	Famous site for new vulnerabilities and l0pht crack (the famous NT password cracker)	http://www.atstake.com/research/redirect.html
Hacking Exposed	Once a book, now a Web site; also has a good links page	http://www.securityfocus.com
Antionline	Once a site that was devoted to death and destruction, now a good informational resource	http://www.antionline.com
HackersClub	This site is different from the site above because it contains a good number of articles	http://www.hackersclub.com
Razor	An elite cracking team's Web page	http://firestarter.sourceforge.net
Freesoft	The Internet's best collection of RFCs and essays, searchable by a number of fields; a must for people studying for CISSP	http://www.freesoft.org
Secureforge	Home of an easy-to-use Linux GUI for configuring ipchains-based firewalls	http://firestarter.sourceforge.net
PhoneBoy	The home of the unofficial Firewall-1 FAQ	http://www.phoneboy.com
COAST Security Archive	The archive contains several thousand tools and documents in all aspects of security	http://www.cs.purdue.edu/coast/archive/Archive_Indexing.html
CyberArmy	Searchable underground Web directory	http://www.cyberarmy.com
Hack Canada	Security information, archives, news, tips, and tools	http://www.hackcanada.com
Hacker News Network	The news and views affecting the computer security industry	http://www.hackernews.com
InfoSysSec	Security news, links and information	http://www.infosyssec.org/infosyssec/index.html
ListQuest	Hosts searchable archives of the BugTraq mailing list, as well as the possibility to search in RFCs	http://www.listquest.com
Net Security	News about new exploits found, advisories, archive of antiattack tools	
Neworder	Security Web portal	http://neworder.box.sk
packet storm	Really huge and searchable archive of security tools, texts, files, exploits	http://packetstorm.securify.com
rootshell	Exploits and vulnerabilities archive	http://rootshell.com
Securiteam.com	The news and new tools in computer security	http://www.securiteam.com

Exhibit 8. Listing of Other Security Web Sites (Continued)

Site Name	Description	URL
Security Stuff for Beginners	A nice reading, both for newbies and profies; basic security infoormation and advanced stuff	http://www.mpx.com.au/~coupe
Security white papers by Lance Spitzner	White papers covering the methodology of the average script kiddie, what to look for in your logs to determine what tools were used, and most important, how to armor your Linux and Solaris firewalls	http://www.enteract.com/~lspitz/papers.html
SecurityNews.org	Contains in-depth information on a wide range of security topics, including security organizations, education, certification programs, jobs, books, mailing lists, and news groups; the link database contains encryption, UNIX/Linux, NT, underground, and security vendor links	http://www.securitynews.org
TwistedinterneT ServiceS International Inc.	Provides news and tools for your security-related items of interest; fine text library and file archive	http://www.twistedinternet.com
Underground News	Security, cracking, satellite news, nice files archive, and more	http://www.undergroundnews.com
Anti-Hacking	Information about how to try and stop hackers; protection programs	http://antihacking.cjb.net
checksum.org	Tutorials, NT text, UNIX text, anonymity, crypto, defaced, discussion, tools, etc.	http://www.checksum.org
Computer Security Information	Page features general information about computer security	http://www.alw.nih.gov/Security/security.html
Computer security news	Moreover news headlines, daily related news feedback	http://w.moreover.com/computersecurity
Cotse news	Security news, advisories	http://www.cotse.com/newz
Criptonomicon	Internet security and privacy, with information and examples	http://www.iec.csic.es/criptonomicon
CyberArmy hacksearch	h/p/c/v Web directory	http://www.cyberarmy.com/search
Darktide Inc.	The selected and commented news, programming/Linux/encryption help and FAQs, interviews	http://www.darktide.com
Digital Avatar's Matrix	Security tools, information, news	http://snow.icestorm.com/damatrix

Name	Description	URL
DoSHelp Network security	Network security tools, patches, port watchers, firewalls, scanning tools, decryption tools, and attack reporting information	http://www.doshelp.com
Elf Qrin's Hacking Lab	Tools, essays, stories, forum	http://www.elfqrin.com/hack
Exploit X	White papers, computer security news	http://www.exploitx.com
Fight Back	Some tips on how to protect yourself from crackers, and how to secure your data	http://www.antionline.com/fight data
Hack In The Box	Slashdot-style security site	http://www.hackinthebox.org
hackZone [Russian/English language]	Articles, news, forum	http://www.hackzone.ru
halcon	Australian security site	http://www.halcon.com.au
Hideaway.net	Security portal	http://www.hideaway.net
ICSA	Security assurance company, information magazine	http://www.icsa.net
Java Applets security	FAQs	http://java.sun.com/sfaq
KSA Security Bulletin	Security news	http://home13.inet.tele.dk/kruse/bulletin.htm
musicforhackers.com	Online radio with security news and music	http://musicforhackers.com
Networking News Source — Security Protection/Education	Computer Networking News source and Computer Networking Information source	http://www.networkingnews.org/security
	Solutions to virus problems, nuke/war protection. education on how and what to do when online regarding protection and prevention	http://sandpit.caloundra.qld.gov.au/~lionx/helpers99
Rediff On The NeT — saving private data	A computer security primer for technology greenhorns	http://www.rediff.com/computer/1999/mar/24secure.htm
Replay Associates	Data security and network security archives, cryptography	http://www.replay.com
Rewted Network Security Labs	An information nexus, with a fully interactive technical database and FAQs; fine tools archive	http://www.rewted.org
SAFER	A free monthly newsletter distributed in PDF format, security vulnerabilities are presented here, sorted by date and operating system	http://safer.siamrelay.com
Safer-Hex	Daily news on all subjects related to computer, IT, and online security issues	http://www.jrpamc.com/safer
Secureroot	Web directory dedicated to computer security and Internet underground	http://secureroot.m4d.com
Security Associates	Information for protection from fraud, computer security, etc.	http://www.security.com.cy

Exhibit 8. Listing of Other Security Web Sites (Continued)

Site Name	Description	URL
Security Horizon	Updated news on the security world, news, tools and docs	http://www.securityhorizon.com
securitysearch.net	Searchable security portal	http://www.securitysearch.net
SecurityWatch.com	A security portal site	http://www.securitywatch.com
Seven Tenets of Good Security	Some rules that may be useful	http://www.avolio.com/7tenets.html
Student Punkz	Information on common school security systems, such as OnGuard, AtEase, and more	http://www.punkz.com

organizations above "hacking back," but that does not mean it has never happened.] We are not going to get into an exhaustive discussion about protecting yourself on the Internet here. After all, this is a book on vulnerability assessment, not Internet Security basics. Here are a few tips to help put your mind at ease when contacting a Web site dedicated to hacking:

- *Run a personal firewall.* There are several different types that you can either download or purchase at a retail outlet. One of the more popular personal firewalls is Zone Alarm from http://www.zonelabs.com. At the time of this writing, there was still a free version of this personal firewall that you can download. A second option is the BlackICE firewall from http://www.iss.net. While this product has no free version, it is still a very commonly used personal firewall.

- *Use a different ISP account.* To make it more difficult to have someone come back into your home system after visiting a hacker Web site, simply change your ISP. You can use a free service provider like netZero or Juno, or you may also want to sign up for an account with a provider such as Earthlink, which offers a 30-day free trial and just cancel your account before the 30 days expires. If switching your ISP is not for you, then perhaps an Internet kiosk is a better option. Internet kiosks are becoming more and more popular, and can be found in major malls, airport, and restaurants. The downside to the kiosks is price. These services generally charge either a per-minute or per-15-minute connection charge. Another option is to use the Internet access at your public library. The major drawback to the library is similar to that of the Internet kiosk: there is no easily available storage for the files you download.

- *Use an antivirus product.* While most of the files you download from these sites are completely safe and legitimate, you may still encounter files that are infected with Trojan horses or other malicious code. Even if the Web site that posted the code has scanned the files for viruses, it is better to protect yourself than to find out the hard way that someone missed a virus.

- *Use anonymous proxy service.* The anonymous proxy services, such as Anonymizer (available from http://www.anonymizer.com), hide the IP address that you are coming from. This provides a pretty good layer of security from anyone who might try to "hack back" into your system. There are a number of different services on the Internet from which to choose. Some anonymous access services are free or feature limited, and other sites simply charge a monthly access fee.

- *Stop cookies from reaching your machine.* There are a number of ways to stop cookies, which are small pieces of code given to your computer from a Web site, from reaching your machine. You can go into your Internet browser and simply turn off the receipt of cookies but this might cause you to lose functionality with sites such as Hotmail and your online bank. So, if you need to stop most cookies from reaching your machine but still want to let through a selective few, then you need a cookie manager tool. An example of a cookie manager is WebWasher®. WebWasher is available from http://www.webwasher.com, and there is a free version of this

product available for downloading. There are more features to this product
that come in handy when visiting hacking Web sites as well, such as a
webbugs filter and a pop-up window filter. Even if you are running this
product, it is still a good idea to check your system and see the number
of cookies and bugs that have been implanted in your system. To do this
you can use a product such as PestPatrol (from http://www.pestpatrol.com)
or Ad-aware (from http://www.lavasoftusa.com/aaw.html). Both products
search your registry, memory, and hard drive for webbugs, cookies, and
other Internet monitoring programs.

Following the five steps outlined above does not provide bulletproof
security for your home machine. However, it will provide you with a pretty
good layer of defense to protect your system and make it easier to target
another Internet address.

Building the Plan

When building your test plan for the vulnerability assessment, it is great to
have guidelines against which to compare your target network's security. This
may be an easy task if you have legal regulations that outline minimum security
practices for your organization, such as the forthcoming Health Insurance
Portability Accountability Act (HIPAA). However, if your organization does not
have industry-specific security criteria to follow, ISO 17799 (discussed in
previous chapters) provides a general framework for any organization. There
are also other standards that can be applied, including (1) the Common Criteria
standards, which were formed by an international consortium and adopted
by the U.S. government; or (2) the older TCSEC guidelines developed by the
U.S. Department of Defense. There are also industry *de facto* standards such
as the Common Body of Knowledge (CBK) from the International Information
Systems Security Certification Consortium (ISC[2]). Finally, if you are not going
to use any of the guidelines listed above — and it is recommended that you
do — the last measure that you can use is your own personal experience.
While the last measure is the least subjective standard, you will often be asked
for your opinion of the security of the target network.

Here are some very basic points to test when performing your technical
NVA. As a bare minimum, your test plan should look for the following:

- *Do configurations support policies?* This is an important point because
  network and security administrators often have to "do their best" when it
  comes to installation and configuration of security devices without the
  advantage of any formal training.
- *Do configurations, patch levels, service packs, and revision levels protect
  against known vulnerabilities?* Keep in mind that the applications that run
  on top of the network systems that you are analyzing may not work with
  the latest service pack. You might have to make the recommendation to
  upgrade to the latest service pack only if the applications support it.

- *Do backdoors or inappropriate chains of trust exist?* There are a number of different ways that this could be happening. Is an end user running pcAnywhere as a means of getting around the corporate virtual private network (VPN)? Another inappropriate chain of trust could exist inside UNIX systems in the /etc/rhosts and the /etc/hosts.equiv files.
- *Is there evidence of intrusion?* Keep your eyes open when performing the tests. If you see results that really make you believe that an intrusion has occurred, stop your testing and alert the responsible party immediately. Any further security testing that you do at this point could overwrite the forensic evidence of how the system was compromised.
- *Are detection measures effective?* There are two primary ways to perform an NVA. The first method is to use "stealth mode," where your testing is known only to the management teams involved for approval. This allows you to catch the network administrators "napping" and also gives you a great opportunity to test the intrusion detection systems of the target network. The other method is the "plain sight" method. In this method, everyone involved in the network and security staff knows that you are coming and can provide you with documentation and access to the systems that you may not get when using the stealth method.

Step 3: Building the Toolkit

This is the step that always gets the most interest — the tools. We are going to tie Steps 3 and 4 of the six-step process pretty tightly together because they are very closely related. An important fact to keep in mind is the overlying methodology of performing the network vulnerability assessment testing, and not a specific focus on the exact tool or tools that you run. The reason for this is that tools will change — manufacturers will go out of business, tools will stop being supported, tool will be purchased by different manufacturers, and better tools emerge all the time. It is also noteworthy that the tools discussed here are not an exhaustive list of all the tools available, but rather a representation of the tools in each particular area. The tools that we discuss range from freeware tools, to shareware tools, to purchase-only products. And because the tools and information about them changes so rapidly, the best we can say is that the information is current as of this writing.

Exhibit 9 denotes the expense of the different tools that we will be looking at in subsequent subsections:

The vulnerability assessment model illustrated in Exhibit 10 shows the process that you will be going through when conducting a vulnerability assessment. The horizontal line denotes the number of hosts that test level will be run against in comparison to the level that follows. The vertical line denotes the length of time it takes to run each successive test level. The model shows that you will run the tests that take the least amount of time against the largest number of hosts, and the tests that take the most time against the fewest number of hosts. As we complete each level of the model, we will use the output from the previous layer as seed information for the next layer

Exhibit 9. Pricing Chart

Symbol	Price
Free	Free for anyone
$	Up to $500
$$	$500 up to $5000
$$$	$5000 up to $15000
$$$$	Greater than $15000

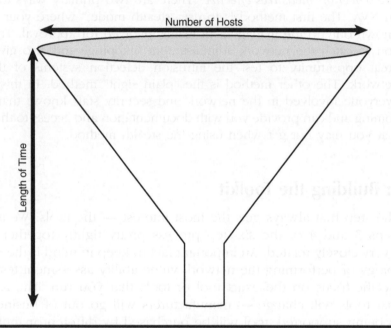

Number of Hosts

Length of Time

Exhibit 10. The Vulnerability Assessment Model

in the model. Remember, as previously discussed, that we have put up a "Chinese wall" and we will begin these tests as any hacker would. In the example we use in this book, we only begin with the name of the company that we are looking to compromise.

The types of tools we discuss include:

- Zero-information-based tools
- Network enumeration tools
- OS fingerprint tools
- Port scan tools
- Scanning tools
- Types of specialty tools
- NetBIOS tools
- Web security tools
- Firewall auditing tools
- Trojan detecting tools

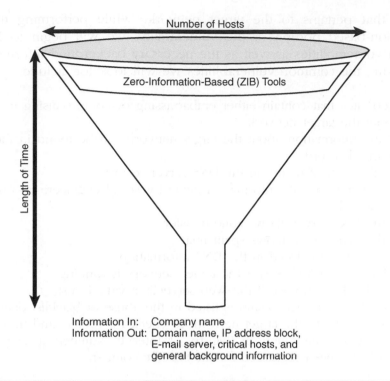

Number of Hosts

Zero-Information-Based (ZIB) Tools

Length of Time

Information In: Company name
Information Out: Domain name, IP address block,
                 E-mail server, critical hosts, and
                 general background information

Exhibit 11.   The Vulnerability Assessment Model: Zero Information Layers

- War dialing tools
- Miscellaneous tools
- Application tools
- Wireless network testing tools
- Network sniffers
- War dialers

Zero-Information-Based Tools

The zero-information-based tools (see Exhibit 11) are tools that help us understand the basic information about the target network we will assess. In this layer we are looking for information that has been posted to a number of publicly available Internet sources. Common sources that we will search are:

- Internet
- SEC
- ARIN
- DNS servers
- IRC channels
- News servers

The end result of the zero-information-based tools will be a network diagram and printed copies of any alarming information uncovered on the

Internet that pertains to the target network. While performing the zero-information-based portion of the vulnerability, we will begin to look for common vulnerabilities as well as the necessary background information. At a minimum, the common vulnerabilities we will look for include:

- Web sites that contain either embarrassing or compromising information about the target network
- If any information about the target network can be found in the posted financial records
- Single point of failure in the DNS server record
- Too much accurate information given for social engineering in the "Who Is" record
- If the DNS server allows zone transfer
- If the mail server allows spam relay
- If a Web site is listed in the DNS information
- What type of Web server the target network is running
- Simple checks to see if the Web server is a virtual host
- Look to see if the domain is listed in the abuse or blacklist databases
- A traceroute to the target network to check for routers and firewalls
- A check of the American Registry of Internet Numbers to see if the IP block has been registered for the specific company

This information will then be used in the next layer of the vulnerability assessment model — network enumeration.

The first tool we will use is a standard Web browser. We begin by checking the http://www.sec.gov Web site (see Exhibit 12) for information about our company. The two major documents of interest are the 10-K and 10-Q documents. These report the major financial transactions for the company we are assessing. We are mostly looking for information on mergers and acquisitions because when two companies merge, the primary focus seems to be on sharing the information, and a secondary concern involves the security controls that will be set between the two networks. This can also be true for the announcement of a "strategic business partnership." Either of the situations can lead to any easy backdoor in the target network for an Internet attacker. Information is generally only posted on publicly held companies and not those that are privately held. So, if you are assessing a privately held company, you can skip this step.

The second Web site we will search contains profanity in the title. We will search http://www.fu**edcompany.com (Exhibit 13) for any references to the target network. This Web site contains a number of different types of postings. In general, these postings pertain to poor financial decisions by a company or to lay-offs. However, frustrated employees often "dish the dirt" after they have been let go. Any dirt that may be useful to a potential attacker is something we need to check. The unfortunate part of the Web site is that you need to pay for premium services to get access to all information about the company you are assessing. The positive side of this is that the Web site will let you know if there is information posted, but just will not let you into

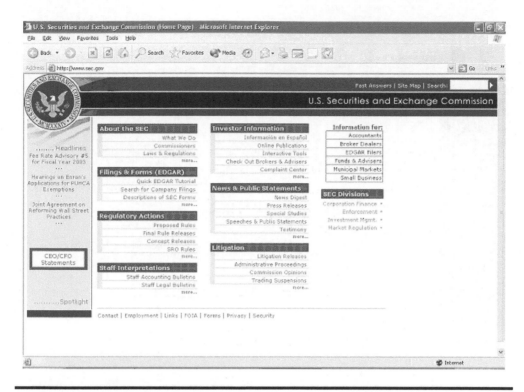

Exhibit 12.   The SEC.gov Web Site

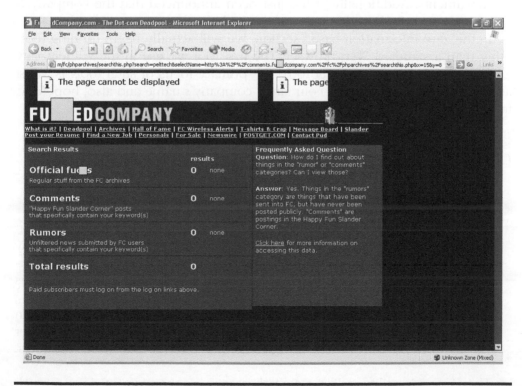

Exhibit 13.   The Fu**Edcompany.Com Web Site

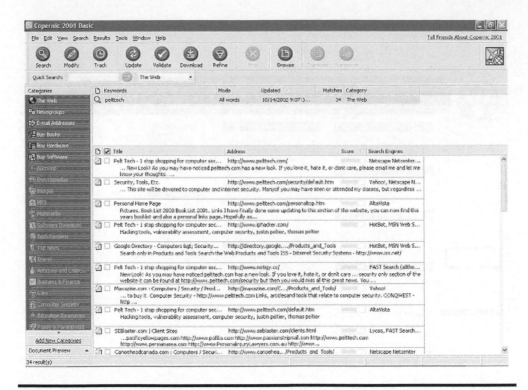

Exhibit 14.   Copernic Basic

the documents. Additionally, it has just been announced that the company is now shipping a PC-based version of the Web site.

In the zero-information-based section, we will actually begin running tools other than a standard Web browser. The first tool we use in the vulnerability assessment is an Internet ferret tool. The primary focus of such tools is to list all of the Web sites that link to our target company's name and also, hopefully, to uncover the domain name for our target network.

Copernic Basic

> *URL:* http://www.copernic.com (Exhibit 14)
>
> *Price:* Free
>
> *OS:* NT
>
> *Vendor's comments:* This entry-level Web search tool, used and trusted by millions of users worldwide, combines many search enhancement features along with an intuitive user interface, making your Web searches faster and easier than ever. Moreover, it is free!
>
> *Opinion:* This is a great all-around tool. It can be used in place of common Internet search engines. The added features of search sources other than the Internet make it a more definitive ferret than other products.

The Copernic utility is like a "search engine on steroids;" it does a much more exhaustive search for any and all references to your target company.

This tool helps by eliminating the need for us to guess what the Internet domain for our company is; it shows us any Web sites that contain the name of our company; and finally, it allows us to look over the search results to see if there are any potentially compromising Web sites postings about our target network. We will be looking in the search results for Web site postings that may be an HTML version of an e-mail posting to a newsgroup. We would be looking for postings made by internal employees, past or present, that may have information such as the types of systems the target network is running. Sometimes, it is possible to find Web sites with postings such as:

> Hi I'm Bob from Pelttech. We just got a new CheckPoint Firewall-1 in our organization, and I'm having some trouble trying to configure split-level DNS. Can anyone offer suggestions?
>
> Thanks in advance,
>
> Bob

Sam Spade

> *URL:* http://www.samspade.org/ssw (Exhibit 15)
> *Price:* Free
> *OS:* NT
> *Vendor's comments:* Sam Spade does the majority of the work in the zero-information-based section. It does a great job of taking UNIX command-line tools and making them easier through the point-and-click interface.

There are a couple of key points to note about the Sam Spade utility. The first item is that, by default, no nameserver is listed and no e-mail address is listed. To do the spam relay check later on, you will need to put an e-mail address in the e-mail address field. The nameserver field does not have to build completed; however, if you are going to be using the tool frequently, it is a time saver to have a nameserver already listed. Exhibit 15 reveals these options.

The second point of note with Sam Spade is that some of the functionality is disabled by default. To turn on all of these functions, you need to go to the "Edit" menu and then select "Options" (Exhibit 16) and "Advanced" (Exhibit 17).

Once you have the options set in Sam Spade, you are ready to begin using the tool. The best way to begin is to simply plug the domain name uncovered in the Copernic search into the target field and either click on the "Whois" button on the left-hand side or simply hit the Enter key. The tool runs a standard "Whois" lookup on the domain name that you specified in the target field. Exhibit 18 illustrates these fields.

There are several pieces of useful information that you can get from the simple "Whois" search in Sam Spade. The first and possibly most useful piece of information is the location of the company that registered the domain.

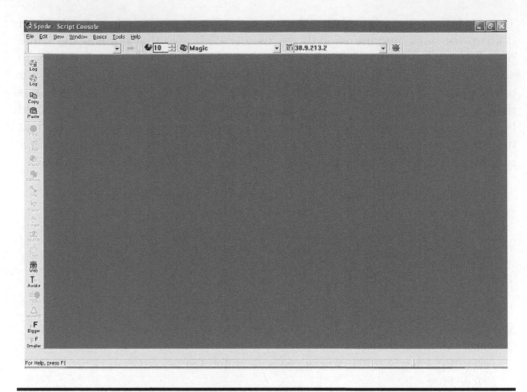

Exhibit 15. The Default Sam Spade Workspace

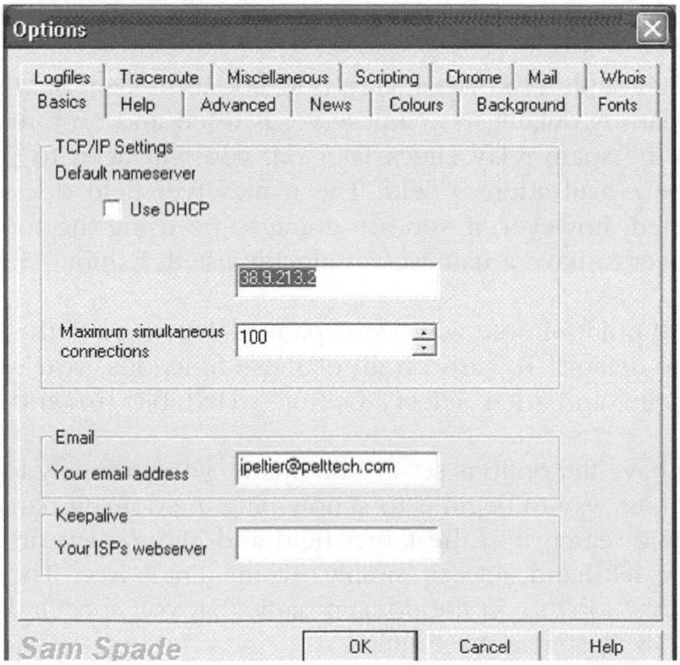

Exhibit 16. The Sam Spade Options Screen

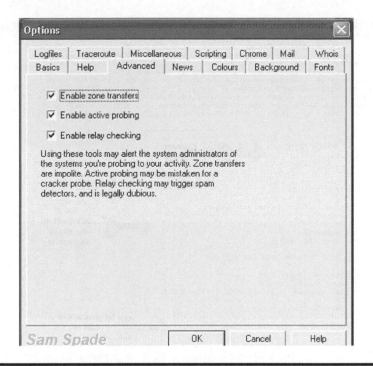

Exhibit 17.   The Sam Spade Advanced Options Screen

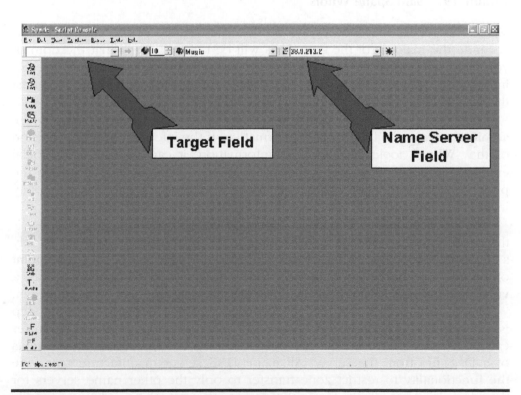

Exhibit 18.   The Sam Spade Default Fields

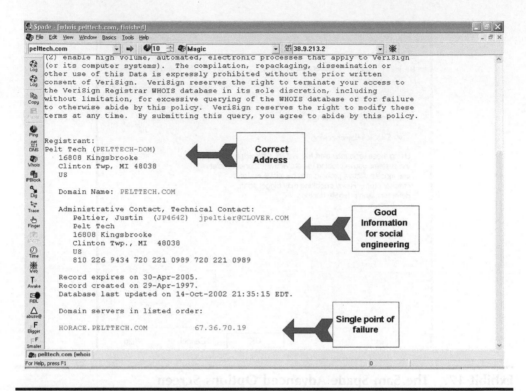

Exhibit 19. Sam Spade Whois

While this record may not always be the true address of the company, it is accurate the majority of the time. This will be the first check that the domain you have selected is the correct target network. It is beneficial to find out this information now, before you spend days running vulnerability tests against the wrong target domain. A mistake that you only make once!

The second piece of information you will get from the "Whois" is the administrative and billing contact information. If the information in this portion of the "Whois" looks like accurate information, it can be useful for social engineering testing later on. If the information is accurate right down to the phone extensions for the contacts, it might be time to list it as a vulnerability in the final report.

The third piece of information that we find from running the "Whois" is the primary and secondary nameserver for our target domain. If there is only a single DNS server listed in the domain, it could potentially be a single point of failure for the target network, and it might warrant a mention as a vulnerability in the final report. Exhibit 19 provides an average "Whois" screen.

Having finished the "Whois" lookup on the target domain, the next step is to attempt a "zone transfer" (see Exhibit 20 and Exhibit 21). Zone transfer can be a vulnerability because it allows a client to download the entire contents of a DNS file from the server. All major DNS server manufacturers provide the functionality to restrict zone transfer to only the other name servers for that domain. After all, those are the devices that actually need to perform a zone transfer, to keep the database information current and synchronized.

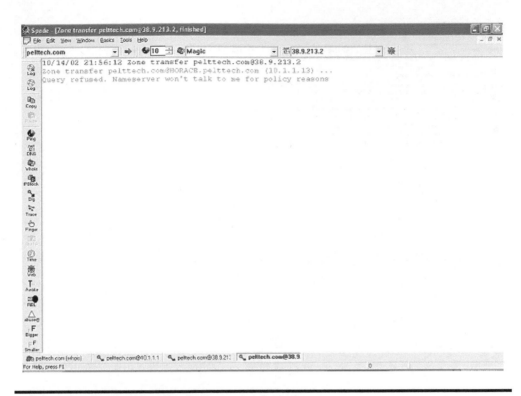

Exhibit 20. Sam Spade Failed Zone Transfer

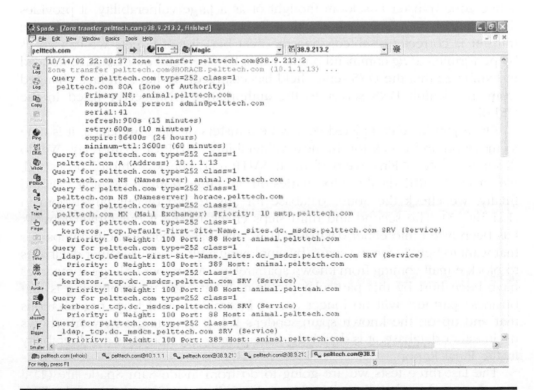

Exhibit 21. Successful Zone Transfer

Exhibit 22. Sam Spade Dig

While zone transfer is seldom thought of as a large vulnerability, it provides the potential Internet attacker with a list of targets to choose from. If zone transfer is correctly disabled, then the next best list of targets we can get is by performing a *dig* command on the target DNS server. You may have noticed in Exhibit 22 that the DNS server field has changed. We have, in fact, changed from the default DNS server to the authoritative DNS server listed in the "Whois."

Once you have completed your zone transfers or *dig* commands, it is time to move on and check for the next vulnerability: SMTP or spam relay. We do this in three steps. First, we perform an SMTP relay check (Exhibit 23); second, we check the RBL database for entries on our target domain (Exhibit 24); and finally, we check the abuse database for any record of our target domain (Exhibit 25). The second and third steps check to see if our target network has been listed into either database. These databases exist to help companies that want to fight incoming spam, by employing a filter that uses their databases to block e-mail coming from known spam relays. A number of large companies have been hurt by this particular problem. What ends up happening is that business partners will no longer accept incoming e-mail from organizations that end up on the known spam sender's list. If your target network shows up in either database, it is definitely something worth noting as a vulnerability in the Final Report.

The last three tests we are going to do from inside Sam Spade are (1) a traceroute to see if we can determine critical devices, (2) a check of the Web

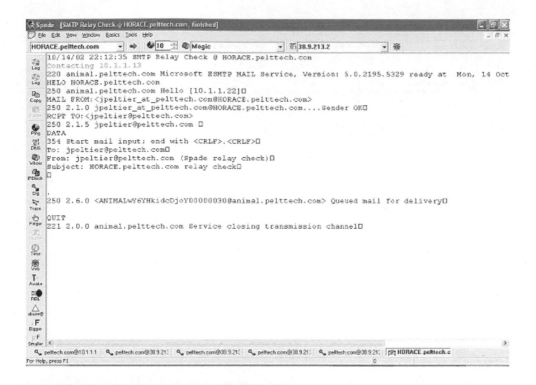

Exhibit 23.   The SMTP Relay Check

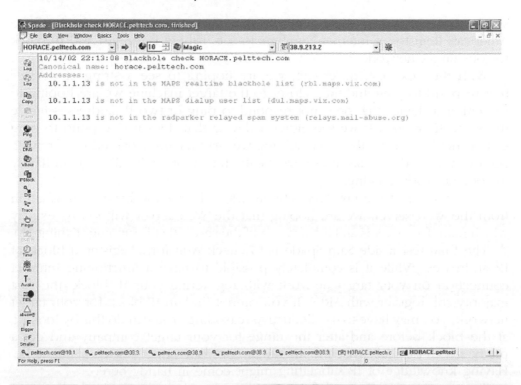

Exhibit 24.   The RBL Database Check

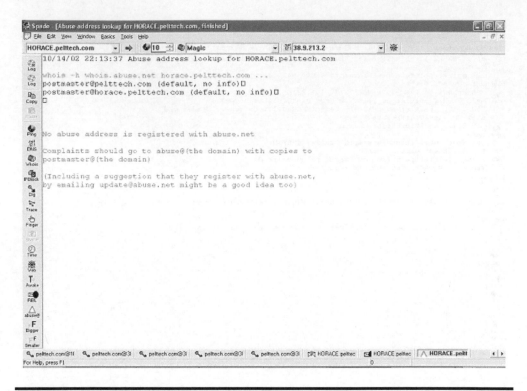

Exhibit 25.   The Abuse Database Check

server to see if we can determine the manufacturer, and (3) a check of the American Registry of Internet Numbers to see if there is a registered IP block for our target network.

With the next test, traceroute, we are hoping to see a string of devices that respond to ping and then closer to the target machine we are hoping to see either a device that does not respond to ping or two IP addresses inside the same IP subnet. If we see either a device that does not respond to ping or two devices inside the same subnet, we may have uncovered the firewall. But even if we do not see these events, the traceroute will still come in handy for our network drawing.

The viewing of the raw Web site allows us to see the header information from the Web server. We are hoping that the Web server will tell us exactly which manufacturer it is and the revision of the server that is running (Exhibit 26).

The final test inside Sam Spade is to check Arin for a registered block of IP addresses. While it is completely possible to have a functioning Internet connection on your target network with registering your IP block, the vast majority still register with ARIN. If you cannot find an IP block for your target network, you may have to use deductive reasoning. You can do this by looking at the block before and after the range for your target company and get a pretty good idea of what the IP range for your target network might be. Having knowledge of IP subnetting might come in handy here.

The next group of zero-information-based tools is the network discovery tools. We will look at two tools in particular: NetFormx and Network Inspector.

Exhibit 26.   The Sam Spade Raw Web Site

These tools are more often run to verify the information in the site survey rather than here in the actual testing component. Because both tools do a complete discovery on their own, they are still considered zero-information-based tools.

NetFormx

> *URL:* http://www.netformx.com
>
> *Price:* $$$
>
> *Vendor's comments:* NetFormx Enterprise AutoDiscovery (see Exhibit 27) lets you quickly identify the assets and structure of any audited network, so designers can propose compatible solutions, deployment teams can track implementation status, and support teams can monitor changes for use in future migration. Add the benefits of our MultiVendor Device Library, and modifying solutions becomes easier than ever.
>
> *Opinion:* NetFormx is an easy-to-use tool that does a very respectable job of enterprise discovery and network mapping. This tool is almost a *de facto* standard for network discovery. NetFormx works best in a wide area environment due to the network discovery capability. The output from this tool can be exported into a Visio document or into HTML format. Another advantage is that this tool also pulls double duty in helping network administrators keep up with the devices on the network.

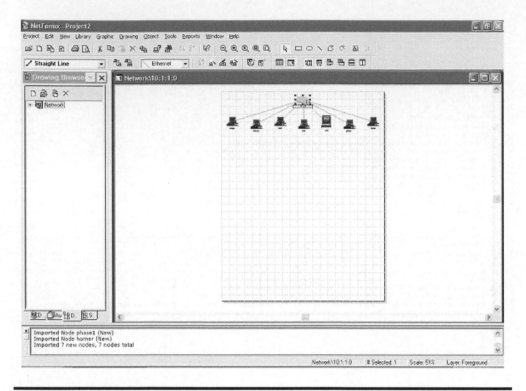

Exhibit 27.   NetFormx

Fluke Network's Network Inspector

> *URL:* http://www.flukenetworks.com
>
> *Price:* $$$
>
> *Vendor's comments:* Designed for switched Ethernet LANs, Network Inspector (NI) actively monitors and diagnoses problems in TCP/IP, IPX, and NetBIOS environments (see Exhibit 28). It rapidly identifies whether the problems lie on the server, client, switch, router, or printer through its quick discovery process, and provides an extensive suite of reports identifying all devices in the LAN, the services they provide, and an array of tools and reports for data analysis.
>
> *Opinion:* Network Inspector is a very good tool for network discovery on a single local area network (LAN). The tools diagram the network to the physical switch port that each device is plugged into. It can also take a histogram and show the network usage statistic over a period of time.

Network Enumeration Tools

Network enumeration tools take the IP block information ascertained in the zero-information-based tools section, and continue to refine the number of hosts to test (see Exhibit 29). It is possible for the target network to be a

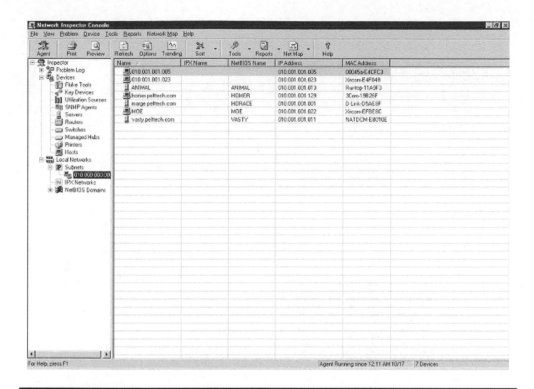

Exhibit 28. Network Inspector

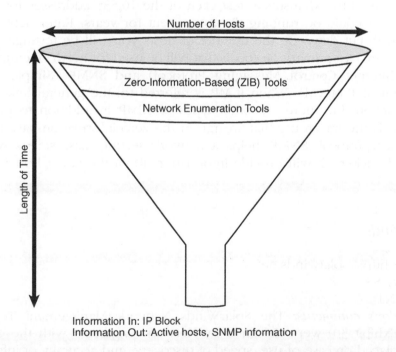

Number of Hosts

Zero-Information-Based (ZIB) Tools

Network Enumeration Tools

Length of Time

Information In: IP Block
Information Out: Active hosts, SNMP information

Exhibit 29. The Vulnerability Assessment Model: Network Enumeration Layer

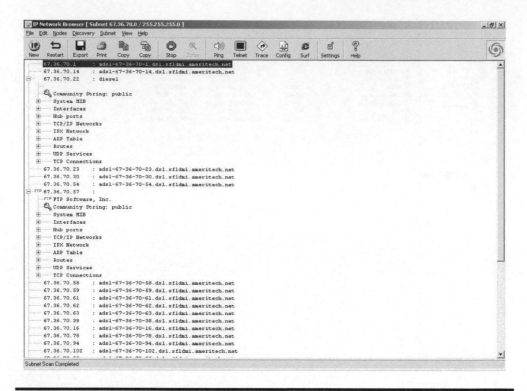

Exhibit 30. The SolarWinds IP Network Browser

"Class B" network, which means that there are 16,535 possible hosts to test. If you wanted to exhaustively test each of the 16,535 addresses for vulnerabilities, you could be running the assessment for years. Enter network enumeration to cut down on the number of hosts you will be testing.

There are two primary protocols that will be used for network enumeration: ICMP (Internet Control Messaging Protocol) and SNMP (Simple Network Management Protocol). When ICMP is referred to, the general link is to the ping function, but there are other types of ICMP in addition to ping. One example is the traceroute that we ran in the zero-information-based section. The other protocol, SNMP, helps a network security assessor as well as a potential hacker. It will provide information about the target host indiscriminately.

SolarWinds

> *URL:* http://solarwinds.net
> *Price:* $$
> *OS:* NT
> *Vendor's comments:* The SolarWinds Network Management Tools (see Exhibit 30) were designed by Network Engineers with the emphasis placed on ease of use, speed of discovery, and accuracy of information displayed. This can best be experienced by running the IP Network

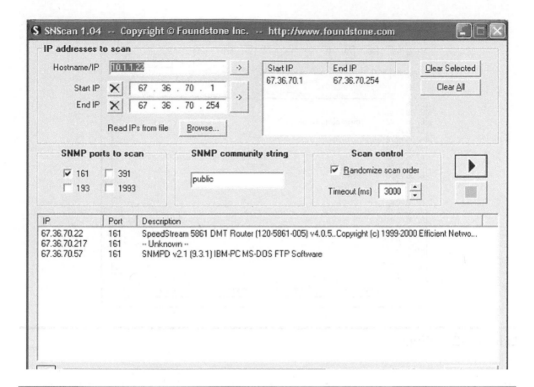

Exhibit 31.   SNScan

Browser. This tool uses ICMP and SNMP to perform a very fast network discovery. The detailed information it returns includes details of each interface, port speed, IP addresses, routes, ARP tables, accounts, memory, sysObjectIDs, and much more.

Opinion: The SolarWinds toolkit has a number of great tools. The IP Network Browser Tool that we use for network enumeration is fast and easy to use. Other tools in the toolkit include a network traffic generator, an SNMP brute-force password crack, and countless Cisco management tools. A great toolset for the price.

SNScan

URL: http://www.foundstone.com

Price: Free

OS: NT

Vendor's comments: SNScan is a Windows-based SNMP detection utility that can quickly and accurately identify SNMP-enabled devices on a network (see Exhibit 31). This utility can effectively indicate devices that are potentially vulnerable to SNMP-related security threats such as those released on February 12, 2002.

Opinion: A similar tool to IP Network Browser, but with a few less features. However, it has a much smaller price tag.

Exhibit 32.   Pinger

Pinger

> *URL:* http://www.pelttech.com
> *Vendor's Web site:* http://www.leto.net/docs/mhd.html
> *Price:* Free
> *OS:* NT
> *Opinion:* A handy network tool to have, it makes performing ping sweeps
> very easy (see Exhibit 32). Just plug in the network range and proceed.

ICMPEnum

> *URL:* http://razor.bindview.com
> *Price:* Free
> *OS:* Linux
> *Opinion:* Great all-around ICMP tool, but can take some time to get installed
> depending on the Linux distribution.

Operating System Fingerprint Tools

At this layer of the network vulnerability assessment model, you build on the
information learned in the previous tool layers. What you hope to accomplish
is to determine the operating system (OS) running on the hosts found to be
active. The tools in this layer fingerprint the operating system in one of two
ways. First, the OS can be fingerprinted by the applications and subsequent

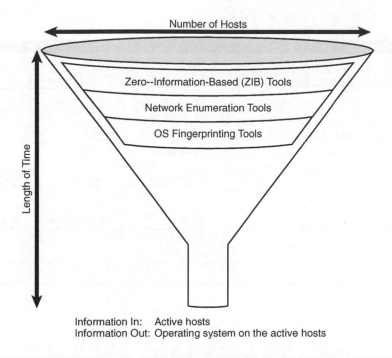

Number of Hosts

Length of Time

Zero--Information-Based (ZIB) Tools

Network Enumeration Tools

OS Fingerprinting Tools

Information In: Active hosts
Information Out: Operating system on the active hosts

Exhibit 33. The Vulnerability Assessment Model: OS Fingerprint Layer

ports that respond (see Exhibit 33). For example, TCP ports 137, 138, and 139 correspond to the Microsoft network access. While some Linux systems will respond on these ports, it is generally the domain of only Microsoft machines. The other way in which the tools can fingerprint the OS is through TCP sequence prediction. Inside TCP communications, a sequence number is used on the packets to help keep the information flow moving smoothly and in the correct order. However, certain OSs respond to TCP communication with an easy-to-predict TCP sequence number, and through the sequence number increment the tools can make a good guess at the OS.

Nmap for Linux

URL: http://www.insecure.org
Price: Free
OS: NT or Linux
Vendor's comments: Nmap is a utility for network exploration or security auditing. It supports ping scanning (determine which hosts are up), many port scanning techniques (determine what services the hosts are offering), and TCP/IP fingerprinting (remote host operating system identification). Nmap also offers flexible target and port specification, decoy or stealth scanning, sunRPC scanning, and more.
Opinion: Nmap is probably the most commonly used tool in network vulnerability assessments due to the feature richness of the product and its lack of cost.

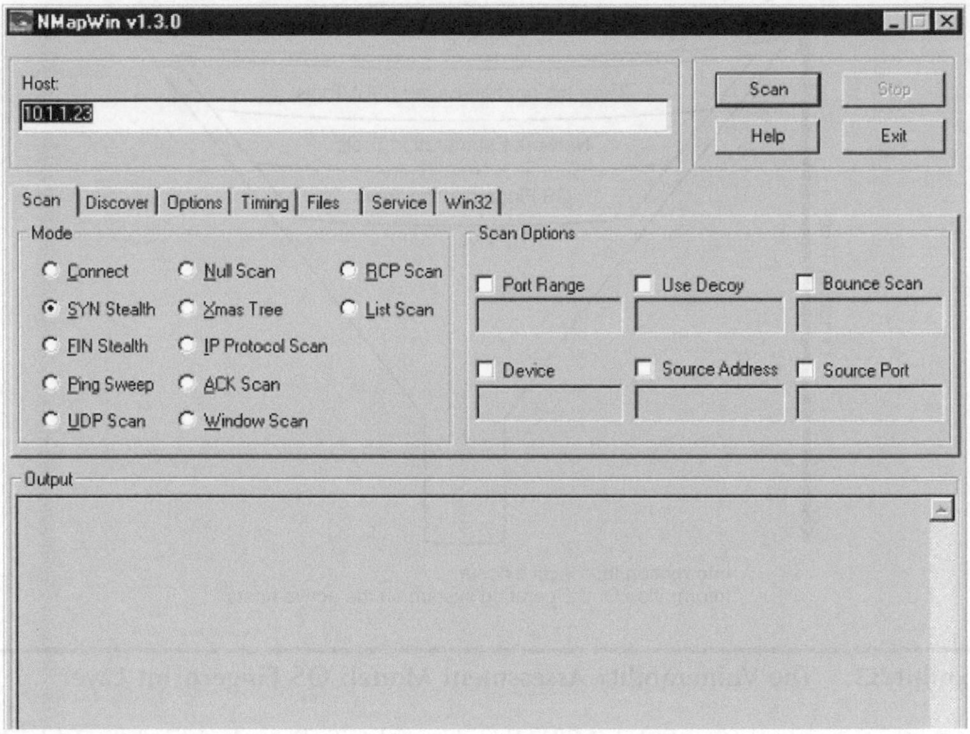

Exhibit 34. Nmap for Windows

Nmap for NT

URL: http://www.eeye.com
Price: Free
OS: NT
Opinion: Nmap for NT is still not as stable or as fast as the Linux version, but has come very far in a very short period of time. This suite of tools is a real credit to the talent of the people at eeye (see Exhibit 34).

Application Discovery Tools

At this layer in the network vulnerability assessment model, we are looking to determine the specific applications that are running on the active hosts (see Exhibit 35). At this point, you really should start to get a good idea of what the target network looks like. To ascertain the applications running on the active hosts, we use port scan tools. Port scanners attempt to identify any services that are open on the network device. There are several different mechanisms that port scanners can use — TCP, UDP, or ICMP — to request open ports. Many port scanners can be easily detected by intrusion detection systems.

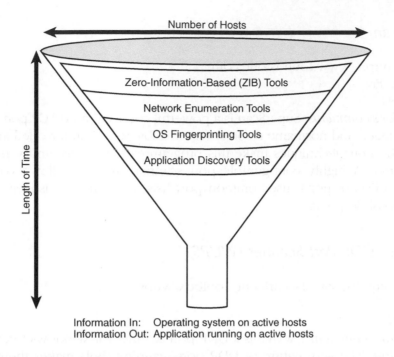

Information In: Operating system on active hosts
Information Out: Application running on active hosts

Exhibit 35. The Vulnerability Assessment Model: Application Discovery Layer

Nmap for Linux

URL: http://www.insecure.org
Price: Free
OS: NT or Linux
Vendor's comments: Nmap is a utility for network exploration or security auditing. It supports ping scanning (determines which hosts are up), many port scanning techniques (determines what services the hosts are offering), and TCP/IP fingerprinting (remote host operating system identification). Nmap also offers flexible target and port specification, decoy or stealth scanning, sunRPC scanning, and more.
Opinion: Nmap is probably the most commonly used tool in network vulnerability assessments due to the lack of cost and the feature richness of the product. Nmap is not only good at fingerprinting an operating system, but it is also a very good port scanner.

Nmap for NT

URL: http://www.eeye.com
Price: Free
OS: NT
Opinion: Nmap for NT is still not as stable or as fast as the Linux version, but has come very far in a very short period of time. It is a real credit to the talent of the people at eeye.

SuperScan

URL: http://www.foundstone.com
Price: Free
OS: NT
Vendor's comments: SuperScan is a powerful connect-based TCP port scanner, pinger, and hostname resolver (see Exhibit 36). Multi-threaded and asynchronous techniques make this program extremely fast and versatile.
Opinion: A highly configurable port scanner, this tool allows you to set up lists of ports, use common port lists, or scan exhaustively from all possible ports.

Windows UDP Port Scanner (WUPS)

URL: http://www.ntsecurity.nu/toolbox/wups
Price: Free
OS: NT
Vendor's comments: WUPS is a UDP port scanner for Windows (Exhibit 37).
Opinion: The very nature of UDP port scanning tools makes them unpredictable. You may find that any time you run this UDP port scan that it gets responses on every port. This, however, is in the implementation of UDP and not the tool.

Port Scanner

URL: http://www.megasecurity.org/Scanners.html
Price: Free
OS: NT
Opinion: A good generic port scanner (see Exhibit 38).

Ultra Scan

URL: http://packetstormsecurity.nl/UNIX/scanners
Price: Free
OS: NT
Opinion: Fastest port scanner around (see Exhibit 39).

Queso

URL: http://www.apostols.org
Price: Free
OS: Linux
Opinion: Queso performs operating system identification like NMAP does, but because it is included most often in the tool listed below i.e., cheops), it is left in as a port scanner. This tool by itself is an OS fingerprint tool.

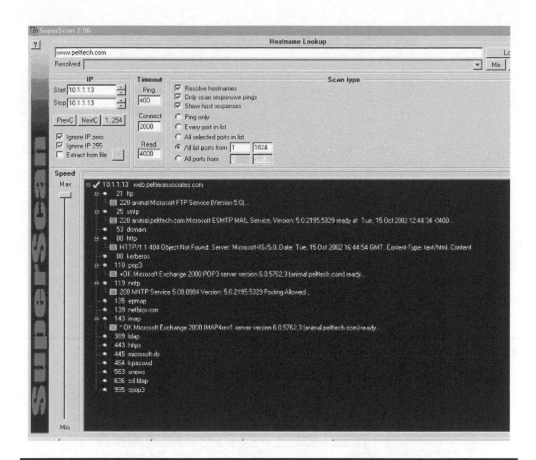

Exhibit 36. Super Scan

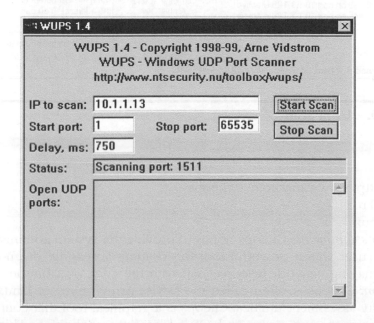

Exhibit 37. WUPS

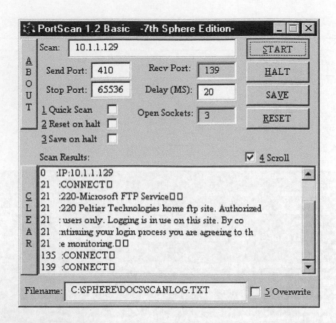

Exhibit 38.   Port Scanner

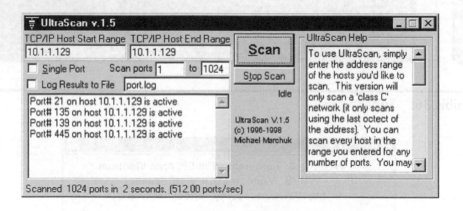

Exhibit 39.   Ultra Scan

Cheops

URL: http://www.marko.net/cheops
Price: Free
OS: Linux

Vendor's comments: Cheops hopes to provide the system administrator and the user with a powerful tool for locating, accessing, diagnosing, and managing network resources, all with the click of a button.

Opinion: Cheops is often called the "Swiss Army knife" of Linux vulnerability assessment utilities. Cheops is a graphical tool that contains ping, traceroute, port scan, and OS fingerprint capabilities. This package contains the tool listed above, Queso, for OS fingerprinting.

Strobe

> *URL:* ftp://ftp.freebsd.org/pub/freebsd/ports/distfiles
> *Price:* Free
> *OS:* Linux
> *Opinion:* A good TCP port scanner for Linux.

Vulnerability Scanning Tools

Vulnerability scanning tools attempt to give the assessor "one-stop shopping" by checking for all vulnerabilities inside the target network, including some of the checks that we performed manually at the beginning of the assessment (see Exhibit 40). These tools take the longest amount of time to run, and have the most options from which to pick and choose. Scanning tools are the most robust of all the vulnerability assessment tools and are often the priciest. While they do most things well, they can be wrong; and they can miss some things. It is recommended that you run at least two tools from this group of scanning tools. The reason for this is to minimize the false positives that you will get as response. Running at least two scanning tools is known as creating a multi-test environment, and is a very positive item to point out to your management or customers.

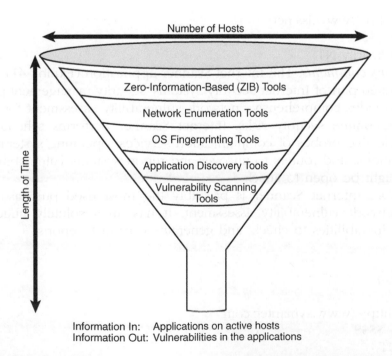

Exhibit 40. The Vulnerability Assessment Model: Vulnerability Scanning Layer

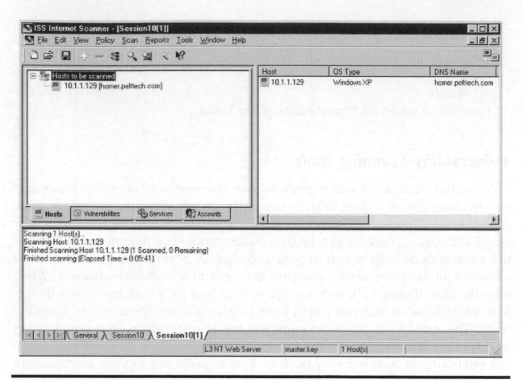

Exhibit 41.   ISS Internet Scanner 6

Internet Scanner

> *URL:* http://www.iss.net
> *Price:* $$$$
> *OS:* Primarily NT
> *Vendor's comments:* The Internet Scanner application (Exhibit 41), an integrated part of Internet Security Systems' security management platform, provides comprehensive network vulnerability assessment for measuring online security risks. Internet Scanner performs scheduled and selective probes of communication services, operating systems, applications, and routers to uncover and report systems vulnerabilities that might be open to attack.
> *Opinion:* Internet Scanner is probably the most used purchase tool in network vulnerability assessment. It has an absolutely huge list of vulnerabilities to check, and generates very nice reports.

NetRecon

> *URL:* http://www.symantec.com
> *Price:* $$$$
> *OS:* NT

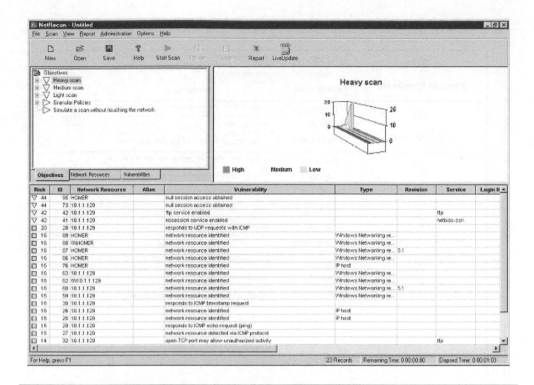

Exhibit 42. NetRecon

Vendor's comments: Symantec NetRecon 3.5 (Exhibit 42) goes beyond just discovering security vulnerabilities to provide a systematic understanding of their causes. It utilizes a unique root-cause and path-analysis engine to illustrate the exact sequence of steps taken to uncover vulnerabilities, thus enabling administrators to identify exactly where to correct vulnerabilities in order to enforce corporate security policies.

Opinion: NetRecon is a great all-in-one scanning tool. It seems to scan as fast if not faster than anything else on the market, and generates the best overall reports.

CyberCop

URL: http://www.nai.com

Price: $$$$

Vendor's comments: Secure your networks against hacker attacks with CyberCop ASaP, an online vulnerability assessment service powered by McAfee Security. CyberCop ASaP saves you time and money by managing your security via the Internet. Our up-to-date, industry-leading technology helps you identify vulnerabilities and proposes fixes that can be quickly implemented — all without the need to hire more staff, or purchase and maintain additional infrastructure. CyberCop ASaP

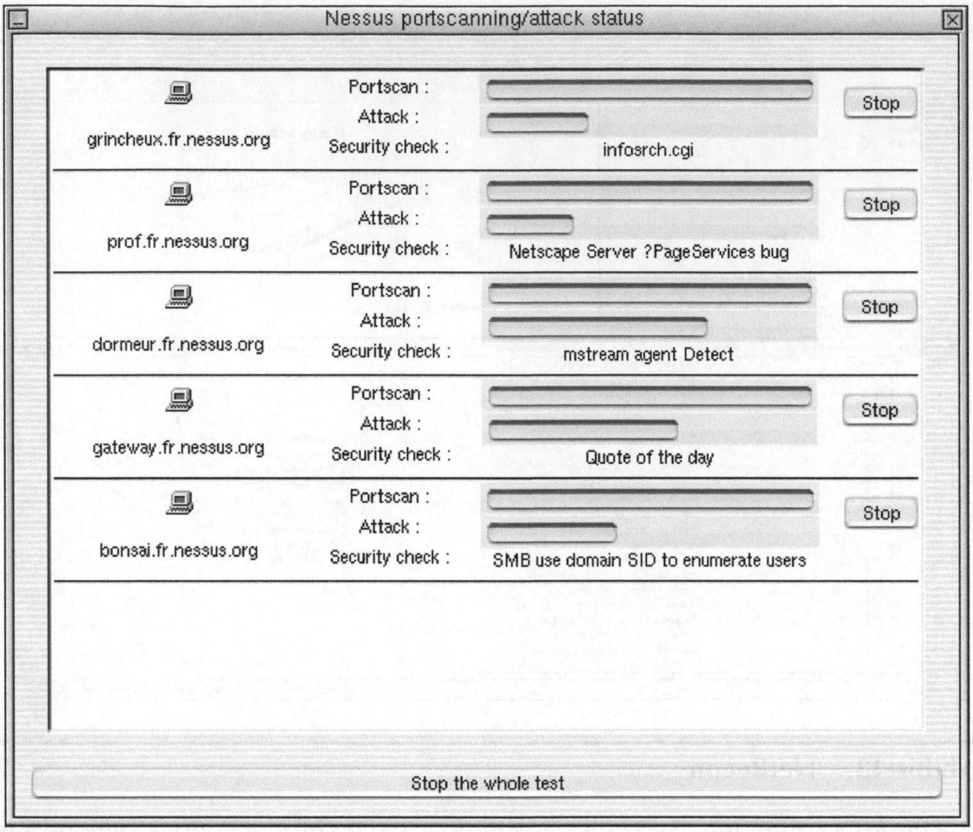

Exhibit 43.   Nessus

remotely evaluates the security of your network perimeter, DMZ, and externally visible assets. In fact, this managed security solution runs over 900 tests to detect vulnerabilities.

Opinion: A very commonly used tool for vulnerability assessment. This tool has a number of additional features, such as a packet building program to create your own vulnerability test.

Nessus

URL: http://www.nessus.org
Price: Free
OS: Linux
Vendor's comments: Unlike many other security scanners, Nessus (Exhibit 43) does not take anything for granted. It will not consider that a given service is running on a fixed port — that is, if you run your Web server on port 1234, Nessus will detect it and test its security. It will not make its security tests regarding the version number of the remote services, but will really attempt to exploit the vulnerability.

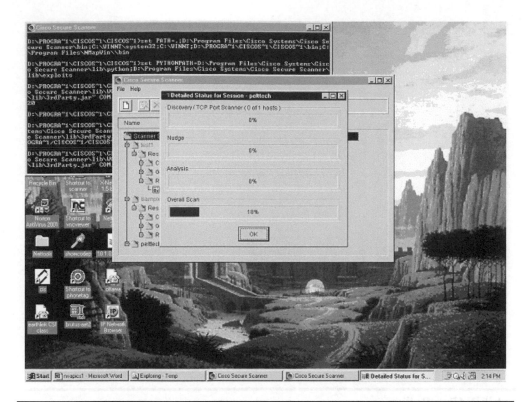

Exhibit 44. Cisco Secure Scanner

> *Opinion:* For the price, the Nessus tool is simply amazing. The upside is that the tool is completely free, but the downside is that there is no one to call for support. This tool has every bit of the functionality of the much more expensive pay tools but none of the cost. Nessus is a must-have tool.

Cisco Secure Scanner

> *URL:* http://www.cisco.com
>
> *Price:* ($–$$$$)
>
> *Vendor's comments:* Cisco Secure Scanner (formerly NetSonar) is an enterprise-class software tool offering superior network system identification, innovative data management, flexible user-defined vulnerability rules, comprehensive security reporting capabilities, and Cisco 24/7 worldwide support (Exhibit 44). Cisco Secure Scanner is a key component in Cisco's comprehensive network security solutions. It allows users to measure security, manage risk, and eliminate security vulnerabilities, thus enabling more secure network environments.
>
> *Opinion:* This tool appears to be young in its life cycle; currently it seems to be a bit cumbersome. As with the rest of Cisco's products, it will soon be a top-notch product.

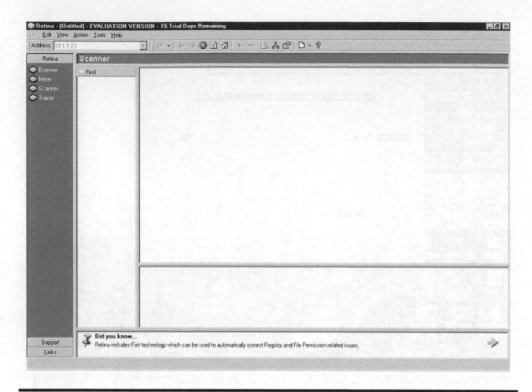

Exhibit 45. Retina

Retina

> *URL:* http://www.eeye.com
>
> *Price:* $$$
>
> *Vendor's comments:* Retina (Exhibit 45) is the award-winning network vulnerability scanner and remediation management system that discovers and helps fix all known security vulnerabilities on Internet, intranet, and extranet systems. Retina is easy to navigate and includes advanced reporting tools to help prioritize and isolate necessary fixes. Retina provides total control over auditing open gateways, user security policies, registry settings, as well as a long list of known security vulnerabilities.
>
> *Opinion:* This product is another good, all-around vulnerability scanner. The people at eeye have really put together an amazing product line with Retina, Secure IIS, Iris, Nmap for NT, etc.

Specialty Tools

Specialty tools do one thing and do it well. The use of these tools can be decided after the site assessment (see Exhibit 46).

- NetBIOS tools
- Web security tools
- Firewall auditing tools

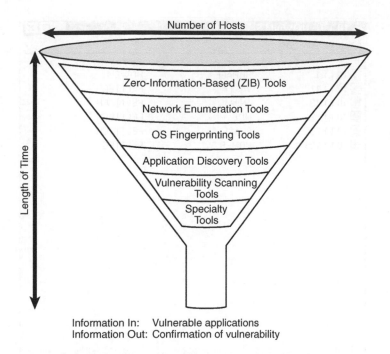

Information In: Vulnerable applications
Information Out: Confirmation of vulnerability

Exhibit 46.   The Vulnerability Assessment Model: Specialty Tool Layer

- Trojan detecting tools
- War dialing tools
- Miscellaneous tools
- NetBIOS tools
- Wireless tools
- War dialers
- Network sniffers

NetBIOS Tools

NetBIOS tools look at the security of Microsoft Windows networking. The tool reform these check by searching for open shares, available user accounts, and remote registry access.

Networld Scanner

> *URL:* http://www.pelttech.com
> *Price:* Free
> *OS:* NT
> *Opinion:* A fun, free, and easy-to-use utility that allows you to scan a large network quickly for open Microsoft shares (Exhibit 47). It can be a lot of fun to see what other Internet users are sharing out from their local hard drive.

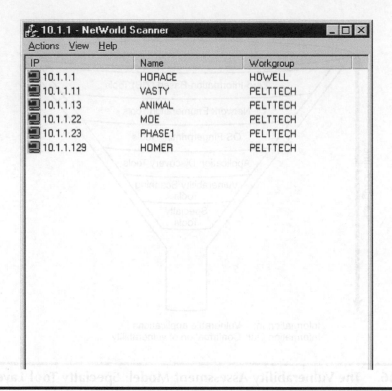

Exhibit 47.   NetWorld Scanner

Nat10

> *URL:* http://www.tux.org/pub/security/secnet/tools/nat10
> *Price:* Free
> *OS:* NT
> *Opinion:* The NetBIOS Auditing Tool (NAT) is designed to explore the NetBIOS file-sharing services offered by the target system (Exhibit 48). It implements a stepwise approach to gather information and attempt to obtain file system-level access as if it were a legitimate local client.

Legion

> *URL:* http://www.pelttech.com — for download
> *Price:* Free
> *OS:* NT
> *Opinion:* This tool is an easy-to-use GUI that will scan a Class C IP address space for open NetBIOS shares (Exhibit 49). The 2.1 version of the tool comes with a brute-force password cracker as well.

Essential Net Tools 3

> *URL:* http://www.tamos.com
> *Price:* $
> *OS:* NT

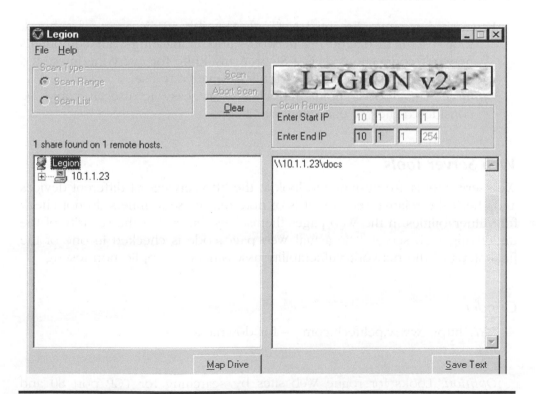

```
C:\WINNT\System32\cmd.exe - nat 10.1.1.23                           _ □ ×
[*]--- Attempting to connect with Username: `' Password: `TEMP'
[*]--- Attempting to connect with Username: `' Password: `SHARE'
[*]--- Attempting to connect with Username: `' Password: `WRITE'
[*]--- Attempting to connect with Username: `' Password: `FULL'
[*]--- Attempting to connect with Username: `' Password: `BOTH'
[*]--- Attempting to connect with Username: `' Password: `READ'
[*]--- Attempting to connect with Username: `' Password: `FILES'
[*]--- Attempting to connect with Username: `' Password: `DEMO'
[*]--- Attempting to connect with Username: `' Password: `TEST'
[*]--- Attempting to connect with Username: `' Password: `ACCESS'
[*]--- Attempting to connect with Username: `' Password: `USER'
[*]--- Attempting to connect with Username: `' Password: `BACKUP'
[*]--- Attempting to connect with Username: `' Password: `SYSTEM'
[*]--- Attempting to connect with Username: `' Password: `SERVER'
[*]--- Attempting to connect with Username: `' Password: `LOCAL'
[*]--- Attempting to connect with Username: `ADMINISTRATOR' Password: `'
[*]--- Attempting to connect with Username: `ADMINISTRATOR' Password: `ADMINISTR
ATOR'
[*]--- Attempting to connect with Username: `ADMINISTRATOR' Password: `GUEST'
[*]--- Attempting to connect with Username: `ADMINISTRATOR' Password: `ROOT'
[*]--- Attempting to connect with Username: `ADMINISTRATOR' Password: `ADMIN'
[*]--- Attempting to connect with Username: `ADMINISTRATOR' Password: `PASSWORD'

[*]--- Attempting to connect with Username: `ADMINISTRATOR' Password: `TEMP'
```

Exhibit 48.   NAT 10

Exhibit 49.   Legion

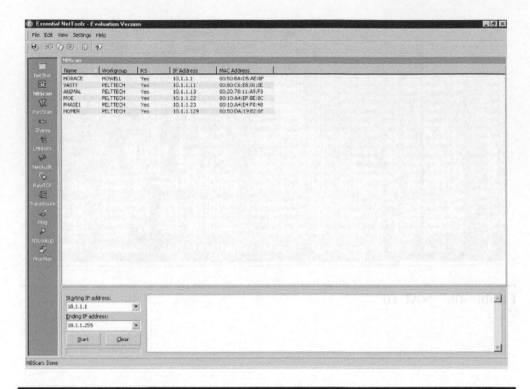

Exhibit 50. Essential Net Tools 3

> *Vendor's comments:* Essential NetTools (Exhibit 50) is a set of network
>   tools useful in diagnosing networks and monitoring your computer's
>   network connections. It is a Swiss Army knife for everyone interested
>   in a set of powerful network tools for everyday use.
> *Opinion:* This tool is point and click, very easy to use. It could be
>   considered the NT equivalent of Cheops.

Web Server Tools

Web server tools are designed to look at the http services of different devices
and check the relative security. It is of note that these scanners do not check
for vulnerabilities in the Web pages themselves, but rather the security of the
underlying Web server. The actual Web page code is checked in one of the
final steps of the network vulnerability assessment — application testing.

Grinder

> *URL:* http://www.pelttech.com — for download
> *Price:* Free
> *OS:* NT
> *Opinion:* Looks for rogue Web sites by searching for TCP port 80 and
>   grabbing the banner information (Exhibit 51). This tool scans large
>   ranges quickly, and has a very simple to user interface.

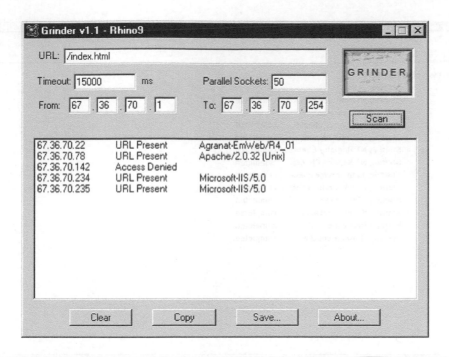

Exhibit 51. Grinder

VLAD the Scanner

URL: http://razor.bindview.com/tools/desc/VLAD_readme.html
Price: Free
OS: Linux
Vendor's comments: Welcome to VLAD the Scanner, a freeware scanner that checks for common security problems. VLAD checks for the items referenced in the SANS Top Ten list of common security problems, found at http://www.sans.org/topten.htm.
Opinion: Because a large number of the top vulnerabilities are against Web servers, this tool fits well here in the Web server tool section.

Cerberus Internet Scanner

URL: http://www.cerberus-infosec.co.uk/cis.shtml
Price: Free
Vendor's comments: Cerberus Internet Scanner (CIS; Exhibit 52) is a free security scanner written and maintained by Cerberus Information Security, Ltd., and is designed to help administrators locate and fix security holes in their computer systems. This tool is a must!
Opinion: A nice, all-in-one scanner that does an especially good job looking for vulnerabilities in Web servers. This tool will probably be a purchase product soon.

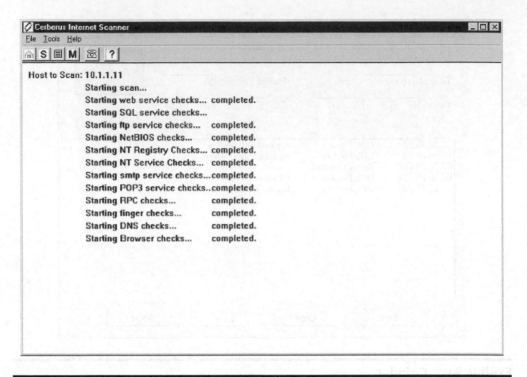

Exhibit 52.   Cerberus Internet Scanner

Password Cracking Tools

Password cracking tools uncover passwords to check for policy compliance. The process of cracking the passwords will be very processor intensive so it is best to try to run the password cracking utility on your laptop. However, some organizations may not permit this, so the next best step is to run the password cracking after hours when fewer people are on the system. As a rule-of-thumb, to get a good sample of network password compliance, run the dictionary attack through to completion and then run the brute-force crack for about an hour before stopping the process. This will get all passwords that are dictionary words, and most passwords that are dictionary words with a special character stuck on to the beginning or the end.

LC4

> *URL:* http://www.atstake.com/research/lc/index.html
> *Price:* $
> *OS:* NT
> *Vendor's comments:* LC4 (Exhibit 53) is the latest version of the award-winning password auditing and recovery application, L0phtCrack. It provides two critical capabilities to Windows network administrators: LC4 helps administrators secure Windows-authenticated networks through comprehensive auditing of Windows NT and Windows 2000

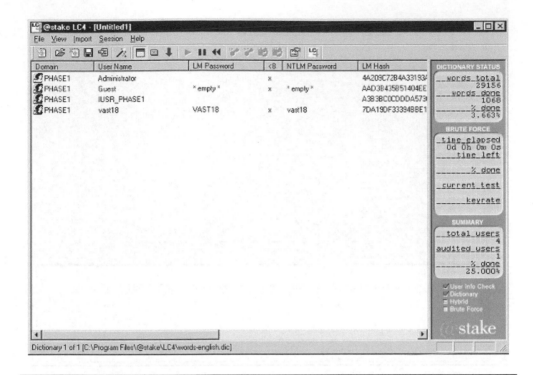

Exhibit 53. LC4

user account passwords; and LC4 recovers Windows user-account passwords to streamline migration of users to another authentication system
or to access accounts whose passwords are lost.

Opinion: This is one of the founding tools in both hacking and vulnerability
assessment. It is easy to use and very fast. As of this writing, a free
command-line version was still available.

John the Ripper

URL: http://www.openwall.com/john
OS: NT
Price: Free
Opinion: This tool requires cgywin to be installed on the system. It is not
as straightforward as it could be. Better help files would really help
this tool.

Pandora

URL: http://www.nmrc.org
Price: Free
OS: NT
Opinion: This is a good password cracker for Novell NDS passwords
(Exhibit 54).

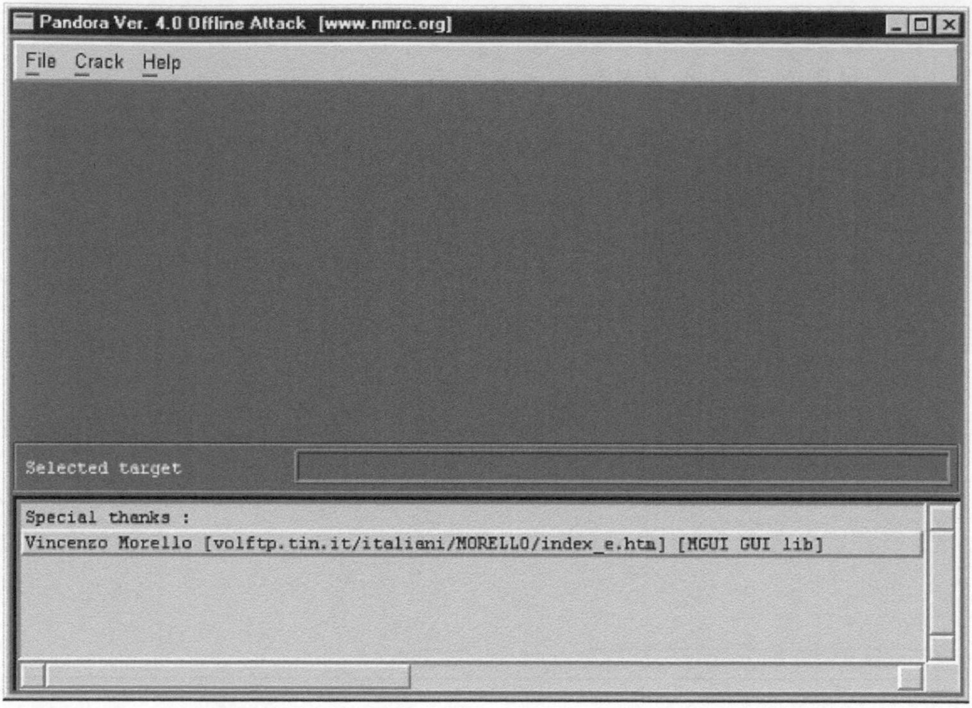

Exhibit 54.   Pandora

Brutus

> *URL:* http://www.hoobie.net/brutus
> *Price:* Free
> *OS:* NT
> *Opinion:* A great brute-force password cracker for common applications
> (Exhibit 55). It is often necessary to use as a network administrator.

Application Tools

At this layer of the vulnerability scanning model (see Exhibit 56), you are testing the Web-enabled application in the target network for vulnerabilities in the customer-written code. These tools check for cookie manipulation, URL modification, HTML comments with inappropriate content, and also underlying vulnerabilities in the Web server itself.

SANCTUM AppScan

> *URL:* http://www.sanctuminc.com
> *Price:* $$$$
> *OS:* NT

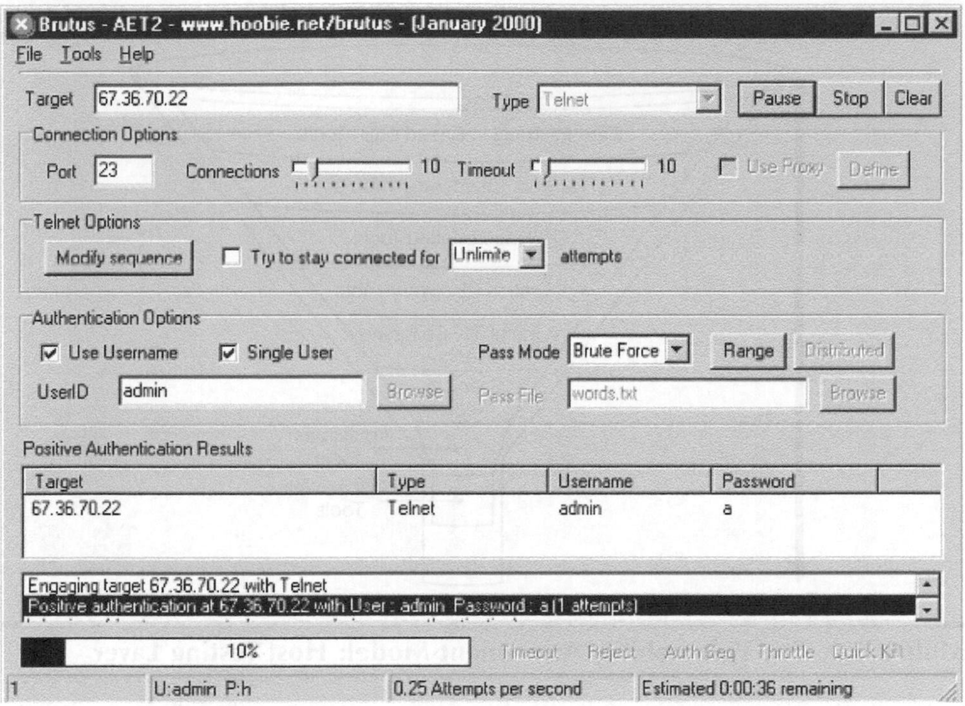

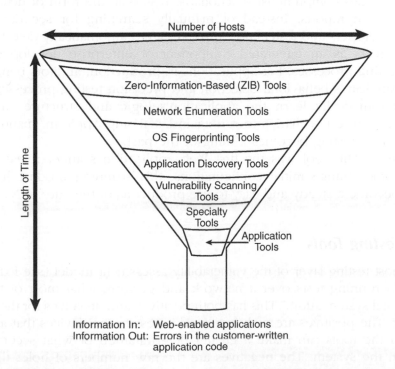

Exhibit 55.   Brutus

Number of Hosts

Length of Time

Zero-Information-Based (ZIB) Tools

Network Enumeration Tools

OS Fingerprinting Tools

Application Discovery Tools

Vulnerability Scanning Tools

Specialty Tools

Application Tools

Information In: Web-enabled applications
Information Out: Errors in the customer-written
                  application code

Exhibit 56.   The Vulnerability Assessment Model: Application Scanning Layer

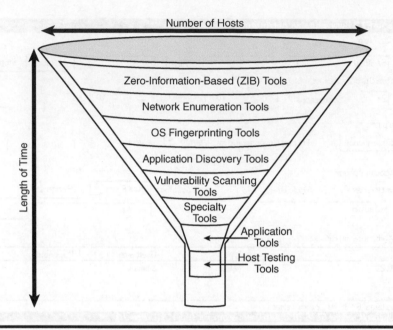

Exhibit 57.   The Vulnerability Assessment Model: Host Testing Layer

> *Vendor's comments:* AppScan is the most comprehensive Web application
> security testing and vulnerability assessment tool available today. It
> explores applications, automatically creates and customizes tests, and
> provides comprehensive actionable results in the form of detailed and
> custom reports. Instead of manually searching for security defects,
> developers and testers use AppScan 3.5 to automatically detect security
> defects as an integrated component of enterprise development and
> testing processes. For applications in production, auditors benefit from
> AppScan's behavioral detection and precision testing processes, which
> automatically learn the application's logic and structure, and build
> custom test scenarios to run against it. Using AppScan, manual appli-
> cation testing becomes a thing of the past.
>
> *Opinion:* This tool was the first Web application scanner released. After
> some strange initial configurations, this scanning product has really
> become a steady and easy-to-use product as of the current NT version.

Host Testing Tools

At the host testing layer of the vulnerability assessment model (see Exhibit 57),
you stop running tests over a network and perform what most of the tools
call a "local system audit." This has both positives and negatives for the security
assessor. The positives are with increased access to the devices that are being
assessed the tools can make a greater determination of what security holes
reside in the system. The negatives are the raw numbers of holes that these
systems can uncover. It is not uncommon for some of these tools to uncover
more than 1700 vulnerabilities on a single system. So, when running the host-

based tools, remember to verify each finding and be prepared to sort through a huge number of vulnerabilities.

Enterprise Security Manager

> *URL:* http://www/symantec.com
>
> *Price:* $$$
>
> *Vendor's comments:* Symantec Enterprise Security Manager 5.5 provides comprehensive security policy compliance management of mission-critical E-business applications and operating systems across the enterprise. From a single location, it manages the discovery of policy deviations and vulnerabilities for services housing mission-critical applications and data on the network, enterprisewide. With its intelligent tools, administrators can quickly and cost effectively create baselines and measure performance against those baselines to identify systems that are not in compliance and correct faulty settings to bring systems back into compliance.
>
> *Opinion:* This tool allows the assessor to monitor several devices from one central console. Agents can be installed and removed from systems without requiring a reboot, and the number of operating systems is spectacular.

SecurityAnalyst

> *URL:* http://www.intrusion.com
>
> *Price:* $$
>
> *Vendor's comments:* Intrusion SecurityAnalyst software is an agent-less assessment tool that does not require the installation of software agents on target systems. It is designed to provide centralized audit data of all key Windows security features. With its built-in policy definition and comprehensive reporting capabilities, SecurityAnalyst can help administrators analyze network risks so they can take immediate corrective action to safeguard network integrity.
>
> *Opinion:* This is a good product for evaluating the effective security of a Windows NT system.

Netlq's Security Analyzer

> *URL:* http://www.netiq.com
>
> *Price:* $$$$
>
> *Vendor's comments:* NetIQ's Security Analyzer is a flexible, enterprise-scale vulnerability assessment product for Windows, Solaris, and Linux platforms that protects your systems from costly downtime and security

breaches. This industry-leading product scans computers in your network for vulnerabilities, providing reports that help you correct problems and comply with company security policies. The extensible architecture and flexible deployment options make Security Analyzer your best choice among enterprise vulnerability assessment tools.

Opinion: A multiple award-winning tool, this tool does exactly what it is supposed to do.

Miscellaneous Tools

These tools are good to have around but do not fit firmly into any category. It could be argued that some of these tools are not vulnerability assessment tools, but having some of them on hand "just in case" may not be a bad idea.

The Coroner's Toolkit

URL: http://www.porcupine.org/forensics/tct.html
Price: Free
OS: Linux
Opinion: This tool is used for local system forensics. It actually is comprised of a number of separate tools, such as a MD5 hash generator utility. The tools in this kit often come in handy.

Fireball

URL: http://www.pelttech.com — to download
Price: Free
OS: NT
Opinion: This tool checks for well-known Trojan applications running on a system. The tool is somewhat limited because it does not scan a network range; it scans a single IP instead.

NetProwler

URL: http://www.symantec.com
Price: $$$
Vendor's comments: Symantec NetProwler 3.5 complements existing security countermeasures and fortifies any company's E-business initiatives by offering dynamic network intrusion detection that transparently examines network traffic. It instantly identifies logs and terminates unauthorized use, misuse, and abuse of computer systems by internal saboteurs and external hackers.
Opinion: This tool may be going away or migrated into the newer Symantec product. NetProwler filled the role of a traditional network sniffer in a

vulnerability assessment. The greatest feature of this tool was the intelligence built in to discard the normal network traffic and still alert you to your scans getting past network security devices that were supposed to stop them.

WinCrash

URL: http://www.pelttech.com — to download

Price: Free

Opinion: This is the tool that has the script to allow you to try the fragmentation or data leakage attacks against Cisco and CheckPoint network devices. It works well with NetProwler (listed above).

Wireless Tools

If you are going to be assessing wireless network security in your vulnerability assessment, you will need a few things:

- Wireless network cards
- A prism chipset card for some utilities
- An Orinoco chipset card for other utilities
- An external antenna or two. One of the best places to get 802.11b antennas on the Internet is at http://www.antennasolutions.com. A good 5-dB, multi-directional antenna is a must, but you can go up to a 72-dB omni-directional antenna and cover a range of a few city blocks
- Time to keep abreast of the latest changes to the wireless networking standards
- Software — discussed below

Netstumbler

URL: http://www.netstumbler.com

Price: Free

OS: NT

Opinion: This is a very fun tool with which to play. You could fire up your laptop, plug in your antenna, and go walking around looking for wireless access points that are giving away free Internet access. Then you are supposed to draw a crazy symbol with a piece of chalk, but that really does not seem to make sense to us.

WEPCrack

URL: http://wepcrack.sourceforge.net

Price: Free

OS: Linux

Vendor's comments: WEPCrack is an open source tool for breaking 802.11 WEP secret keys. This tool is an implementation of the attack described by Fluhrer, Mantin, and Shamir in their article "Weaknesses in the Key Scheduling Algorithm of RC4" at http://www.eyetap.org/~rguerra/toronto2001/rc4_ksaproc.pdf.

Air Snort

URL: http://airsnort.shmoo.com/
Price: Free
OS: Linux

Network Sniffers

These products monitor network segments for traffic. There is a discussion of network sniffing in the "Site Survey" section.

Ethereal for Linux or Windows

URL: http://www.ethereal.com
Price: Free
Vendor's comments: Ethereal is a free network protocol analyzer for UNIX and Windows. It allows you to examine data from a live network or from a capture file on disk. You can interactively browse the capture data, viewing summary and detail information for each packet. Ethereal has several powerful features, including a rich display filter language and the ability to view the reconstructed stream of a TCP session.

Opinion: A tremendous product for free.

Iris

URL: http://www.eeye.com
Price: $$
OS: NT
Opinion: A very capable network sniffer with lots of bells and whistles, Iris does a very good job decoding and breaking down the packet information.

Sniffer Pro

URL: http://www.nai.com
Price: $$

Vendor's comments: Sniffer Investigator is an affordable, turnkey 10/100 Ethernet network management solution. It addresses the unique troubleshooting needs of small and medium-sized enterprises by combining six essential network management functions into a single, easy-to-manage appliance. The fully integrated appliance eliminates downtime and limits productivity loss caused by abnormally behaving applications. Sniffer Investigator is a flexible solution for managing network traffic between the Internet and corporate networks, or between network segments and users. When problems are reported, Sniffer Investigator can jump into action and provide a bird's-eye view of the situation instantly, assisting with defining whether the origin of the problem occurs on the present segment or if the Sniffer Investigator needs to move to a different segment.

Opinion: Sniffer Pro is almost a *de facto* standard for network sniffing. It does everything well, and is one of the first to incorporate new features.

War Dialing

Phonetag

URL: http://packetstorm.widexs.nl/wardialers
Price: Free
Opinion: Our favorite war dialer (Exhibit 58). It has a very easy-to-use Visual Basic interface that makes it just like dialing a telephone.

The Hackers Choice

URL: http://packetstorm.widexs.nl/wardialers
Price: Free
OS: DOS
Opinion: A very commonly used war dialer.

Telesweep

URL: http://www.securelogix.com
Price: $$
Opinion: This is the best product if you have the capital to spend. This product has many more features than the other war dialers.

Step 4: Conduct the Assessment

Because we discussed most of conducting the assessment in the tools section, we do not have a lot of ground left to cover here (see Exhibit 59). There are,

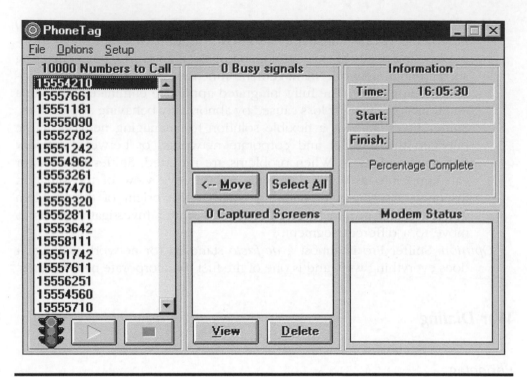

Exhibit 58.   PhoneTag

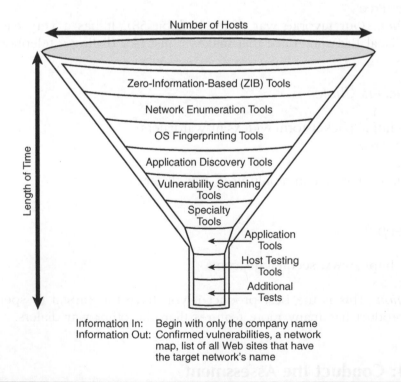

Exhibit 59.   The Vulnerability Assessment Model

however, a few key points to remember. First, beware of the tools that you run. There are primarily two types of tests: active and passive. The following are examples of active testing:

- Probes using scanners:
  - Nessus — broad view
  - Webtrends Security Analyzer — focused view
  - SolarWinds tools — Cisco devices
- Use of exploit scripts and "underground" tools:
  - Password crackers — on all platforms and by sniffing
  - War dialers — remote access
  - Web exploit tools — Web server specific
  - Wireless testing

It is important to note that using any of the tests above will degrade network performance in one aspect or another. Some tools have a very small footprint on network performance while others can cause nearly total interruption. So be aware that any active tool will increase network traffic, processor utilization, or both. On most networks this will not be a problem; however, you should study the network with the tools cited in the network sniffer section or the tools cited under the network discovery section of the zero-information-based attacks.

In addition to increasing network traffic or processor load, your testing can have other negative impacts on the target network. Several of the tools we examined have the ability to run denial-of-service (DoS) testing. Here is a handy rule-of-thumb:

Denial of service tests tend to deny service.

So be aware of the effects of DoS testing a production network. This is especially true if you are testing during peak production times. Remember that if you are not sure, do not guess on a production network. If you are afraid of the consequences of running a test, take it home and run it against your home network, or against another test network. However, your test network should be a network that you have permission to test. This leads us to another point: only test network systems that you have permission to test. Do not say that we did not warn you. Testing systems that you are not authorized to can get you in a world of trouble. So be cautious.

The second type of testing that you will do during a network vulnerability assessment is passive testing. During a passive test, you seldom have any impact on network performance (see Exhibit 60). The following tests are examples of passive tests:

- SNMP and RMON "listening":
  - General network sniffing
  - Wireless sniffing

Exhibit 60. Testing Chart

Type of Test	Active	Passive
Host	Any host scanner	TCP dump or RMON listening
Network	Any vulnerability scanner tool	Network sniffing

- Attack signature "sniffing":
  - Symantec NetProwler
  - ISS RealSecure — network
  - Symantec Intruder Alert (ITA) — host/server

The only type of testing not listed above is quality assurance testing. This is a very important step in the process. As we discussed previously, by using a multi-test environment (MTE), we will help to minimize both false positives and false negative reports. While all the software we looked at in the tools section is great software, there are just too many network conditions that can interfere with accurate testing. So always double-check the tests that you run and keep records of that tests that you run as you run them. There will be more discussion on this in the section on documentation.

The following is a brief checklist of items to watch out for while performing local or host testing:

- *Device configuration:* Does it support corporate policies?
- *Local exploits:* Signs of intrusion?
- *Uneven administration:* Do some systems stand out as easy targets?
- *Named after products:* for example, Exchange, Catalyst, or ColdFusion
- System is not named according to the corporate naming convention
- System is named after the user who works on it
- *Logging:* Is logging enabled and read?

The following is a brief checklist of items to watch out for while performing network or remote testing:

- Sniffing for attack signatures to see if security devices are passing packets that should be stopped
- Look for less secure entry points to the network (backdoors), such as:
  - WAN connections
  - Rogue connections
  - Corporate VPNs to other networks
- *Access Controls:* are they adequate, and are they enforced?
- *Social engineering:* using nontechnical means to get access to systems, but that is another book entirely
- *Quality assurance:* always double-check

Step 5: Analysis

This leads us to Step 5 of the six-step model. In this layer of the model, there is not too much that you can learn about in books. The best way to get better at analysis is to practice. You should download the tools you are interested in and use them to test your home network and test networks again and again. The more times you run through vulnerability assessments, the better you will become at analysis. Here are a few key points of the analysis:

- Analysis can take up to four days for every day of data gathering. This is not an exact science but it is a pretty good rule-of-thumb.
- Analysis can be done after each set of tools is run. As a matter of fact, it is best to analyze the data after each set of tools. This is the only way to get the important seed information for the next level of tests.
- Analysis will give you feedback during testing. This will help you understand the structure of the target network, as well as additional places to look for vulnerabilities.

Step 6: Documentation

Welcome to the final step of the six-step model — documentation. This is probably the most important component of an NVA. It was once said that you can never get in trouble for having too much documentation. There are a few reasons to keep such detailed documentation. First, in many cases, one person may not run the complete vulnerability assessment, and with good documentation it is easier for a second person to continue the vulnerability assessment. Another reason to keep good documentation is what we call "the lights are dimmer in my office today; is there any chance that your tests have anything to do with that?" rule. Most people who work on the target network will not understand what you are doing, and as such will have a tendency to blame your tests for everything that is happening on the network. To combat having to answer these questions again and again, the best way to defeat this process is with a good test log of what you are doing and when you are doing it. To keep track of this, simply build a spreadsheet in Excel. Here is what should be in your test logs at a minimum:

- Logging needs to occur as each test is being done
- Log the tests — tool name or tool component
- Include the start and stop times
- Connection diagram with IP
- Brief description of the results for your memory and to help others who may follow

Summary

In this chapter we looked at both the methodology and the tools for conducting a network vulnerability assessment. We used a six-step model to help depict what we will be doing, and also to allow us to maximize the time spent. We began by conducting a site survey to determine what we would be encountering on our target network. Next, we researched the most current vulnerabilities from common Internet sources and began to formulate a plan for what we absolutely needed to test. After that, we actually went about building our toolkit, and we discussed the network vulnerability assessment model and how each group of tools would be used in our assessment. We also looked at a sampling of popular tools that we could select for each level of the model. Then we looked at some good ideas for minimizing our impact on the target network while running our tools. Next, we discussed the analysis process, the length of time necessary to do the analysis, and ideas for how to improve doing the analysis portion of a vulnerability assessment. Finally, we looked into the documentation and exactly what we need to log and how to protect ourselves while running the assessment. Now all you need to do is go out and practice.

Chapter 7

Network Vulnerability Assessment Sample Report

The following material is a sample network vulnerability assessment (NVA) report. It will give you the basics that should be included in your report back to your management or client. Be sure to review Appendix C to see a complete NVA report.

Table of Contents

To help the reader of the report search for the section that he or she is interested in, make certain to include a table of contents. Use the formatting process available in the word processing product you use. You will see the sections that should be included in your report. Remember that ease of reading will improve the acceptance of your team's findings.

Executive Summary

The executive summary should not be longer than one page, double sided. The sections that are typically included are:

- Introduction
- Methodology
- Results and Conclusions
- Recommendations

A sample of the executive summary is shown in Exhibit 1.

Body of the NVA Report

Methodology Overview

The Overview in Exhibit 2 describes the methodology used by the NVA team to gather the information upon which the recommendations are based. The NVA follows the Facilitated Risk Analysis Process (FRAP) for risk analysis.

Security Profile

This section (see Exhibit 3) contains documents and data collected during Phase I (Data Collection) and Phase II (Interviews, Information Reviews, and Hands-On Investigation) of the NVA process:

- *Background information:* baseline information about Bogus Corporation
- *Company documents:* policies, procedures, processes, training materials, and network topology; copies of relevant company documentation are included in Appendix A of the report
- *Summaries of relevant information* gathered during interviews with engineers, administrators, and other users of network services
- *Reports from hands-on investigation* of the Bogus Corporation's network operations

Analysis

This section (see Exhibit 4) details the vulnerabilities and risks discovered in the organization's network operations during Phase I (Data Collection) and Phase II (On Site). This analysis is divided into the functional areas of policy, management, architecture, and safeguards. Emphasis is placed on the impact that these problems, vulnerabilities, and unmitigated risks have (or could have) on the organization's ability to do business.[1]

For each indicated area or element, the following issues are addressed:

- Current problems, threats, and related vulnerabilities
- Potential vulnerabilities
- Perceived risk level
- Recommendations

Key Safeguards for Providing Information Security

See Exhibit 5 for a sample of this section.

Conclusions

This section (Exhibit 6) provides recommendations for minimizing the vulnerabilities and mitigating the risks detailed in Phase III (Analysis). These recommendations are ranked in order of their critical importance. This section concludes with a summative table listing all recommendations in order of importance (risk levels).

Final Comments

See Exhibit 7 for a sample of Final Comments.

Summary Table of Risk, Vulnerabilities, and Recommendations

See Exhibit 8 for a sample Summary Table of Risk, Vulnerabilities, and Recommendations.

Glossary

See Exhibit 9 for a sample Glossary.

Summary

When developing your findings and recommendations, stick to the facts. Try not to let your opinions and those of the team color the findings. It is important to stay as neutral as possible. Listen to the people in the interviews and get their concerns and opinions. Do not go into an assessment with a preconceived idea of what the results will be.

The sample report is presented as a guide to what you might want to consider including in your report. Check Appendix C to see a complete report.

Notes

1. In a real network vulnerability assessment, this section is quite detailed, quite technical, and covers all aspects of the organization's computing systems. For the purposes of this example document, only a few vulnerabilities and risks in each category arecovered.

Exhibit 1. Sample Executive Summary

Important Note: This report contains sensitive and highly confidential information that could be used to the detriment of Bogus Corporation. It is strongly recommended that this report is classified as confidential and distribution is restricted. All copies should be numbered and kept in a secure location when not in use.

Introduction

The Network Vulnerability Assessment Team (NVA Team) reviewed the security policy and practices of the Bogus Corporation network. This effort revealed that the network supports critical functions with sensitive data that, in turn, support manufacturing, finance, and product design and development. Through documentation reviews, in-depth interviews with key Bogus staff and testing of portions of the network and network devices, the team drew conclusions regarding the security of the network and the integrity of the data it supports for Bogus Corporation. An investigation of these critical systems revealed serious risks to corporate data and communications, which can be mitigated by countermeasures recommended by our team of specialists.

Methodology

The NVA Team spoke with the managers and technicians of the network systems as well as the information security practitioners who provide the custodial protection for both critical and sensitive data in the organization's network. The team collected available documentation, regardless of status (draft, preliminary outline, etc.) and conducted individual interviews with staff associated with several business units. By paying close attention to actual practice, and with the cooperation of the Bogus staff who contributed to our understanding of both policy and practice, we have been able to identify areas of security concern and to determine appropriate measures that the Bogus Corporation can take to improve the security of its data and systems.

Results and Conclusions

The Bogus Corporation depends on a vast, complex network that supports a significant amount of critical data. The NVA Team investigated several aspects of the organization's security and discovered that sensitive and critical data has been exposed to a number of risks, as follows:

- Lack of a coordinated security policy that addresses the protection of business-critical data (ISO 17799, Item 3.1)
- Physical security of main servers and computer facilities (ISO 17799, Item 7.2)
- Lack of awareness of basic data security practices among most Bogus staff (ISO 17799, Item 6.2)

Exhibit 1. Sample Executive Summary (Continued)

- Lack of a cohesive and coordinated disaster recovery and business continuity plan (ISO 17799, Item 11.1)
- Inadequate controls on access to the corporate network and confidential corporate data (ISO 17799, Item 5.1)
- Lack of a clearly defined security administration role (ISO 17799, Item 4.1)
- Inadequate oversight of additions and deletions of applications and equipment to the network (ISO 17799, Item 10.5)
- Lack of established procedures for handling security incidents (ISO 17799, Item 10.2, 10.5)
- Inadequate logging of security-related events (ISO 17799, Item 6.3)

Recommendations

The results of the NVA indicate that Bogus Corporation needs to address network security issues from a business systems aspect. The lack of coordination for security issues leads to serious gaps in the security of the organization that could be exploited by a hacker or an unauthorized user.

- Establish a security oversight committee that is tasked with developing a comprehensive security plan and implementation schedule. To be effective, it must be evident that this committee receives complete support from senior management (ISO 17799, Item 4.1.1).
- The ability to recover the network from a man-made or natural disaster needs to be assured. The organization needs to develop a comprehensive disaster recovery/business continuity plan that can ensure that business-critical operations can be brought back online rapidly in the event of a security incident or business interruption (ISO 17799, Item 11.1.3).
- Network and system administrators should be trained in the principles and common practices of network security. They should be given the opportunity for ongoing security training because the security field is constantly responding to new threats to data security and integrity (ISO 17799, Item 6.2.1).
- The Bogus Corporation should develop security policies that define access criteria matrixed by function and data sensitivity. At the least, anomalous network events should be logged and audited on a regular basis (ISO 17799, Item 9.1.1).
- The physical security of the physical plant needs to be reviewed. Access to critical hardware (servers, routers, and cables) must be limited to those who have been approved for access based on their job functions (ISO 17799, Item 7.1.1).
- Shredders need to be provided for secure disposal of confidential and sensitive documents and other media. Staff needs to be trained to distinguish between confidential data that requires special handling and ordinary trash (ISO 17799, Item 5.2.2).
- All staff needs to be trained in appropriate password control and use, and password checking needs to be implemented on the network (ISO 17799, Item 9.2.3).

Exhibit 2.   Methodology Overview

Introduction

Originally, the utility of computers lay in their ability to accelerate business processes. If the system went down, it was inconvenient, but it was not catastrophic. Today, computers and networks are used for much more than automating our business processes. If the network is down, we are not working. If the data in the customer database is not available, we are losing business. If a safety-critical system is down, lives may be endangered. This enterprise depends on our computers and networks; they are integral to the success of the business objective and mission.

Business decisions are based on information stored, generated, and presented electronically. An effective information protection program is measured by whether the organization exercised due diligence in seeking to prevent and detect criminal conduct by its employee and other agents. In the event of a security breach, corporate officers must be able to show that reasonable care could avert charges of negligence.

The NVA provides management with the information they need to determine the security, availability, and integrity of the information and processes stored on their network(s). The NVA outlines the existing vulnerabilities in the system and identifies strategies for mitigating those vulnerabilities.

Because every organization has different security requirements, the NVA is implemented to meet the specific security needs. The NVA evaluates the systems and the data in the context of the client's operating environment, business practices, and strategic goals. The goal is to reach the right balance among security, effective system utilization, and cost for the enterprise.

Methodology

The NVA team met with Bogus Corporation staff to review your goals and objectives for this NVA. Once the scope was established, a plan was developed for gathering relevant information from major business units. The NVA team identified the key functions in network operations that were critically important to interview, and provided the NVA team with the names of the people that should be contacted for these interviews. The Point of Contact (POC) assisted the team in contacting the people who needed to be interviewed. After reviewing the documentation and the interview information, the team determined areas that required additional information, which were requested. The team then analyzed all the data received, with particular attention to the needs and concerns of the network staff and network customers that were interviewed, and produced a Draft Report of findings, which was given to the NVA sponsor. This Draft Report becomes final after the sponsor reviews the findings and their comments are noted in the Final Report. The NVA team investigated all the areas that exemplify how the network is managed. The NVA team spoke with people who are familiar with the policies and practices in effect at the time of the visit.

Exhibit 2.   Methodology Overview (Continued)

The review of Bogus Corporation's environment included the following steps:

- Phase I: Data Collection
  - Collected and began review of business objectives, strategic business directions, mission statements, etc.
  - Collected and began review of existing policies, procedures, standards, applicable regulations, laws, guidelines, circulars, letters, memos, audit comments, etc.
- Phase II: Interviews, Information Review, and Hands-On Investigation
  - Interviewed key department and business unit representatives
  - Interviewed internal customers of network services
  - Evaluated security performance of key hardware, network, and software implementations
- Phase III: Analysis
  - Identified existing security concerns and analyzed possible mitigating practices
  - Identified critical data issues and sensitive data practices
  - Formulated actions to facilitate a successful implementation of a comprehensive security program
- Phase IV: Draft Report
  - Assessed Bogus' existing security policies and procedures and made recommendations, where appropriate
  - Evaluated risks implicit in Bogus' existing network implementation and made recommendations for improved security practices, where appropriate
  - Assessed the effectiveness of currently implemented safeguards (including firewalls) and made recommendations for improvement, where appropriate
  - Presented the *Draft Report* to members of the Information Technology Group and solicited their comments, which will be included in the Final Report
- Phase V: Final Report
  - A white paper and presentation to senior management (COO, CIO, and executive managers); the NVA Team is available to answer questions and clarify issues as needed

Exhibit 3. Security Profile

Background Information

Bogus Corporation is a large (15,000+) manufacturing organization with interests in the United States and several Middle Eastern countries. Founded in 1962 as a major supplier of oil drilling equipment to U.S. oil companies, Bogus expanded to Saudi Arabia and Iraq during the late 1960s. Despite occasional disruptions to business operations in the Arabian Gulf, Bogus Corporation continues to have significant business interests in the Middle East. Bogus Corporate Headquarters are in Houston, Texas; and the Engineering and Manufacturing Divisions operate primarily from their facilities in Galveston, Texas.

Seven Bogus regional offices in Europe and the Middle East provide sales and consulting services only. All parts are shipped from U.S. ports and transshipped through various Arab ports, depending on final destination. U.S. business relies heavily on networked operations, especially between HQ and Manufacturing. Communications between regional sales offices and HQ are conducted by phone and fax, and increasingly by electronic communications over fast modems. The Houston and Galveston facilities are connected by a dedicated high-speed WAN. The Information Technology Group supports 15,000+ users, and all hardware and software implementations. Supported platforms include MVS, UNIX, Win95, and NT. Supported applications include office productivity tools, GroupWare (Lotus Notes), specialized engineering and finance applications, and complex databases for Sales and Human Resources.

List of Company Documentation

The team collected the following documents during our review of the organization's environment:

- Network Diagram
- System Administrator Operations Manual
- Blueprints of the Houston Central Computer Services Facility
- Human Resources Guidelines for Terminating Staff
- Bogus Policies and Procedures
- New User Account Request Form
- Nondisclosure Agreements (for visitors and consultants)
- Backup Recovery Guidelines
- Bogus Organizational Chart
- Employee Directory
- "Quick-Reference" Card for password policy given to all new employees
- Recent network auditing logs

Exhibit 3. Security Profile (Continued)

Interview Reports*

The following is a summary of the interviews conducted with representatives of Bogus Corporation. Significant outcomes of the interviews only are presented; however, detailed questions and answers can be made available as required.

Interviewees were asked questions regarding their job description, number of years in their positions, scope of their duties, their relationship to data and to the network, what critical or sensitive data knowledge they possessed, and what areas of concern with the protection of corporate information they had identified.

- *Network architect.* A team of network specialists maintains the network and monitors its usage. They are responsible for ensuring network availability and observing anomalies. Network implementation and practice is not governed by policies. Knowledge of network operations is often *ad hoc* and undocumented. The emphasis is upon ease of access rather than on protection of information. No automated tools are available to monitor intrusions or spoofing.
- *Executive assistant to the operations manager.* Houston facilities access is controlled by card key readers and by the receptionist in the main lobby. Exterior doors are often propped open during the day but the security guards ensure that all doors are closed and locked after 5 p.m. All employees are issued photograph-bearing identification badges that must be worn in a visible position. Contractors and other temporary workers are also issued photo IDs, and visitors to the facility must display temporary passes. New employees are issued card keys and passes as part of the new employee orientation facilitated by HR. When an employee loses a card key or an ID badge, he or she must request replacements in person from the building security office.
- *Help desk supervisor.* Requests for computer accounts for new employees come to the help desk in writing from HR. Access rights are determined by job classification and job function. Often, modifications must be made to access rights based on requests from the employee's supervisor. Because of the volume of work, computer accounts for new employees are often created several days before the employee starts. The default password for new users is widely known throughout the organization. When employees forget their passwords, they call the help desk to have their password reset to the default. The only identification is the employee name on the telephone display at the help desk. Password sharing does happen, although the company applies sanctions whenever it is discovered.

---

* In a real Security Impact Analysis, many more interviews would be recorded. In an organization of the size of Bogus Corporation, the NVA team would probably conduct between 15 to 25 interviews.

Exhibit 3.   Security Profile (Continued)

- *Product development administrator.* This person is responsible for managing the paperwork and data for the engineering department. He maintains configuration information in an engineering database, and handles the physical storage of blueprints and other engineering design documents. Design documents and blueprints are checked out to staff as needed, but careful logging of check-outs and check-ins is *not* maintained. When someone requests a document that is not in the document cabinets, the administrator sends an e-mail asking for the document. Most documents turn up, although a few have disappeared over the years. The cabinets are usually locked at 5 p.m. when the administrator leaves, but he does leave them unlocked if an engineer needs after-hours access.
- *Network system administrator. Houston.* This person's primary responsibility is to keep the network up and running. The network uses Novell's NetWare v4.1, with Windows NT, Sun, and HP platforms. The multi-segmented network is backed up daily, and recovery of any server is based on specific configuration and installation criteria and data maintained in the Backup Recovery Guidelines. Some critical systems are mirrored, so that those servers can be taken offline for maintenance and upgrades without disrupting ongoing work.
- *Sales administrator.* This person provides support services to the U.S. sales team, which mostly works off-site. Each remote employee has a laptop with a modem to communicate with HQ. All sales people are given training in remote dial-in, and part of the training covers dial-in and laptop security.

Hands-On Investigation Reports

The following is a summary of information gathered from probing the network, visiting primary servers, and investigating system and network configurations. Critical systems and vulnerable elements are emphasized here; details are available as required.

Network Access and Practices

Bogus Corporation recognizes that network access needs to be controlled, although the controls are currently not administered consistently throughout the organization. The NVA team was able to gain access to the network through a guest account. Users are required to change their passwords every 90 days, and they are given examples of good and bad passwords, but the system does not screen the passwords for inappropriate choices. Access control logs are maintained on the system but can easily be accessed by minimally savvy users. It would be difficult to detect unauthorized changes made to the access control logs.

Access to the corporate intranet is controlled by a firewall router that filters packets coming from the Internet. The firewall configuration is rather basic, permitting mail and address-specific data to pass into the intranet from outside. The firewall places few restrictions on packets that may contain viruses.

Exhibit 3.   Security Profile (Continued)

Sensitive information (e.g., competitive bid quotations) is sent via e-mail, an unsecured method that could be vulnerable to attack. While some cryptographic protocols are available (e.g., Pretty Good Privacy [PGP]), these are rarely used. Most of the people we interviewed were not even aware that PGP capability existed on their system.

Computer Operations and Telecommunications Areas

Physical access to servers and systems is partially protected but some critical networking facilities are vulnerable. For example, although servers are kept in a locked room with controlled access (card keys), we observed "tailgating," in which one employee followed another through the door to the computer room. Fire protection in the computer room was inadequate, and emergency exits were not clearly marked. There is a key safe in the computer room that contains keys to offices, other computing facilities (e.g., wiring closets), and servers. The lock on the key safe had been disabled, some of the keys were not marked, and no key inventory was available. This key safe also contained a hardcopy list of server passwords. The names, addresses, and phone numbers of IT employees were posted on a bulletin board outside the computer room.

The wiring closet on the second floor of the HQ building was unlocked; leaving network connections completely unprotected.

The Computer Services supervisor has been employed at Bogus Corporation for nearly 20 years and carries the institutional computer history in his head. No other employee has the knowledge he has, and few efforts have been made to document his knowledge of Bogus' system operations.

System and Network Configurations

The NVA team probed various aspects of the Bogus network, using a local workstation with the NetWare client installed. Several guest accounts were accessed from the network, and some machines were found with either no password or the default password. Several directories were incorrectly configured to allow public access, rather than access restricted to system administrators with root privileges only. Some system configuration information was in public directories; an intruder could use this information to gain access to root functions or to change critical system settings. We were able to obtain the following system information:

- Directory service map
- Complete list of NetWare objects (users, devices, groups, and servers) with IP addresses
- Access control logs

Some audit logs were maintained but system administrators seldom checked them for system anomalies. Some of the auditing functions were incorrectly configured, so those unsuccessful attempts to gain access to the system were not recorded.

Exhibit 3.   Security Profile (Continued)

These vulnerabilities allow for an intruder to easily map out the network and more readily identify critical targets and plan their attack. The lack of consistent security auditing will allow an intruder to go unnoticed.

Exhibit 4.   Analysis

Nontechnical Management

Strategic Direction

Bogus Corporation's senior management has indicated strong support for the implementation of a comprehensive security policy. Based on our experience, effective security requires senior management support, sufficient corporate resources, and documented security policies and procedures. While the commitment is there, we recommend that senior management create a security policy team charged with creating a comprehensive security policy for the organization.

Management support for the implementation of a security policy must be clearly articulated (ISO 17799, 3.1.1). The business case for security should be communicated to all employees, and their responsibility for supporting security should be emphasized. Because security is often viewed as "an impediment" to productivity, it is important that management makes sure that all staff members understand that security is a corporate requirement. And, of course, management needs to model appropriate security-aware behavior.

Organizational Issues

Responsibility for system and physical security is scattered throughout the organization. Security oversight (ISO 17799, 4.1.1) needs to be consolidated in one office to ensure consistent policies and practices. In addition, the organization needs to develop a consistent view of what needs to be protected — that is, to define what data is critical to the continued existence of the organization, what is significant, and how best to limit the vulnerability of the network to protect critical and sensitive data.

Once a corporatewide security function has been established, that office or person should develop a comprehensive security training program for all employees (ISO 17799, 6.2.1). This training should cover all the relevant security policies developed by the security policy team, and all employees should be held accountable for following the security policies. It is also

Exhibit 4.   Analysis (Continued)

important that employees receive ongoing training in proper security practices, including proper disposal of hardcopy sensitive and critical material. System and network administrators also need additional specialized training in system and network security. They need to know your systems better than a hacker, and this level of knowledge requires training. Currently, such advanced training is optional — it should be mandatory.

Personnel

Bogus Corporation's system administrators provide the management behind access to data. It is important that all staff members have a consistent understanding of what data is critical (ISO 17799, 5.2.1), what data is sensitive, and how the overall administration of access to data is managed. This understanding does not appear to be consistent; variances in practice exist concerning password management and administration, auditing and logging, network access of temporary and permanent employees, and access to data based on job function alone. Overall, each individual charged with the management or administration of access to information needs to be aware of established policy, the principles of information security, and how to implement information security effectively.

Furthermore, all practices need to be documented (ISO 17799, 6.1.1). At present, too much essential system knowledge is in the heads of employees. If a senior system administrator were to leave or become unexpectedly disabled, you would not be able to easily replace his or her knowledge of your systems, and system functioning could be severely impacted.

Technical Management and Network Practices

Reporting Structure

Risk = *medium*. Some system administrators report to managers within the IT organization; others report to the manager of the functional group to which they provide systems support. Such an arrangement tends to provide better service to IT customers but often fails to provide consistent administration of security practices.

Recommendation. Matrixed reporting might provide for more consistency in network security administration A permanent Information Security Steering Committee (ISSC) (ISO 17799, 4.1.1) should be established, with members drawn from IT and major user groups. This group's charter would be to approve and support the vision and goals of Bogus Corporation's information protection program. The members of this group should provide guidance in the consistent implementation of security throughout the organization, ensure that the resources are adequate for the successful implementation and maintenance of this program, and provide training for all users in security practices.

Exhibit 4.   Analysis (Continued)

Policies and Procedures

Risk = high. Few of the policies and procedures that we reviewed covered information security. Policies are usually mandated to make them effective and universally applied. It will be a challenge for Bogus Corporation to mandate stringent security practices throughout the organization.

We believe that the lack of an enterprisewide information protection policy hinders Bogus' ability to make effective and secure use of its networks and systems. Explicit security policies and procedures must be implemented. This is the first step in providing secure information systems. Without such explicit policies and practices, it is difficult to choose the appropriate security functions to provide cost-effective protection to your critical and sensitive data.

Recommendation. A set of comprehensive policies, standards, procedures, and guidelines mapped to the *International Standard for Information Security* (ISO 17799) must be developed and implemented (see ISO 17799, 3.1.1).

System Administrators

Risk = medium. There is currently no one person appointed to the task of assisting management to develop, implement, and maintain an information protection program consistent with Bogus objectives.

Recommendation. An Information Protection Coordinator (ISO 17799, 4.1.4) should be appointed by management to assist in the creation of security policy documents, working in concert with the ISSC. This person should report directly to senior management and should be responsible for the day-to-day oversight of information protection practices at Bogus Corporation.

Physical Controls

Risk = high. Physical access controls restrict the entry and exit of personnel (and often equipment and media) for an area, such as an office building, suite, data center, or a room containing system equipment (e.g., modem banks for dial-in customers). Unlocked doors and cabinets, of course, are not secure, and automatic doors that close slowly (such as the main entrance to the central computer services room) can offer opportunities for unauthorized access. Unmarked keys in an unlocked key safe are especially vulnerable. Without an inventory, there is no way to determine if keys have been taken.

Exhibit 4.   Analysis (Continued)

Recommendation. Access to computing facilities should be strictly controlled (ISO 17799, 7.1). Only authorized personnel should be able to enter the computing facilities, and entrance and exit should be monitored. Automatic doors are a bad idea, unless they can be modified to close quickly. Access to cables, routers, and other network devices should be limited as well. Doors to the outside should not be propped open. These exits should be wired so that an alarm sounds in the security office when the door is held open for a specified length of time. Employees should have to request new key cards in person, and positive identification should be required. It is also good practice to check the employee's name against a list of recently terminated employees provided on a daily basis by the HR department.

Any publicly posted material that indicates employee names, building addresses, job titles, or phone numbers should be removed (ISO 17799, 5.2.2). This kind of information can be used by a hacker to spoof one of the employees. For the same reason, information about your systems, system identifiers, IP addresses, network configuration, and network architecture should never be stored where an unauthorized person can view it. Critical and sensitive design documents should also be kept under lock and key, and access should be monitored.

Fire Safety Factors

Risk = high. Building fires represent a serious threat to security because of the potential for complete destruction of hardware and software, the risk to human life, and widespread damage, even from a localized fire. Smoke, toxic and corrosive gases, and high humidity from even a localized fire can damage systems throughout the building.

We noticed several fire hazards in our inspection of your central computing services facility. There were no smoke detectors, and we saw only one fire extinguisher. Several stacks of old magazines were haphazardly stored in the back of the facility, along with foam computer packing material (highly toxic when burned).

Recommendation. We recommend that computing facilities throughout the organization be carefully evaluated for fire hazards (National Fire Prevention Association code [NFPA 75]). Your local fire department can help you to identify existing fire hazards and ensure that you are in compliance with existing fire protection standards.

Exhibit 4.   Analysis (Continued)

Contingencies and Disasters

Risk = high. Contingency planning directly supports an organization's goal of continued operations. Bogus Corporation has no comprehensive contingency plan for the data center or the network. Although backup tapes are stored off-site, no plans exist for obtaining these materials in the event of a disaster.

Recommendation. Bogus Corporation should implement a Business Continuity Plan with all possible speed (ISO 17799, 11.1.1). The first task should be to develop a data center recovery plan in which critical business processes are identified. It is critically important that Bogus Corporation knows what its critical business processes are and how to reestablish them elsewhere in the event of a serious business interruption.

Computer Incident Response Team

Risk = medium. Computer incidents are defined as unauthorized intrusions into one or more of your network services. The most commonly reported incidents are Web site vandalism, viruses, and theft of financial information. In reality, many more incidents occur than are actually reported. Most organizations prefer to keep their vulnerabilities as quiet as possible. Bogus Corporation currently does not have a designated incident response coordinator, and what incidents that have occurred have been handled in an *ad hoc* fashion.

Recommendation. Because most incidents involve several management domains (i.e., security, public relations, IT, operations), it is important to have a coordinated response to any incidents (ISO 17799, 6.3). Whether or not your organization chooses to inform the authorities (the police) of an attempted or successful intrusion, you need to be sure that you know how you are going to respond to different levels of damage, who is responsible for media relations, and how you will ensure that such a vulnerability is not exploited by others. If you do decide to charge a perpetrator, you will need to have documentation of the alleged system events (i.e., audit logs). The NVA has provided our "Incident Handling Guidelines" in the Appendix to assist you in developing your own computer incident response guidelines.

Network Administration

Risk = medium. System administrators are the backbone of your skilled computing security resource. At present, although they know a lot about your network and a lot about maintaining it and keeping it available for your users, they know very little about the technical practice of

Exhibit 4. Analysis (Continued)

information security. The help-desk personnel possess significant authority to set up and terminate user accounts and "reset" passwords but
these activities are not logged or audited. Most system administrator
activities on the network are not logged either.

Recommendation. Although these individuals are "trusted" to protect the
interests of Bogus Corporation, their activities should be monitored and
logged (ISO 17799, 9.7). These employees have a broad view of the
network and its capabilities, so it makes good business sense to monitor
all or most of their change activities. Currently available logging tools
should be enabled, and new monitoring tools should be deployed as
needed. Your Internal Audit department should be responsible for
monitoring compliance.

Network Architecture and Connectivity

Network Topology

Bogus Corporation's network consists of several optical fiber local area networks (LANs) that serve the Houston and Galveston networks. The wide area
network (WAN) that connects the two sites has high-speed connections (T1
and T3). Dial-up capacity to modems connected to the corporate network
provides connectivity for regional sales staff.

Partitioning and Administration

The partitioning and administration of the network is primarily based on operational divisions. Because there is no central oversight, equipment can be added
to a particular segment without clearance from the IT group. Security is often
not considered when decisions about hardware and network upgrades are made.

We believe that a more coordinated approach to network management
would provide the oversight that is critical to maintaining secure network
operations. Changes to the network should be reviewed by the Information
Security Steering Committee (ISSC) (ISO 17799, 4.1.1) to make sure that
arbitrary network additions and deletions do not jeopardize system security.

Network Operating Systems

Novell NetWare

Risk = high. Novell NetWare is the primary network operating system.
Version 3.xx is the deployed version. This version has many known
bugs that affect overall system security. These bugs were fixed in v4.xx.
It is highly recommended that you upgrade to 4.xx or higher as soon
as possible.

Exhibit 4.   Analysis (Continued)

The lack of security-oriented default user profiles on Novell servers means that critical data can be accessed from a noncritical system.

Recommendation. A firewall or segment configuration policy is needed that defines the users who are allowed to access particular segments of the network (ISO 17799, 9.2). Access to subnets can be achieved with screened subnet architecture, proxy services, or interior routers.

User Accounts without Passwords

Risk = high. We discovered several accounts with no assigned passwords. The lack of a password assigned to an account means that no authentication of the actual person using the account exists. If the account is misused, that misuse cannot be traced to a specific person. An account without a password is highly vulnerable to hackers.

Recommendation. Run a NULL password checker on the network and remove all NULL password accounts or assign passwords. For maximal security, delete guest accounts. Use a password generator to generate one-time random passwords for users when issuing a new password. Force users to change that password immediately (ISO 17799, 9.2.3).

Passwords in Cleartext

Risk = high. Passwords are mechanisms used to identify individual network users. If the password can be found, observed, or otherwise noted, the user account can be used by an unauthorized person.

Passwords may exist in batch files for automated log-in and for resetting multiple passwords within a list of user IDs. These passwords are stored on the system unencrypted and can be easily discovered. Passwords may be found in .bat files that execute log-in processes. They may also be found in profiles (MAC) for RUMBA connections to the mainframe or other systems.

Passwords were also found at user workstations. Users sometimes post their account and application passwords within their immediate work environment.

Recommendation. Employees need to be trained in good security practices (ISO 17799, 10.3). A program should be implemented to ensure employee adherence to good security practices. Passwords should never be stored or transmitted in cleartext. Bogus Corporation needs to encrypt stored passwords whenever user programs supersede the access control mechanisms provided by the network. Also, Bogus Corporation needs to protect stored passwords by access controls provided by the network. These controls protect the password database from unauthorized modification and disclosure.

Exhibit 4.   Analysis (Continued)

TCP/IP

Risk = medium. A security vulnerability called the "Land Attack" has been posted to a security mailing list. This attack can "freeze" operating systems, networks, and network devices. An attacker can send a SYN packet, which is normally used to open a connection, to the host under attack. The packet is spoofed to appear to the machine that it is coming from itself, from the same port. When the system or device tries to respond to it multiple times, it crashes.

Recommendation. Packet filters that protect against IP address spoofing (ISO 17799, 8.5) will be effective in preventing Internet-based "Land Attacks." Cisco has released information on how to configure its hardware to provide system security against this attack.

Remote Network Access

Risk = high. These practices are risky. Because the 800 number is well known, unauthorized users can attack the system and attempt to gain access by guessing dial-in passwords. Because the passwords are passed in the clear over the telephone line, anyone seeking dial-in passwords can "sniff" the wire. These passwords could then be used in a replay attack.

Members of the sales force routinely dial in to the Bogus Corporation network, using a well-known 800-access number. Dial-in users have an additional dial-in password that allows them to connect to the *system, and then they can access the network with their system ID and password information.*

Recommendation. Secure the dial-in process with either token card or smart card access (ISO 17799, 9.8). These provide an additional layer of security, and both methods avoid sending passwords over the telephone line in cleartext.

Systems — Client/Server, Mainframes

MVS

Risk = medium. RACF has the ability to log and record actions that are taken when creating accounts and changing access to specific files and applications. This logging facility is not being used in the administration of mainframe-based account management. If a security incident did occur, Bogus Corporation would be unable to recreate the sequence of activities.

Recommendation. RACF should be configured to take advantage of its audit and logging abilities (ISO 17799, 9.2).

Exhibit 4.   Analysis (Continued)

Miscellaneous

Applications: UNIX

Telnet is not secured. This means that all information, including user name and password, is sent and received across the wire in cleartext (ISO 17799, 8.2.7).

Secure Paper and Physical Media Disposal

In all of the offices we visited, few employees knew how or where to dispose of critical or sensitive information. No shredders were available, and no guidelines on the secure disposal of information have been provided to staff (ISO 17799, 5.2.2).

Exhibit 5.   Key Safeguards

Authentication

Authentication is the principle of identifying the user to the network. Once users understand their responsibilities to follow Bogus security policies, they should then be given user names and passwords. Some applications require additional passwords for user access. Password management, under these circumstances, becomes problematic. Different applications impose different password criteria.

Passwords need to be established and maintained in a manner that provides the greatest security, without causing undue burden and loss of productivity for users. Single sign-on password applications offer the ability to sign on to the network and a variety of applications with one password entry.

Recommendation. The NVA recommends deployment of Single SignOn clients. This will provide strong authentication to Bogus' multiple environments with effective and secure password management. Bogus system developers can also use Bart's Security Software Development Kit (SDK) to customize Bogus applications to support Kerberos or public key authentication and encryption.

Nonrepudiation

Nonrepudiation allows the digital signing of electronic documents and authorizations. Neither sender nor receiver can repudiate such documents.

Recommendation. We recommend deployment of the Homer Security Server and Single SignOn clients for secure network log-ons. Kerberos and public key encryption can be utilized for ensuring data confidentiality and integrity between the client and the network service. Bogus applications can be further secured using Marge's Security SDK.

Exhibit 5.   Key Safeguards (Continued)

Secure Messaging

It is important that all messages containing confidential information be sent by a secure means within the network environment. This is true even for information that is being kept within the corporate network. Because the major threat to your data comes from within the network, it is important that your data be protected from internal threats. Protection for data that is passed across the network can be made available through the use of file encryption software of "link encryption," where the path the data takes is protected.

Recommendation. Protection for network data can be provided through the use of file encryption software or "link encryption," where the path the data takes is protected. Virtual private networks (VPNs) are an additional means of protecting data at the network layer.

Access Control (Authorization)

Access control is the process of determining what actions a properly authenticated individual user can take on the network. "Read, write, and execute" are access control rights. We found little formal evidence that Bogus has any explicit access control policies. What access control is there is mostly anecdotal. "Everybody knows that manufacturing personnel cannot access the finance database." Everyone who is responsible for providing access to internal network data is expected to "do the right thing." Access control is the method used to control access at a very granular level and can be managed by a number of products.

Recommendation. Bogus should deploy Authorization Software to enhance access control on Bogus' UNIX and NT systems.

Auditing

Auditing allows an organization to determine what actions have been taken in the network environment. With this information, it is possible to determine what happened, when it happened, and who did it. This information is essential for investigations into breaches of data security. Gathering evidence and establishing events leading up to a security incident require that network, file, and application data is available. All significant events should be monitored by detective controls.

Recommendation. The Homer Security Server logs all relevant authentication events according to system default settings for security logging in a distributed environment. Even without strict audit implementation, network management should consider using a variety of auditing software to better monitor network activities. Logging of significant events in the network needs to be identified and recorded. The NVA recommends additional deployment of Intrusion Detection's KANE products (Monitor and Analyst) or ISS's SAFE-suite products (System Security Scanner and RealSecure) for system monitoring and analysis.

Exhibit 5.   Key Safeguards (Continued)

Firewalls

Firewalls are designed to restrict the ability of network users to pass and to access data between nodes or within certain spheres of data on a network. They are also used to restrict access to data for persons or systems not within the Bogus environment. Basically, firewalls use a variety of methods for performing their functions. Some deal with "listening" on specific port addresses, while others are designed to pass only data that meets an address requirement. The current "firewall" mechanism at Bogus is intended to restrict access to systems via network address recognition and authorization. With this configuration, IP address filtering can be spoofed; it is not a secure method for isolation or protecting data. Bogus systems are exposed to attacks from the Internet.

Recommendation. We believe that there are other means available and other design considerations for restricting access to the network and from external networks. Each environment within Bogus must be considered an entity, and restrictive subnetworks should be established to prevent access to the most critical data or processes. This is similar to a set of concentric fences that serve as increasingly secure barriers as a network user approaches critical or sensitive data. CheckPoint's Firewall-1 product can control and restrict access within the network and from the outside.

A firewall alone cannot protect network resources from attack by an internal user of the private network. The firewall is a gateway that simply intercepts the traffic between a private network and the Internet. An intra-company firewall can intercept traffic among different parts of an organization, but an insider might steal critical information or damage resources without any awareness by the firewall. This threat can be addressed by implementing appropriate authentication and access control mechanisms. The Homer product is designed to authenticate all users to a network, thereby restricting access to unauthorized applications.

Although additional products can be installed that more properly restrict access, the policy basis for firewalls constitutes the greatest initial step because it determines how the restrictions will be established in the router or firewall mechanism. Finally, this recommendation suggests that an overall network architecture be explored and implemented.

Exhibit 6. Recommendations to Mitigate Risks

Policy Development (ISO 17799, Item 3.1.1)
A comprehensive and clearly articulated security policy needs to be developed. Such a policy would provide the guidelines and define the practices that must be followed to protect Bogus' critical and confidential information and to provide security to the network.

Information Protection Oversight (ISO 17799, Item 4.1.1)
The responsibility for information security should be consolidated into one office or person that reports directly to senior management. This allows for the development and implementation of one set of security policies and practices throughout the organization.

Network Facility Security (ISO 17799, Item 7.1.1)
Physical access to the facility needs to be restricted to authorized employees only. Fire hazards need to be removed, and the entire facility needs to meet fire safety codes. Keys should be inventoried and stored in a secure place, and password information should not be recorded. All electronic information that gives information about computing facilities and architecture should be stored in a secure place on the network, and physical data about personnel and network access should be stored out-of-sight.

Disaster Recovery/Business Continuity (ISO 17799, Item 11.1.1)
No coordinated disaster recovery plan exists. Although data is backed up and stored off-site, no plans for recovering servers or facility systems in the event of a disaster or business interruption are available. Such a comprehensive plan needs to be put together as soon as possible, starting with a comprehensive IT systems recovery plan.

Information Security Awareness (ISO 17799, Item 6.2.1)
All employees need to understand their responsibilities in protecting Bogus systems and information. This requires orientation training for new employees and ongoing training for existing employees. Those employees with more responsibility for protecting information resources, such as system administrators, need to receive ongoing training so that their skills remain up-to-date.

Computer Incident Response Team (ISO 17799, Item 6.3)
Denial of access to system operations could seriously impede Bogus' ability to use and sustain business operations. With prepared Computer Incident Response strategies, a coordinated response to an incident could be provided.

Logging and Auditing (ISO 17799, Item 9.7)
There is insufficient logging of system event data in the network environment to identify and reconstruct incidents or attempts to penetrate the internal network. The internal audit department has not implemented sufficient controls to protect system administration personnel from creating accounts and subverting access to critical and sensitive data.

Exhibit 7.   Final Comments

All employees who were interviewed were helpful and extremely cooperative in their assessment of present information system conditions. The purpose of this report is to identify potential vulnerabilities to serve as a foundation for future corrective action. Such corrections can form the basis for the company's information management decisions.

Computer networks are dynamic and notoriously subject to change. This means that information protection strategies must include frequent assessments of existing data storage and handling practices. Once policies have been established, the practices can be implemented to fulfill the policy goals of network and information protection. The NVA team believes that such attention to policy and practice will result in significant reduction in cost and risk to Bogus Corporation.

Exhibit 8. Summary Table of Risk, Vulnerabilities, and Recommendations

Risk	Vulnerability	Recommendation
High		
Security policy	Without policy, information protection is not supported	Create security policies and processes (ISO 17799, 3.1.1)
Oversight	Security is breached because no one is responsible for preventing it	Provide centralized oversight of policy and processes (ISO 17799, 4.1.1)
Facility access	Unauthorized personnel can gain access to the computing facility	Provide enhanced access control to computing facility (ISO 17799, 7.1.1)
Disaster recovery	Business may be unable to recover from a serious business interruption	Create a Disaster Recovery/ Business Continuity plan (ISO 17799, 11.1.1)
Medium		
Security awareness	Confidential data is not protected because employees do not know what their responsibilities are	Train all staff in information protection practices (ISO 17799, 6.2.1)
Documentation	A knowledgeable employee leaves, taking a lot of system knowledge with him	Document IT processes (ISO 17799, 6.3)
Logging and auditing	The network is attacked and no one realizes it	Log and audit all change activities on the network (ISO 17799, 9.7)
Paper disposal	Critical and sensitive data is discarded in a publicly available Dumpster	(ISO 17799, 5.2.2) Provide necessary furniture to properly protect information
Low		
Security incident	A security incident is inadvertently divulged to the media	Create a Computer Security Incident Response Team (ISO 17799, 6.3)

Exhibit 9.   Glossary

Business continuity plan: A coordinated set of activities designed to reestablish an organization's information system function after experiencing a man-made or natural disaster that destroys or partially inhibits normal functioning.

Countermeasure: A safeguard implemented against a specific threat or in reaction to a specific incident.

Critical data: The data, the loss of which would have a direct impact upon the company's survival.

Data classification: The development of classes of data depending on sensitivity and the access, control, and management standards for each class.

Disaster recovery plan: A coordinated set of rules, practices, and responses that are designed to identify the most critical information system applications to an organization for safeguarding in the event of a man-made or natural disaster that threatens the organization.

Risk: The likelihood that a vulnerability might be exploited, or that a threat may become harmful.

Safeguard: Measure taken to negate or reduce a threat.

Sensitive data: That data, the release, misuse, or loss of which could cause direct embarrassment to the organization or result in significant legal proceedings against the organization.

Threat: The potential for exploitation of a vulnerability.

Trust: A confident reliance on the integrity, honesty, or justice of another. Trust refers to the ability of the application to perform actions with integrity, to keep confidential information private, and to perform its functions on a continuing basis.

Vulnerability: A weakness in a system that can be exploited to violate the system's intended behavior.

Chapter 8

Summary

This book has been designed to assist the security professional in understanding what must be done to conduct a network vulnerability assessment (NVA). Because no organization has unlimited resources to devote to security, we attempted to divide the tasks into manageable portions. Because budgets are always strained, we attempted to show the security and audit professional where to get the tools that would be effective and as cheap as possible.

Most failed projects come to grief because the scope of the project was poorly defined to begin with, or because the scope was not managed well. We attempted to discuss Project Overview Statements and the Project Scope Document for a Network Vulnerability Analysis. We looked at the processes needed to gather the information for the Project Overview Document. We also presented how to manage scope change.

To be successful, the NVA team will have to identify what network security concerns have the highest priority. This will allow the team to focus on those threats and risks that can cause the enterprise the most damage. Understanding that the security concerns include personnel and the physical as well as technical issues will ensure the most comprehensive assessment prospect.

Establishing a team that represents the enterprise will also add to the creditability of the assessment results. Using enterprise personnel will ensure that those individuals with the most intimate knowledge of how the network works and how it is supposed to work will have input into the report. Our goal in assessing needs was to ensure that the assembled team had the greatest chance for success. Establishing a team that represents the enterprise will also add to the creditability of the assessment results. Using enterprise personnel will ensure that those individuals with the most intimate knowledge of how the network works and how it is supposed to work will have input into the report. Some of our best and most knowledgeable network users come from business units.

Use all the resources available to plot out what threats will be addressed. Do your research to gather significant issues and then prioritize these risks based on probability of occurrence and impact to the enterprise or network. Concentrate on those issues that will bring the biggest impact to your organization. Use your team to identify additional items and measure their specific impact.

Developing a checklist will assist the NVA team in ensuring that basic security controls are examined. Do not just use the checklist. Listen and ask questions and be ready to include additional information into the examination process.

A network vulnerability assessment can take a considerable amount of time to complete. Divide the total mission into manageable chunks and then begin the process. Complete one phase before moving on to the next. Be sure to get support from the infrastructure groups; this will make the task easier. Remember that it is not your NVA, it is the NVA of the organization.

ISO 17799 Self-Assessment Checklist

How to Use This Self-Assessment Checklist

This checklist is designed to assist you in taking "snapshots" of your organization's security status. Answer each question, checking Y or N. The blank column is designed for comments.

When you have finished each section, add the points — one for each question answered Y.

Finally, total score (Sections 3 through 12): _____

Superior:	> 95 "yes" answers
Fair:	82 – 95 "yes" answers
Marginal:	68 – 81 "yes" answers
Poor:	54 – 67 "yes" answers
At Risk:	< 54 "yes" answers

3	**Security Policy**			
	Note: ISO17799, Sections 1 and 2 are nonaction items, and are not included in this checklist.			
3.1	Information Security Policy	Management direction and support for information security must be clearly established.		
3.1.1	*Information Security Policy Document Development*	Has an information security policy document been developed?	Y ___	N ___
3.1.2	*Information Security Policy Document Publication*	Has an information security policy document been published?	Y ___	N ___
		Score (number of questions answered Yes):		
4	**Organizational Security**			
4.1	Information Security Infrastructure	A management framework must be established to initiate and control the implementation of information security within the organization.		
4.1.1	*Management Information Security Forum*	Has a forum been established to oversee and represent information security?	Y ___	N ___
4.1.2	*Information Security Coordination*	Has a process been established to coordinate implementation of information security measures?	Y ___	N ___
4.1.3	*Allocation of Information Security Responsibilities*	Are responsibilities for accomplishment of information security requirements clearly defined?	Y ___	N ___
4.1.4	*Authorization Process for Information Processing Facilities*	Has a management approval process been established to authorize new IT facilities from both a business and technical standpoint?	Y ___	N ___
4.1.5	*Specialist Information Security Advice*	Has a capability been established that provides specialized information security advice?	Y ___	N ___

4.1.6	*Cooperation between Organizations*	Is there a liaison with external information security personnel and organizations, including industry and government security specialists, law enforcement authorities, IT service providers, telecommunications authorities?	Y___ N___
4.1.7	*Independent Review of Information Security*	Has an independent review of information security practices been conducted to ensure feasibility, effectiveness, and compliance with written policies?	Y___ N___
4.2	*Security of Third-Party Access*	The organizational IT facilities and information assets that control the access of nonorganizational third parties must be kept secure.	
4.2.1	*Identification of Risks from Third-Party Access*	Have third-party connection risks been analyzed?	Y___ N___
	Combating Risks from Third-Party Connections	Have specific security measures been identified to combat third-party connection risks?	Y___ N___
4.2.2	*Security Conditions in Third-Party Contracts*	Are security requirements included in formal third-party contracts?	Y___ N___
4.3	*Outsourcing*	The security of information should be maintained even when the responsibility for the processing has been outsourced to another organization.	
4.3.1	*Security Requirements in Outsourcing Contracts*	Have the security requirements of the information owners been addressed in a contract between the owners and the outsource organization?	Y___ N___
		Score (number of questions answered Yes):	
5	**Asset Classification and Control**		
5.1	*Accounting of Assets*	Appropriate accounting of organizational assets must be established.	
5.1.1	*Inventory of Assets*	Have inventories of major assets associated with each information system been created?	Y___ N___

5.2	Information Classification	Security classifications should be used to indicate the need for, and priorities for, security protection of information assets.		
5.2.1	*Classification Guidelines*	Have security classification guidelines been established to indicate the need for, and priorities for, security protection?	Y ___	N ___
5.2.2	*Information Labeling and Handling*	Has a process been implemented for labeling information that requires security protection?	Y ___	N ___
		Score (number of questions answered Yes):		
6	**Personnel Security**			
6.1	Security in Job Definitions and Resourcing	Security should be addressed at the recruitment stage, included in job descriptions and contracts, and monitored during an individual's employment.		
6.1.1	*Security in Job Descriptions*	Are security responsibilities included in employee job descriptions?	Y ___	N ___
6.1.2	*Personnel Screening and Policy*	Are employment applications screened for jobs that require access to sensitive information?	Y ___	N ___
6.1.3	*Confidentiality Agreement*	Are nondisclosure agreements required?	Y ___	N ___
6.1.4	*Terms and Conditions of Employment*	Do the terms and conditions of employment include the employee's responsibility for information security, including duration after employment and consequences of failure to fulfill these terms?	Y ___	N ___
6.2	User Training	Users should be trained in security procedures and the correct use of IT facilities.		
6.2.1	*Information Security Education and Training*	Before they are granted access to IT facilities, are users trained in information security policies and procedures, security requirements, business controls, and the correct use of IT facilities?	Y ___	N ___

6.3	Responding to Security Incidents and Malfunctions	Incidents affecting security should be reported through management channels as quickly as possible.	
6.3.1	Reporting of Security Incidents	Do formal reporting and incident response procedures exist to identify action to be taken on receipt of an incident report?	Y__ N__
6.3.2	Reporting of Security Weaknesses	Are users required to note and report all observed or suspected security weaknesses in or threats to systems or services?	Y__ N__
6.3.3	Reporting of Software Malfunctions	Are users required to note and report to IT support any software that does not function correctly?	Y__ N__
6.3.4	Learning from Incidents	Are mechanisms in place to monitor the types, volumes, and costs of incidents and malfunctions?	Y__ N__
6.3.5	Disciplinary Process	Does a formal disciplinary process exist for dealing with employees who violate security policies and procedures?	Y__ N__
		Score (number of questions answered Yes):	
7	**Physical and Environmental Security**		
7.1	Secure Areas	IT facilities supporting critical or sensitive business activities belong in secure areas.	
7.1.1	Physical Security Perimeter	Does physical security protection exist, based on defined perimeters through strategically located barriers, throughout the organization?	Y__ N__
7.1.2	Physical Entry Controls	Are entry controls employed over secure areas to ensure only authorized personnel can gain access?	Y__ N__
7.1.3	Securing Offices, Rooms, and Facilities	Is physical security for data centers and computer rooms commensurate with threats?	Y__ N__

7.1.4	Working in Secure Areas	Are additional controls used for personnel or third parties working in the secure area?	Y___	N___
7.1.5	Isolated Delivery and Loading Areas	Are the computer room/data center delivery and loading areas isolated to prevent unauthorized access?	Y___	N___
7.2	Equipment Security	Equipment must be physically protected from security threats and environmental hazards.		
7.2.1	Equipment Location and Protection	Is equipment located to reduce risks of environmental hazards and unauthorized access?	Y___	N___
7.2.2	Power Supplies	Is electronic equipment protected from power failures and other electrical anomalies?	Y___	N___
7.2.3	Cabling Security	Is power and telecommunications cabling protected from interception or damage?	Y___	N___
7.2.4	Equipment Maintenance	Have procedures been established to correctly maintain IT equipment to ensure its continued availability and integrity?	Y___	N___
7.2.5	Security of Equipment Off-Premises	Is equipment used off-site, regardless of ownership, provided the same degree of protection afforded on-site IT equipment?	Y___	N___
7.3	General Controls	Information and information processing facilities should be protected from disclosure to, modification of, or theft by unauthorized persons, and controls should be in place to minimize loss or damage.		
7.3.1	Clear Desk and Clear Screen Policy	Has a clear desk/clear screen policy for sensitive material been adopted to reduce risks of unauthorized access, loss, or damage outside normal working hours?	Y___	N___
7.3.2	Removal of Property	Are personnel required to have documented management authorization to take equipment, data, or software off-site?	Y___	N___
		Score (number of questions answered Yes):		

8	**Communications and Operations Management**		
8.1	Responsibilities and procedures must be established for the management and operation of all computers and networks.		
8.1.1	*Documented Operating Procedures* — Are operating procedures clearly documented for all operational computer systems to ensure their correct, secure operation?	Y___	N___
8.1.2	*Operational Change Control* — Is there a process for controlling changes to IT facilities and systems to ensure satisfactory control of all changes to equipment, software, or procedures?	Y___	N___
8.1.3	*Incident Management Procedures* — Are incident management responsibilities and procedures in place to ensure a quick, effective, orderly response to security incidents?	Y___	N___
8.1.4	*Segregation of Duties* — Are sensitive duties or areas of responsibility kept separate to reduce opportunities for unauthorized modification or misuse of data or services?	Y___	N___
8.1.5	*Separation of Development and Operational Facilities* — Are development and operational facilities segregated to reduce the risk of accidental changes or unauthorized access to operational software and business data?	Y___	N___
8.2	System Planning and Acceptance — Advance planning and preparation can ensure the availability of adequate capacity and resources.		
8.2.1	*Capacity Planning* — Are capacity requirements monitored, and future requirements projected, to reduce the risk of system overload?	Y___	N___
8.2.2	*System Acceptance* — Has acceptance criteria for new systems been established, and have suitable tests been performed prior to acceptance?	Y___	N___
8.3	Protection from Malicious Software — Applying precautions to prevent and detect the introduction of malicious software can safeguard the integrity of software and data.		
8.3.1	*Controls against Malicious Software* — Have virus detection and prevention measures and user awareness procedures been implemented?	Y___	N___

			Y ___	N ___
8.4	Housekeeping	Routine procedures should be established for making backup copies of data, logging events and faults, and where appropriate, monitoring the equipment environment.		
8.4.1	Information Backup	Has a process been established for making regular backup copies of essential business data and software to ensure that it can be recovered following a computer disaster or media failure?	Y ___	N ___
8.4.2	Operator Logs	Are computer operators required to maintain a log of all work performed?	Y ___	N ___
8.4.3	Fault Logging	Do procedures exist for logging faults reported by users regarding problems with computer or communications systems?	Y ___	N ___
8.5	Network Management	The security of computer networks that may span organizational boundaries must be managed to safeguard information and to protect the supporting infrastructure.		
8.5.1	Network Controls	Do appropriate controls ensure the security of data in networks, and the protection of connected services from unauthorized access?	Y ___	N ___
8.6	Media Handling and Security	Computer media should be controlled and physically protected to prevent damage to assets and interruptions to business activities.		
8.6.1	Management of Removable Computer Media	Do procedures exist for the management of removable computer media such as tapes, disks, cassettes, and printed reports?	Y ___	N ___
8.6.2	Disposal of Media	Is a process in place to ensure that computer media is disposed of securely and safely when no longer required?	Y ___	N ___
8.6.3	Information Handling Procedures	Do procedures exist for handling sensitive data to protect such data from unauthorized disclosure or misuse?	Y ___	N ___
8.6.4	Security of System Documentation	Is system documentation protected from unauthorized access?	Y ___	N ___

			Y	N
8.7	Exchanges of Information and Software	Exchanges of data and software between organizations should be controlled to prevent loss, modification, or misuse of data.		
8.7.1	Information and Software Exchange Agreements	Do formal agreements exist, including software escrow agreements when appropriate, for exchanging data and software (whether electronically or manually) between organizations?	Y___	N___
8.7.2	Security of Media in Transit	Are controls applied to safeguard computer media being transported between sites to minimize its vulnerability to unauthorized access, misuse, or corruption during transportation?	Y___	N___
8.7.3	Electronic Commerce Security	Are security controls applied where necessary to protect electronic commerce (electronic data interchange, electronic mail, and online transactions across a public network such as the Internet) against unauthorized interception or modification?	Y___	N___
8.7.4	Security of Electronic Mail	Are controls applied where necessary to reduce the business and security risks associated with electronic mail, to include interception, modification, and errors?	Y___	N___
8.7.5	Security of Electronic Office Systems	Do clear policies and guidelines exist to control business and security risks associated with electronic office systems?	Y___	N___
8.7.6	Publicly Available Systems	Is there a formal authorization process before information is made publicly available?	Y___	N___
8.7.7	Other Forms of Information Exchange	Are procedures and controls in place to protect the exchange of information through the use of voice, facsimile, and video communications facilities?	Y___	N___
		Score (number of questions answered Yes):		
9	**Access Control**			
9.1	Business Requirement for System Access	Policies for information dissemination and entitlement should control access to computer services and data on the basis of business requirements.		
9.1.1	Access Control Policy	Are business requirements defined and documented for access control?	Y___	N___

9.2	User Access Management	Formal procedures are needed to control allocation of access rights to IT services.		
9.2.1	*User Registration*	Is there a formal user registration and deregistration procedure for access to all multi-use IT services?	Y___	N___
9.2.2	*Privilege Management*	Are there restrictions and controls over the use of any feature or facility of a multi-user IT system that enables a user to override system or application controls?	Y___	N___
9.2.3	*User Password Management*	Has a formal password management process been established to control passwords?	Y___	N___
9.2.4	*Review of User Access Rights*	Does a formal process exist for periodic review of users' access rights?	Y___	N___
9.3	User Responsibilities	Users should be made aware of their responsibilities for maintaining effective access controls, particularly regarding the use of passwords and security of user equipment.		
9.3.1	*Password Use*	Have users been taught good security practices in the selection and use of passwords?	Y___	N___
9.3.2	*Unattended User Equipment*	Are all users and contractors made aware of the security requirements and procedures for protecting unattended equipment?	Y___	N___
		Are all users and contractors made aware of their responsibilities for implementing such protection?	Y___	N___
9.4	Network Access Control	Connections to network services should be controlled to ensure that connected users or computer services do not compromise the security of any other networked services.		
9.4.1	*Policy on Use of Network Services*	Does a process exist to ensure that network and computer services that can be accessed by an individual user or from a particular terminal are consistent with business access control policy?	Y___	N___

9.4.2	*Enforced Path*	Have controls been incorporated that restrict the route between a user terminal and the computer services that its user is authorized to access?	Y___	N___
9.4.3	*User Authentication for External Connections*	Are connections by remote users via public or non-organization networks authenticated to prevent unauthorized access to business applications?	Y___	N___
9.4.4	*Node Authentication*	Are connections by remote computer systems authenticated to prevent unauthorized access to a business application?	Y___	N___
9.4.5	*Remote Diagnostic Port Protection*	Does a process exist to control access to diagnostic ports designed for remote use by maintenance engineers?	Y___	N___
9.4.6	*Network Segregation*	Have large networks been divided into separate domains to mitigate the risk of unauthorized access to existing computer systems that use the network?	Y___	N___
9.4.7	*Network Connection Control*	Have controls been incorporated to restrict the connection capability of users, in support of access policy requirements of business applications that extend across organizational boundaries?	Y___	N___
9.4.8	*Network Routing Control*	Have routing controls been incorporated over shared networks across organizational boundaries to ensure that computer connections and information flows conform to the access policy of business units?	Y___	N___
9.4.9	*Security in Network Services*	Have network providers clearly described the security attributes of all services used, and established the security implications for the confidentiality, integrity, and availability of business applications?	Y___	N___
9.5	Operating System Access Control	Access to computers should be strictly limited through the use of: ■ Automatic terminal identification ■ Terminal log-on procedures ■ User IDs ■ Password management ■ A duress alarm ■ Terminal time out ■ Limited connection time		

			Y N
9.5.1	*Automatic Terminal Identification*	Is automatic terminal identification employed to authenticate connections to specific locations?	Y___ N___
9.5.2	*Terminal Log-on Procedures*	Have procedures been designed for logging into a computer system to minimize the opportunity for unauthorized access?	Y___ N___
9.5.3	*User Identification and Authentication*	Do all users have a unique identifier (user ID) for their personal and sole use, to ensure that their activities can be traced to them?	Y___ N___
9.5.4	*Password Management System*	Is an effective password management system employed to authenticate users?	Y___ N___
9.5.5	*Use of System Utilities*	Are the system utility programs that could be used to override system and application controls strictly controlled and their use restricted?	Y___ N___
9.5.6	*Duress Alarm to Safeguard Users*	Based on an assessment of risk, is a duress alarm provided for users who might be the target of coercion?	Y___ N___
		Are responsibilities defined for responding to duress alarms?	Y___ N___
9.5.7	*Terminal Time Out*	Are terminals in high-risk locations set to time out when inactive to prevent access by unauthorized persons?	Y___ N___
9.5.8	*Limitation of Connection Time*	Has a limit been set on the period during which terminals can be connected to sensitive application systems?	Y___ N___
9.6	*Application Access Control*	Logical access controls should be enacted to protect application systems and data from unauthorized access.	
9.6.1	*Information Access Restriction*	Is access to applications system data and functions restricted in accordance with defined access policy and based on individual requirements?	Y___ N___
9.6.2	*Isolation of Sensitive Systems*	According to identified risks, do sensitive application systems operate in an isolated processing environment?	Y___ N___

			Y	N
9.7	Monitoring System Access and Use	Systems should be monitored to ensure conformity with access policy and standards, to detect unauthorized activities, and to determine the effectiveness of security measures adopted.		
9.7.1	*Event Logging*	Have audit trails that record exceptions and other security-relevant events been produced and maintained to assist in future investigations and in access control monitoring?	Y___	N___
9.7.2	*Monitoring System Use*	Have procedures been established for monitoring system use to ensure that users are only performing processes that have been explicitly authorized?	Y___	N___
9.7.3	*Clock Synchronization*	To ensure the accuracy of audit logs, have computer or communications device clocks been set to an agreed-upon standard?	Y___	N___
9.8	Mobile Commuting and Teleworking	When using mobile computing and teleworking, the organization should examine the risks and apply appropriate protection to the equipment or site.		
9.8.1	*Mobile Commuting*	Has a formal policy been developed that addresses the risks of working with mobile computing facilities, including requirements for physical protection, access controls, cryptographic techniques, backup, and virus protection?	Y___	N___
9.8.2	*Teleworking*	Have policies and procedures been developed to control teleworking, encompassing existing facilities, the proposed teleworking environment, communications security requirements, and the threat of unauthorized access to equipment or the network?	Y___	N___
		Score (number of questions answered Yes):		
10	**Systems Development and Maintenance**			
10.1	Security Requirements of Systems	To ensure that security is built into IT systems, security requirements should be identified, justified, agree to, and documented as part of the requirements definition stage of all IT system development projects.		
10.1.1	*Security Requirements Analysis and Specification*	Is an analysis of security requirements part of the requirements analysis stage of each development project?	Y___	N___

10.2	Security in Application Systems	Security controls that conform to commonly accepted industry standards of good security practice should be designed into applications systems to prevent loss, modification, or misuse of user data.	
10.2.1	Input Data Validation	Is data that is input into applications systems validated to ensure that it is correct and appropriate?	Y___ N___
10.2.2	Control of Internal Processing	Have validation checks been incorporated into systems to detect corruption caused by processing errors or deliberate acts?	Y___ N___
10.2.3	Message Authentication	Has message authentication been considered for applications that involve the transmission of sensitive data?	Y___ N___
10.2.4	Output Data Validation	Is data that is output from applications systems validated to ensure that it is correct and appropriate?	Y___ N___
10.3	Cryptographic Controls	To protect the confidentiality, authenticity, or integrity of information, cryptographic systems and techniques should be used for complete protection of information that is considered at risk.	
10.3.1	Policy on the Use of Cryptographic Controls	Has management developed a policy on the use of cryptographic controls, including management of encryption keys, and effective implementation?	Y___ N___
10.3.2	Encryption	Is data encryption used to protect highly sensitive data during transmission or in storage?	Y___ N___
10.3.3	Digital Signatures	Are digital signatures in use to protect the authenticity and integrity of electronic documents?	Y___ N___
10.3.4	Nonrepudiation Services	Are nonrepudiation services in place where disputes might arise based on the use of encryption or digital signatures?	Y___ N___
10.3.5	Key Management	Is a management system in place to support the organization's use of cryptographic techniques, including secret key techniques and public key techniques?	Y___ N___

10.4	Security of System Files	To ensure that IT projects and support activities are conducted in a secure manner, the responsibility for controlling access to application system files should be assigned to and carried out by the owning user function or development group.		
10.4.1	Control of Operational Software	Is strict control exercised over the implementation of software on operational systems?	Y___	N___
10.4.2	Protection of System Test Data	Is all application system test data protected and controlled?	Y___	N___
10.4.3	Access Control to Program Source Library	To reduce the potential for corruption of computer programs, is access to program source libraries strictly controlled?	Y___	N___
10.5	Security in Development and Support Environments	Project and support environments must be strictly controlled to maintain the security of application system software and data.		
10.5.1	Change Control Procedures	Have formal change control procedures been implemented?	Y___	N___
10.5.2	Technical Review of Operating System Changes	Are application systems reviewed when changes to the operating systems occur?	Y___	N___
10.5.3	Restrictions on Changes to Software Packages	Are modifications to vendor-supplied software discouraged; and when such modifications are necessary, are they strictly controlled?	Y___	N___
10.5.4	Covert Channels and Trojan Code	To avoid covert channels or Trojan codes, does the organization: ■ Buy programs only from a reputable source ■ Buy programs in source code that is verifiable ■ Use only evaluated products ■ Inspect all source code before operational use ■ Control access to, and modification of, installed code ■ Use trusted staff to work on key systems	Y___	N___

			Y	N
10.5.5	*Outsourced Software Development*	When software development is outsourced, have details been arranged to protect the project from intellectual property to pre-installation testing?	Y___	N___
		Score (number of questions answered Yes):		
11	**Business Continuity Management**			
11.1	Aspects of Business Continuity Planning	Business continuity plans should be available to counteract interruptions to business activities.		
11.1.1	*Business Continuity Management Process*	Is there a managed process for developing/maintaining business continuity plans across the organization?	Y___	N___
11.1.2	*Business Continuity and Impact Analysis*	Has a strategy been developed to determine the overall approach to business continuity, and endorsed by management?	Y___	N___
11.1.3	*Writing and Implementing Continuity Plans*	Has the business continuity planning process encompassed identification and agreement of all responsibilities and emergency procedures?	Y___	N___
11.1.4	*Business Continuity Planning Framework*	Is a single business continuity plan framework maintained to ensure that all levels of the plan are consistent?	Y___	N___
11.1.5	*Testing, Maintaining, and Reassessing Business Continuity Plans*	Are business continuity plans tested regularly to ensure that they are current and effective?	Y___	N___
		Score (number of questions answered Yes):		
12	**Compliance**			
12.1	Compliance with Legal Requirements	All relevant requirements for each IT system should be identified and documented.		
12.1.1	*Identification of Applicable Legislation*	Are all relevant statutory, regulatory, and contractual requirements specifically defined and documented for each information system?	Y___	N___

			Y	N
12.1.2	*Intellectual Property Rights*	Is there compliance with legal restrictions on the use of copyright material, ensuring that only software developed by the organization, or licensed or provided by the developer to the organization, is used?	Y ___	N ___
12.1.3	*Safeguarding of Organizational Records*	Are important organizational records securely maintained to meet statutory requirements, as well as to support essential business activities?	Y ___	N ___
12.1.4	*Data Protection and Privacy of Personal Information*	Do applications that process personal data on individuals comply with applicable data protection legislation?	Y ___	N ___
12.1.5	*Prevention of Misuse of Information Processing Facilities*	Are IT facilities to be used only for business purposes?	Y ___	N ___
12.1.6	*Regulation of Cryptographic Controls*	Has legal advice been sought on the organization's compliance with national and international laws on cryptographic controls?	Y ___	N ___
12.1.7	*Collection of Evidence*	When an action against a person involves the law, have the rules for evidence been followed for admissibility, quality, and completeness?	Y ___	N ___
12.2	*Reviews of Security Policy and Technical Compliance*	To ensure compliance of IT systems with organizational security policies and standards, compliance reviews should be conducted regularly.		
12.2.1	*Compliance with Security Policy*	Are all areas within the organization considered for regular review to ensure compliance with security policies and standards?	Y ___	N ___
12.2.2	*Technical Compliance Checking*	Are IT facilities regularly checked for compliance with security implementation standards?	Y ___	N ___
12.3	System Audit Considerations	There should be controls over operational systems and audit tools during system audits to minimize interference to and from the system audit process, and to protect the integrity and prevent the misuse of audit tools.		

12.3.1	*System Audit Controls*	Are audits and activities involving checks on operational systems carefully planned and arranged?	Y ___	N ___
12.3.2	*Protection of System Audit Tools*	Is access to system audit tools controlled?	Y ___	N ___
		Score (number of questions answered Yes):		

Appendix A-2

Windows NT Server 4.0 Checklist

Security Requirement	Y, N, or N/A	Description of How the Requirement Is or Will Be Met, or Why It Cannot Be Met
A. Mandatory security configuration settings		
1. Server must be in a physically secure location		
2. An Emergency Recovery Disk must be prepared and updated		
3. Latest service pack and hot fixes must be installed		
4. Anonymous log-on users must be restricted		
5. Minimum password age must be set to two (2) days		
6. Password uniqueness must be set to 24		
7. Account must be locked out after 5 attempts		
8. Lockout duration must be set to 30 minutes		
9. The NTFS file system must be used (not FAT)		
10. Standard file system permissions must be replaced by stricter security settings		

11. The system page file must be wiped during shutdown		
12. Security logs must be protected (all servers)		
13. Auditing must be implemented on all NT servers		
B. High-level security configurations (for high-risk systems)		
1. Floppy disk and CD-ROM drives must be disabled		
2. Server must be hidden from the network neighborhood and browsing tools		
3. Administrative shares must be removed		
C. Optional security settings for stronger security		
1. Disable or minimize caching of log-on credentials		
2. Rename administrator account; create a user account with the name Administrator but with no rights		
3. Set boot sequence to start with the hard drive "C"		
4. Use NTFS for all applications and user data		
5. Enforce the use of strong passwords (registry portion) by enabling use of the passfilt.dll utility		
6. Only systems operators will have the privilege to enter the scheduling commands		
7. Consider limiting of hours when users can log on		
8. Administrators should not be allowed to log on from the network		
9. The "Everyone" group should be replaced with "Authenticated Users"		
10. Saved passwords must be disabled		
11. Avoid granting "Administration" and "Full Control" permissions to users		
12. Limit "Change" access to users who need to delete or modify files and directories		
13. Deny requests for shared accounts		

14. Encrypt the password database with 128-bit encryption		
15. Do not grant "Force Shutdown From Remote System"		
16. Limit "log-on locally" on servers to administrators and to server and backup operators only		
17. Limit "shut down the system" on servers to administrators and server operators only		
18. Turn off all unneeded network services		
19. Implement virus protection software		
20. Force Shutdown from Remote System restricted to Admin. Only		

Appendix A-3

Network Vulnerability Assessment Checklist

Security Checklist

Security Requirement	Y, N, or N/A	Description of How the Requirement Is or Will Be Met, or Why It Cannot Be Met
1. Unique user ID and confidential password required		
2. Additional identification required for remote access		
3. "Help" screen access available to logged-on users only		
4. Last session date and time message back to user at sign-on time		
5. Exception reports for disruptions in either input or output		
6. Session numbers for users/processors that are not constantly logged in		
7. Notification to users of possible duplicate messages		
8. Threshold of errors and consequential re-transmission on the network related to management via automatic alarms		

9. Encryption requirements		
10. Encryption key management controls		
11. Message Authentication Code requirements for nonencrypted sensitive data transmission		
12. System authentication at session start-up (wiretap controls)		
13. Confirmation of host log-off to prevent line grabbing		
14. Downloading controls for connected intelligent workstations		
15. User priority designation process		
16. Transaction handling for classified communications		
17. Trace and snapshot facilities requirements		
18. Log requirements for sensitive messages		
19. Alternate path requirements between nodes		
20. Contingency plans for hardware as well as all usual system requirements		
21. Storage of critical messages in redundant locations		
22. Packet recovery requirements		
23. Physical access for workstations when units are not in use		
24. Control units, hubs, routers, cabinets secured		
25. Environmental control critical requirements		
26. Segregation for sections of the network that are deemed "untrustworthy"		
27. Gateway identification for authorized nodes		
28. Automatic disable of a user/account, line or port if evidence an attack is underway		
29. Naming convention to distinguish test messages from production		
30. User switching application controls		
31. Time-out reauthorization requirements		
32. Password changes (time/length/history) requirements		

33. Encryption requirements for passwords, security parameters, encryption keys, tables, etc.		
34. Shielding requirements for fiber-optic lines		
35. Controls to prevent wiretapping		
36. Reporting procedures for all interrupted telecommunication sessions		
37. Identification requirements for station/ terminal access connection to network		
38. Printer control requirements for classified information		
39. Appropriate "welcome" connection screens		
40. Dial-up access control procedures		
41. Anti-daemon dialer controls		
42. Standards for equipment, applications, protocols, operating environment		
43. Help desk procedures and telephone numbers		
44. Protocol converters and access method converters dynamic change control requirements		
45. LAN administrator responsibilities		
46. Control requirements to add nodes to the network		
47. Telephone number change requirements		
48. Automatic sign-on controls		
49. Telephone trace requirements		
50. FTP access controlled		
51. Are patches tested and applied?		
52. Software distribution current		
53. Employee policy awareness		
54. Emergency incident response plan/ procedure		
55. Internal applications control		
56. Proper control of the development environment		

57. Software licensing compliance review		
58. Portable device (laptop/notebook/PDA) handling procedures		
59. Storage and disposal of sensitive data/ information		
60. Default password controls and settings		
61. Review of off-site storage for disaster recovery resources		
62. Unnecessary services disabled		
63. Client server data transfer analyzed and secured		
64. Restrict telnet and r-commands (rlogin, rsh, etc.)		
65. Configuration management procedures		
66. Tracking port scans		
67. Review monitoring responsibilities		
68. Separation between test and production environment		
69. Strong dial-in authentication		
70. System administrator training		
71. Voice system protection procedures		
72. Tunneling for all remote access (inbound or outbound)		
73. Encryption of laptops		
74. Management awareness		
75. Program and system change control procedures		
76. Open "inbound" modem access for vendor support		
77. Modem usage policy		
78. Incident event coordination (procedures)		
79. Intrusion detection system (IDS) implementation and monitoring		
80. Monitoring Web site from attack (internal and external)		

81. Domain Name Server monitoring		
82. Hardware maintenance requirements		
83. Hard drive repair, maintenance, and disposal procedures		
84. BIOS (Basic Input/Output System) boot order		
85. E-mail content policy and monitoring		
86. E-mail forwarding policy (hopping)		
87. Spamming controls and testing procedures		
88. Employee termination and credential disablement		
89. After-hours sign-in logs		
90. Network sniffer policy, procedures, and monitoring		
91. Validity of e-mail accounts		
92. Background checks before hiring		
93. Administrator accounts and password controls		
94. Time synchronization procedures		
95. Establishment of a Security Committee		
96. Testing process for LAN applications		
97. Business unit security person designated		
98. Log and review of all Administrator changes		
99. Review and resolution of past audit comments		
100. Audit logs secured		

Appendix B

Pre-NVA Checklist

Contacts

NVA Team Members

Identify the personnel who make up the NVA team. Be sure to include the sponsor.

- Sponsor
- Project Lead
- Policy Review Lead
- Policy review support
- Technical Review Lead
- Technical support

Name and Department	Phone Number	E-mail Address

Infrastructure Support Contacts

Identify the personnel who are primarily responsible for system and network development, management, and maintenance. Please include name, job title, responsibilities, phone number, and e-mail address of each person:

- NT Domains
- Netware Trees/Contexts
- UNIX Systems
- MVS Systems
- Security systems (firewalls, key distribution systems, certificate authorities)

Name and Department	Responsibilities	Phone Number	E-mail Address

Identify personnel who are primarily responsible for the following areas:

- Auditing:
  - Physical Security
  - Technical Support Services
  - Contracts and Legislation
  - Corporate Inter- and Intranet
  - Facilities (Physical Plant)
  - Purchasing
  - Human Resources and Payroll
  - Records Maintenance/Retention
  - Security Policy
  - Other Corporate Policy, Guidelines, Standards, and Goals

Name and Department	Responsibilities	Phone Number	E-mail Address

Network

Identify the network elements that are part of the assessment.

Network Elements	Connections	Vendor, Model, Quantity, Name, and IPs
1. Components (e.g., *routers, terminal servers, bridges, hubs):* for numerous components of the same type, provide a typical configuration and the quantity of each.		
Connections: describe the quantity and types of connections for each component.		
2. *Management systems:* describe the systems used to manage the network (including monitoring).		
3. *Network services:* describe the network services provided and where those services are provided. A *network service* is any service used by multiple platforms that traverses the network (e.g., directory/name, mail, time).		
4. *Security systems:* describe any network- or host-based security products currently implemented.		

Network Elements	Connections	Vendor, Model, Quantity, Name, and IPs
5. *Exception reports:* for disruptions in either input or output.		
Service/vendor name, description, and type of connection.		
Description and diagram of current firewall implementation.		
Description and diagram of current remote access implementation (dial-up and VPN architecture).		

Host

Identify the critical host computer systems that are part of the assessment, where "host" refers to mainframes, servers, and workstations.

Network Elements	Connections	Vendor, Model, Quantity, Name, and IPs
1. *Configuration:* describe the configuration of each host; for workstations, provide a typical configuration and the quantity.		
Number of users and types of users.		
Management systems: describe the systems used to manage the network (including monitoring).		
2. *System software:* identify system software (system vendor or third party) used on the host. Of primary interest is security-related software (e.g., assessment and monitoring tools).		
3. *Network services:* identify the network services provided by, or used by, each host.		

Applications

Identify the critical applications that are part of the assessment, including any major applications that execute on the hosts identified above.

Applications	BIA Ranking	Dependencies
1. *Description:* provide a brief description of the application; indicate the criticality of the application and the data used by the application.		
2. *Hosts:* identify the hosts on which the application runs; if a client/server application, identify both the client and server systems.		

Documentation

Priority 1 documents will be needed as soon as possible.

Document	Included	Not Available
Documentation		
Network Topology (Diagram)		
Firewall Architecture		
Remote Access Server Architecture		
Detailed List of Mission-Critical Applications		
Brief description (purpose)		
Data storage method (database)		
Who is the data owner/administrator?		
Who are the users (job title)?		
Security mechanisms		
Sensitive or critical data		

Document	Included	Not Available
Policies and Procedures		
Information Security Policies		
Password & ID policy		
Confidential information policies and procedures		
Data classification		
System Access Policy and Procedures		
Mainframe		
Network		
Internet		
Corporate Communication Policies		
Electronic/paper communications		
Disposal policy		
Internet usage policy		
Organizational Material		
Mission Statements		
Organization Charts		

Priority 2 documents will be needed by <date>.

Document	Included	Not Available
IS Infrastructure		
Detailed System List		
Name and location		
Description of use		
Hardware/software installed		
Actual system owner (dept./persons)		
System admin (dept./persons)		
User access classes		
Backup Methods and Procedures		
Archival Methods & Procedures		
Policies and Procedures		
Corporate Security Policy		
Employee Handbook		
Antivirus Strategy/Policy		
Disaster Recovery Plan and Business Continuity Plan		
Application Development Procedures		
Methodology/SDLC		
Promotion to production		
Additional Information Needs		
Physical Security in Place		
Facilities (operations) Plans		

In the case that a document cannot be delivered, please include an explanation of why (i.e., does not exist).

Appendix C

Sample NVA Report

SANITIZED CLIENT

VULNERABILITY ASSESSMENT FINAL REPORT

By

Version 1.3

YOUR COMPANY

This document contains confidential and proprietary information. It is intended for the exclusive use of the Client. Unauthorized use or reproduction of this document is prohibited.

VULNERABILITY ASSESSMENT REPORT

Presented to: Client
                Michael J. Cannon
Presented by: Your Company
                Consultant Name

Vulnerability Assessment Team Members

Name	Company	Role
Consultant Name	Your Company	Vulnerability Assessment Data Collection
Consultant Name	Your Company	Vulnerability Assessment Data Collection
Consultant Name	Your Company	Regional Security Practice Manager
Consultant Name	Your Company	Client Services Manager
Consultant Name	Your Company	Principal Consultant
Consultant Name	Your Company	Consultant, Security
Michael J. Cannon	Client	Manager of Network Infrastructure
Michael J. Cannon	Client	Network Security Analyst

Version History Information

Name	Description	Date	Version
Consultant Name	Initial Draft for Client and Internal Review	6/20/02	1.0
Consultant Name	Second Draft for Client and Internal Review	7/7/02	1.1
Consultant Name	Third Draft for Internal Review	7/14/02	1.2
Consultant Name	Final Version	7/20/02	1.3

Table of Contents

1.0 Executive Summary

Your Company was engaged to conduct a vulnerability assessment (VULNER-ABILITY ASSESSMENT: VA) on the perimeter and network systems of CLIENT during the month of June 2000. Your Company's objective was to discover significant vulnerabilities within the CLIENT network infrastructure. The findings are to be utilized with a risk analysis to assist in developing an Intrusion Detection System Architecture for CLIENT.

The most significant findings relate to the overall design philosophy behind the CLIENT trust model, the lack of a consistent Identification and Authentication (I&A) scheme, the inconsistent and uneven implementation of and compliance with existing policies and procedures, a lack of sufficient audit controls and procedures, and a significant number of vulnerabilities that result in the network and systems being susceptible to compromise from the internal network. The detailed VULNERABILITY ASSESSMENT findings are described later in this document and have been ordered according to severity.

The culture and philosophy of the company dictate the trust model. The trust model of an organization is the philosophical basis upon which the security architecture is built. The security architecture provides the common framework for all other security tools, policies, and procedures. CLIENT has a trust model that assumes the internal users of the network are to be trusted. This model is designed to meet the business needs of CLIENT in which people routinely change locations within the building and resources need to be allocated dynamically. The model is designed to meet the needs of a fluid and open business environment.

The fluid environment at CLIENT creates a situation in which control measures cannot be easily added to the network infrastructure. Due to the lack of sufficient controls, there is an environment that frequently results in violations of current policies and procedures that are not necessarily prevented or detected. Additionally, there is not a mechanism in place to provide a verified and nonrepudiating identity of individuals in the event an intrusion were to occur. Also, user IDs are locally administered and therefore inconsistent across systems. Finally, there is an uneven administration of the current policies and procedures, and there are insufficient reviews of audit logs and information collected from various systems.

The vulnerabilities found during this assessment present several risks to CLIENT. The most significant of these is that internal intrusions cannot be stopped and that both external and internal intrusions cannot be detected. Information essential to the protection of critical data is not available because it is not recorded. The situation is further exacerbated by the discovery of significant vulnerabilities that would allow an internal user to easily compromise the most critical information resources. In effect, an internal user could access almost any critical aspect of the infrastructure and not only would they succeed, but there would be no record of the intrusion and there would be almost no way of proving if the intrusion occurred or did not occur.

In conclusion, Your Company strongly recommends that CLIENT install an intrusion detection system (IDS) and develop a consistent user Identification and Authentication Service (I&A) inside the network. Your Company also recommends an increase in internal audit controls to ensure compliance with existing policies and to ensure that timely and adequate review of log files is occurring.

2.0 General Opinion

This General Opinion will discuss several overarching concerns that became apparent during the VULNERABILITY ASSESSMENT testing. This discussion is intended to provide more in-depth and detailed analysis of the various issues brought forth in the Executive Summary and provides further illumination on the more significant risks to CLIENT.

Personnel

While several people involved with maintaining the network and systems have expressed concerns over the access given to entities (such as developers), the

CLIENT security architecture does not provide, by design, any means of limiting these individual's or group's network infrastructure access. CLIENT tends to accept the risks associated with having a completely open internal architecture in order to accommodate the fluid and changing nature of the environment. However, a documented rationale should accompany any risks that are accepted.

CLIENT has several knowledgeable and skilled individuals in the Information Technology department. These individuals are aware of security-related issues and understand that their internal systems are completely open and accessible. They differ in their opinions as to the severity of this situation. The situation entrusts a great deal of power and responsibility, to the point that any one of a handful of administrators, acting independently, has the capability to compromise a system without any of the other administrators being aware that any misuse has occurred. This requires a great deal of trust in these administrators, which is evidently well placed; however, future employees who may hold these positions may not be as trustworthy. Without measures in place to monitor the activity of such individuals, current or future intrusions or compromises may not be detectable.

Policies and Procedures

CLIENT has several policies and procedures in place to inform its users of the responsibilities and obligations associated with the use of information resources. While the policies in place are adequate in regard to what they address, there appear to be several missing policies, either policies that are referenced and then are not readily available, or policies considered necessary that do not appear to be present. These policies would generally indicate how standards and procedures are to be created and how compliance with the existing policies, standards, and procedures would be monitored. Your Company also observed and was told through interviews that there is uneven compliance and nonexistent auditing of these policies.

Critical Vulnerabilities

The large number of vulnerabilities discovered, both those that are critical in and of themselves as well as those that can be exploited in concert to become critical vulnerabilities, leave many of the most sensitive systems at CLIENT exposed to internal users. The firewall and perimeter devices are configured in such a way that it would be very difficult for an outside user to successfully attack one of the sensitive systems. This is not the case for an attacker on the inside. Any knowledgeable user could gain complete access to all of the critical systems of the infrastructure, including the Sun Development Servers and the core network components themselves.

Identification and Authentication

CLIENT does not have an Identification & Authentication (I&A) process. With the absence of an I&A service, it becomes very difficult to correlate events across multiple platforms and link them to a single entity. It would also be nearly impossible to trace an event to an individual or group. These events are occurring, as Your Company noted, during some of the VULNERABILITY ASSESSMENT tests. User IDs and passwords only provide single-factor identification. In systems where the value of the resource justifies stronger authentication and the ability to trace a user identity, there must be at least two-factor authentication: one that is unique to the individual and one generated randomly at the time credentials are presented. An I&A service, with a time service such as the one CLIENT already has, can also address one of the more difficult problems that exists in modern networked environments, the issue surrounding time of a change in privilege versus the time of privilege usage.

The problem, known as TOCTOU (Time of Change versus Time of Use) comes from a practice during the old mainframe days where the privilege a user has is granted at log-in. The user privileges were managed by the systems Reference Monitor, which was an integral part of the operating system. Therefore, any change in the user's privilege level was immediately enforced by the operating system, so there was period of time when the user's privileges that were in effect did not match the privileges that the user was invoking. In networked environments, the practice still exists of granting privilege at the time of log-in. However, because there is no centralized Reference Monitor that is directly tied into each and every operating system on the network, a change in the user's privilege level is not registered until the user logs off the network and then logs back on. This is the TOCTOU problem. Identification and Authentication services, when coupled with a time service, can resolve this issue in that they force users to present their credentials before accessing any resource on the network. This provides a chance for the privileges to be checked, as well as ensuring the authenticity of the identity of the user ID accessing the resource.

Intrusion Detection

Because of CLIENT's open and fluid environment and the fact that new network-based threats are identified almost daily, an effective means to detect, react, and manage events is necessary. An IDS (intrusion detection system) to identify suspect activity and alert someone of the risk is becoming an increasingly critical part of security architecture. In most environments, this would be coupled with segmentation of network resources across internal firewalls or centralized I&A services. While segmentation may not be feasible within the current CLIENT trust model and architecture, I&A services as well as increased auditing is possible.

An IDS hat can conduct profiling as well as one that utilizes signatures would most likely be the best fit for CLIENT. The profiling of users, especially after the implementation of an I&A service, would allow for anomalous activity to be detected immediately and would allow for an automated review of various system logs that are not being properly reviewed at this time.

Conclusion

Regardless of the frequency of vulnerability testing, no critical system can be considered acceptably protected unless both the network segments and the critical hosts/servers are monitored constantly for signs of abuse and intrusion attempts. Because new exploits and vulnerabilities within devices and network operating systems are discovered regularly, it is impossible to test a network completely, giving 100 percent assurance of being impervious to penetration either from within or from outside. Additionally, CLIENT has chosen a trust model in which the application of stronger internal controls is more difficult than in a more restrictive trust model. Therefore, the easiest method of detecting misuses would be some type of intrusion detection system that is both network based and can do user profiling. Without appropriate identification and authentication of users, referencing abuses to specific individuals becomes unreliable. Without appropriate audit controls to ensure compliance with policies, the policies and procedures themselves become untenable.

Your Company believes the corrective actions and recommendations in this report will improve CLIENT's ability to avoid breaches of information security. However, Your Company strongly recommends that an Intrusion Detection and Identification and Authentication capability be added to the network to detect misuses and intrusions and provide the information necessary to support forensic investigations. It is also recommended that additional audit controls such as compliance testing, independent log review, or configuration audits be implemented, with the results of these controls incorporated with the results of the IDS capability. A policy and procedure review, combined with a risk analysis, would also be very beneficial at this point in time to streamline and reiterate those policies that are critical to the functioning of the enterprise.

3.0 Finding Rating Levels

In the following Findings section, Your Company uses a rating system using stars (*) to indicate the level of severity of our findings. All findings are vulnerabilities that have a business risk to the client.

5 Stars	*****	Critical importance	This needs immediate attention.
4 Stars	****	Important	This should be addressed as soon as is practical.
3 Stars	***	Moderately important	Address this at your convenience but do not ignore it.
2 Stars	**	Moderately important	Address this the next time you perform minor reconfiguration of the host.
1 Star	*	Information only at this time	Address this the next time you perform major reconfiguration of the host.

4.0 Findings

Security Management

Finding 1: Policy and Procedure Enforcement

CLIENT has various policies designed to protect the information assets of the company. Many of these policies reference other policies that were not readily available to be delivered to PA. Interviews of employees indicated that the existence of some of these policies was unknown. Interviews indicated that compliance with policies was not audited or measured except in extreme and obvious instances of flagrant violations.

The following policies were provided to PA:

- *Commitment to Professional Conduct.* A general guide to professional conduct within CLIENT. This document was not formatted as a usual policy and was presented more as an awareness document.
- *Internet Acceptable Use Policy.* A policy that also contained procedures and guidelines for usage.
- *Confidential, Computer Responsibility, and Professional Certification Agreement.* This policy is actually three policies in one, including a Confidentiality Agreement, a Computer Responsibility Policy, and a reference to the Commitment to Professional Conduct.
- *E-Mail Acceptable Use Policy.* This policy detailed the acceptable use of e-mail.

Policies referenced but not provided include:

- Systems Security Policy and Standards
- Human Resources Manual
- Internet Access Policy

Policies that were not found include:

- Information Classification Policy
- Encryption Policy
- External Network Access Policy
- Operating System Hardening Policy
- Password Policy
- Remote Network Access Policy
- Security Change Management Policy
- Security Organization Roles and Responsibilities
- Separation of Duties Policy
- Strong Authentication Policy
- System Access Policy
- User Identity Policy
- Virus Detection and Management Policy

Other policies were mentioned by employees in interviews but were not presented directly or as references to Your Company's team.

Urgency Rating*****

Risk

Policies define the business rules around a particular area, in this case information protection. Procedures tell employees how to operate within those business rules. They define the boundaries in within which people are to operate. Failure to have policies or procedures, or uneven compliance with the existing policies and procedures, can result in legal liability as well as lower employee morale. It will also result in an increased probability of an incident occurring, as people do not know what is expected of them.

Recommendations

Review existing policies and procedures then update them as necessary for both clarity and completeness, followed by the institution of an Information Security Awareness Program so that employees understand their responsibilities. Additional policies addressing deficit areas mentioned above need to be addressed.

Finding 2: Log Review and Auditability

The review of logs is an integral part of an information security program. Logs produced by systems and applications provide detailed information to the owners of the data as to what has occurred with the data for which they are responsible. Your Company's tests showed that many logs, such as the application logs on the Solaris systems and the event logs on the Web servers, were not collected or reviewed on a routine basis. The employee resources dedicated to this task did not appear to be sufficient to adequately examine all the necessary logs.

Urgency Rating*****

Risk

Failure to properly review log entries presents an opportunity for malicious actions to occur. Many systems are not built to resist malicious actions but they do record the results of those actions in their log files. If the files are not reviewed, then the actions can continue.

Recommendations

Implement an intrusion detection system (IDS) that can review log entries to automate the tedious task of log review. Most IDS systems can accomplish this and then generate an alert when anomalous activity is detected.

Finding 3. Risk Analysis Procedure

In an open model where the internal users are assumed to be trusted, it is imperative that there is a process by which any additional protection measures are applied to resources. This process must include a risk analysis to determine the value of the resource and the cost of the protection measure in order to justify the imposition of additional controls on a user community that is normally trusted. When questioned in interviews, it became apparent that there was no risk analysis occurring prior to the imposition of controls.

Urgency Rating****

Risk

Without performing at least a basic risk analysis, controls may be placed on systems that do not need them, and needed controls may not be applied where necessary. Also, without a formalized process, the existing trust model cannot be accurately evaluated to determine if it is still appropriate, given the level of controls placed upon resources.

Recommendations

Develop a formalized risk analysis procedure and add it to the change control process. Subject all changes to security configurations through some variant of the change control process.

Finding 4: Incident Management and Response

CLIENT has an Emergency Response Team designed to respond to critical situations. From the description provided, the team acts more as an Environmental Disaster Team designed to respond to events affecting the core business of the company such as a fire or other natural disaster. It was stated that this team was designed for anything that had "a major impact on user operations." As such, there is no formalized method for dealing with intrusions or other security-related incidents. There is no one designated with the responsibility of collecting and preserving evidence in the event of a computer crime, and there is no one designated to evaluate an event and determine if it is malicious or nonmalicious. Further, there is not a formalized process to determine who will respond to an incident and what the recovery path should be.

Urgency Rating****

Risk

In the event of an intrusion or computer crime, CLIENT would be unable to properly collect and protect evidence necessary for either termination or prosecution of the offending party. Likewise, failure to protect in the event of a computer crime can have a negative impact on a company and also exposes the company to legal liability. In the event of a nonmalicious, noncriminal event, CLIENT would not have the formalized capability to recover, collect the evidence of what happened, and apply that evidence to the prevention of the event reoccurring.

Recommendations

Develop a formalized incident management and response plan. The plan can include the development of a team internally or a contract with an external entity to provide the necessary services.

Finding 5: Information Awareness Program

CLIENT does not appear to have an Information Awareness Program designed to remind all employees of existing policies and procedures, and to promote the proper use and protection of computing resources.

Urgency Rating***

Risk

Every study has shown that between 75 and 80 percent of all computer-related losses are caused by internal users. The development of an effective Information Awareness Program has traditionally been one of the most effective expenditures for the protection of information assets and, outside of basic security services, one of the greatest methods of reducing computer-related incidents.

Recommendations

Develop an effective Information Security Awareness Program in conjunction with the other recommendations in this report.

Security Architecture

Finding 1: Intrusion Detection System

Although a system or network can be tested and made secure, new vulnerabilities are discovered almost daily. Regardless of the amount of time and effort spent correcting configuration errors, it is still possible for an intruder to discover a new intrusion technique and attempt it on the system. Additionally, internal abuse is very difficult to guard against, and there must be some method of full-time monitoring implemented to catch and appropriately log intrusion attempts.

Urgency Rating*****

Risk

There is no way to guarantee through testing that a system is secure. The best that testing can provide is a snapshot of the security of the system at the time of the tests. Therefore, it is critical, especially for sensitive systems, that full-time monitoring be employed. Only through full-time intrusion detection can CLIENT be certain that the vulnerability assessment majority of attack and abuse attempts, either external or internal, can be caught and traced. More important, should an attempt succeed, only complete intrusion detection will allow the ability to track the root cause that permitted the intrusion, repair the problem, and ensure that it does not happen again.

Recommendations

Proposed intrusion detection systems (IDSs) will be presented as a part of the Facilitated Risk Analysis Process, which is to follow the Vulnerability Assessment and is indicated as Milestone II in the Engagement Agreement under which this document was produced.

Finding 2: Security Architecture

As discussed throughout this document, the CLIENT trust model is one designed for both rapid changes, resource reallocation, and fluidity in business processes. Of the classical information security triad — confidentiality, integrity, and availability — the CLIENT network is designed for availability of resources above all else. Beyond the concepts of the CLIENT trust model, a true formalized Security Architecture does not exist. At this point, it is a nebulous idea that is shared by the IT staff, but it has not progressed beyond that.

Urgency Rating**

Risk

The security trust model is the basis for the entire information security infrastructure. The focus on availability in the CLIENT infrastructure results in the integrity and confidentiality of other components not being addressed. This presents the possibility for vulnerabilities to be present that will not be detected because of the infrastructure itself. Without a formalized architecture, future decisions about information protection will be made based on the current view of the information to be protected, which may not accurately reflect the true situation. A formalized architecture provides a framework upon which all security controls can be based, allowing logical decisions to be made based on the direction chosen as opposed to reacting to existing circumstances.

Recommendations

There are three things the client can do:

1. Install an IDS to monitor the users of the network to be aware of potential intrusion attempts.
2. Consider the risks of the existing business risk model and decide if changes need to be made.
3. Evaluate the existing architecture and make any necessary changes to bring it in line with the business risk model if it is found to be out of line

Access Control Methodologies

Finding 1: User Identification and Authentication

The identification of who is using a resource is a critical component in an information security infrastructure. Having two-factor authentication typically does this. A user presents his identification, usually a user ID, and then asserts who he is, usually through a password or passphrase. This is the system used by CLIENT.

Urgency Rating*****

Risk

Failure to have adequate user Identification and Authentication (I&A), especially where a single ID is used by multiple people — as in the case of the XXX Admin account — causes the situation where an individual cannot be traced to an action. Additionally, CLIENT policy states that users are responsible for the actions taken by their account. If a user cannot be proven to be who he is through a nonreputable method, then that policy cannot be enforced. In the case of a common use account, there is no way for this policy to be legally enforced without additional evidence to determine the individual using the account. Finally, because CLIENT has multiple platforms in use, there is no centralized repository of user information that ties an individual to multiple user IDs as they pass from system to system. A central I&A system provides this capability to map user IDs on different systems to a single individual and therefore trace the actions of that individual if necessary.

Recommendations

CLIENT should install a single Identification and Authentication system that has the capability to authenticate user access across not only all platforms, but also their networking equipment. Such a system would need to be RADIUS or TACACS+ compliant, and would need to use biometrics, a token, or both. Adding a second authentication factor — either through biometrics or a one-time password (such as token devices/software like SecureID or a CryptoCard) — would ensure that the user is who he asserts himself to be. This meets the legal requirements for nonrepudiation that is the basis for any action taken in response to an incident.

Finding 2: Password Strength

Within the CLIENT architecture, user passwords are the primary method of authenticating an asserted identity. Therefore, the security of user passwords is critical. CLIENT policy even states that users will be held responsible for the actions of their accounts based on their passwords. Your Company conducted two types of password reviews. One was an attempt to try a basic dictionary attack against passwords sniffed from the wire with tools that any CLIENT employee could download, and the other was a detailed analysis on policies specified within the systems themselves to see if they match CLIENT policy.

Urgency Rating*****

Risk

Compromise of a user password will allow an attack to masquerade as the user. Your Company was able, in a two-hour period, to crack XXX percent of the passwords captured off the wire. A majority of the passwords were the same as the username. Additionally, a point test on the XXX Admin account (named as such) was successful in 12 hours. Finally, it was discovered that password changes are not required and that many of the admin account passwords have not been changed in a significant amount of time.

Recommendations

The following changes need to be implemented immediately:

- Force an immediate change of all passwords.
- Institute a policy of periodic password changes.

Additionally, the following changes need to occur:

- Install an Identification and Authentication (I&A) system.
- Install an intrusion detection (IDS) system.

Finding 3: Unencrypted Passwords

CLIENT has several systems that utilize the Telnet protocol. This protocol sends usernames and passwords, or the hash of the password, in cleartext across the network.

Urgency Rating*****

Risk

Sending usernames and passwords across the network in cleartext allows an attacker to log onto the resource. The systems affected by this are all routers and switches, as well as all the Sun Solaris systems. Any user with a sniffer could potentially access any resource sending usernames and passwords in cleartext.

Recommendations

There are two recommendations to resolve this issue. The first is to install an Identification and Authentication (I&A) service that supports two-factor authentication. The one-time passwords (tokens) generated by these types of systems mean that even if the password is noticed on the wire, the password will have changed at the next log-in. A second solution is to utilize SSH (Secure Shell) where possible. SSH encrypts all traffic, including user-name and password, as well as supporting the use of public/private key pairs, which negates the need for using a password in the situation where that is supported.

Finding 4: User Account Management

Every NT system tested by Your Company resulted in several user account management issues. These ranged from active guest accounts, to missing account policies, to short passwords. The other problem noticed was that there was no consistent policy enforced across all systems and there were no apparent guidelines as to what those policies should be.

Urgency Rating****

Risk

Failings in user account management is one of the first places a potential attacker will look to gain entry into a system. Nonexistent user account management policies will result in varying system strength across critical systems, leaving significant opportunity for an attacker — either internal or external — to gain unauthorized access.

Recommendations

Develop a User Account Management Policy — including minimum password length, change frequency, account lockout, and password history — and then implement the policy across all platforms.

Physical and Operational Security

Finding 1: Violations of Operations Security Procedures

Access to the CLIENT computer room is through a card key system. Visitors are supposed to then log in on a sign-in sheet when entering and sign-out when exiting. Employees are to swipe their cards when entering or leaving. Your Company noticed employees following the procedure of swiping in and out; however, visitors, such as PA, were not required to sign almost every time the facility was visited. Of the entrances and exits from the computer room, Your Company employees were required to sign out only once. Most of the time, Your Company employees exited the room without someone swiping them out. Also, even when Your Company signed in, the names were never checked. A review of the log should show a recent visit to the CLIENT computer room by Mickey Mouse.

Also, consoles in the computer room were routinely left unlocked with an administrator account logged in. In almost a month of time in the CLIENT computer room, the consoles to all of the NT servers were never locked, and most of them had the XXX Administrative account logged in, an account which has Administrator privileges on the NT system.

Urgency Rating*****

Risk

Control of the central computing facility is critical to the survival of CLIENT. Unauthorized access to the computer facility and unrestricted access to administrative accounts would allow a user to do whatever he wished. Additional investigation revealed that developers have access to the computer room, thereby effectively giving them and anyone else in the computer room administrator access to the NT servers. With this access, anyone can do whatever he wants to the system under his control. Additionally, physical access to the computer room grants physical access to the Sun servers and the network core. Physical access would allow someone to shut down these systems.

Recommendations

The following steps should be taken immediately:

- Enforce strict sign-in and sign-out procedures.
- Lock all NT server screens, thereby requiring a log-in.
- Do not allow developers access to the computer room.

Additional steps should be taken as follows:

- Physically isolate the Sun server room.

- Lock cabinets with NT servers and key them so that only authorized individuals have the necessary keys.
- Install an Identification and Authentication system to verify not only the account in use, but also who logged in as that account.
- Lock the power distribution cabinet so that only authorized personnel can disable power internal to the computer room.
- Physically secure the core network equipment so that someone cannot shut down the network.
- Implement a cable management system so that physical access to core network devices is not required for troubleshooting physical network problems.
- Install more cameras to provide full coverage of the computer room.
- Store camera images for future reference as evidence in the event of an incident.
- Computer room space should not be used as a staging area for deployment hardware.

Finding 2: Violations of Physical Security Procedures

Physical security is described as the "guns, guards, gates, dogs, cameras, and bombs" part of security. It is designed to provide a physical, deterrent control to the behavior of individuals. Your Company observed several critical violations of physical security. They were as follows:

- The front door was unlocked late on the evening of XXX at approximately XXX with no one present at the front guard counter for over 15 minutes.
- The computer room was unmanned several evenings during the week of XXX while operators were out smoking, leaving only Your Company personnel in the computer room or, in one observed case, no one was present while Your Company personnel waited for several minutes for the operator to return from a break.
- Visitor bags were not checked or examined upon entry/exit.

Urgency Rating*****

Risk

These violations could result in the introduction of materials or the removal of information from CLIENT. Part of CLIENT's security trust model is to rely on human intervention in the event of problems, with the absence of operators or guards, no human response was available.

Recommendations

Enforcement of existing policy and procedures.

Finding 3: Physical Access to Critical Workspaces

Various workspaces contain critical media and data, such as the operating system disks for Solaris or the NT recovery disks. In addition, confidential data is also stored in user workspaces. Your Company noticed several workspaces without locking drawers or covers in which critical information and data was stored.

Urgency Rating*****

Risk

The potential exists for critical data to be stolen or for users to bypass system controls with access to critical operating system media.

Recommendations

Provide sufficient locked space for employees with critical or sensitive data or media.

Telecommunications and Network Security

Finding 1: SNMP

SNMP (Simple Network Management Protocol) is a protocol that was developed to ease the management of network devices. However, the protocol was not developed with security in mind. It utilizes community strings to determine which devices belong in a specific community, and SNMP devices can now require a password before accepting commands. However, Your Company discovered that these precautions were not in place at CLIENT. Using a tool called SolarWinds, Your Company was able to use SNMP to map the entire network and to also gain the full status of the core network devices. Further, Your Company would have been able to order the devices to show continuous updates that would have consumed significant cycles of CPU power on the devices and slowed network traffic through the core devices. Finally, Your Company was able to determine that little work would have been required to fully access almost all network switches and issue SNMP commands to alter their configurations.

Urgency Rating*****

Risk

Using SNMP, an attack can discover the entire layout of a network as well as request the device to continually update the attacker on its status. This will result in the device spending CPU cycles to send the updates and can slow network traffic. Some devices can also be reconfigured by SNMP.

Recommendations

Disable all MIB extensions not necessary for management or monitoring of devices, and select community strings and passwords that are cryptographically secure.

Finding 2: TCP Sequence Prediction

When computers communicate using TCP/IP, they utilize a series of numbers known as TCP Sequence Numbers. These numbers tell the communicating computers in what order the conversation is progressing so that a connection can be formed. If an attacker can guess the TCP Sequence Numbers of a device, the attacker can then initiate a man-in-the-middle attack, in which the attacker proceeds to place himself in the middle of the conversation, effectively pretending to be invisible. Almost all NT machines were able to have their TCP Sequence Numbers guessed.

Urgency Rating*****

Risk

Successful guessing of the TCP Sequence allows an attacker to insert himself into the middle of the conversation and eventually knocks one of the devices out of the conversation, stealing its identity.

Recommendations

Install the appropriate service packs and patches to all NT devices.

Finding 3: Outside Availability of Telnet

Devices outside the corporate firewall responded to Telnet from the Your Company test machine, located outside of the firewall as well. The devices were:

- XXX.XXX.XX.XXX
- XXX.XXX.XX.X
- XXX.XXX.XXX.XX
- XXX.XXX.XX.X

Urgency Rating****

Risk

As described above, Telnet sends usernames and passwords in cleartext. Because these devices were available for Telnet outside the firewall, and attacker could attempt to use brute force to guess the passwords and proceed to access these devices. Two of the devices are the boundary router interfaces for CLIENT.

Recommendations

Disable accepting Telnet from all hosts except those who should have access to make configuration changes and consider some type of Identification and Authentication (I&A) service to further protect the boundary devices.

Finding 4: Firewall, DMZ, and Proxying

CLIENT does not have a traditional DMZ. Its DMZ is defined as a set of IP addresses mapped from behind the firewall to be accessible from the Internet. This configuration places the externally reachable servers inside the perimeter with the internal network. CLIENT also does not have any application-level proxying done to inspect inbound or outbound traffic. The firewall does possess some level of application-level proxying for certain command sets such as SMTP and FTP commands. Additionally, without a proxy, the IIS servers are susceptible to malformed IIS API calls, as was demonstrated by PA.

Urgency Rating***

Risk

In this configuration, a compromise of any externally available server would give an attacker access to the entire internal network. Also, without application-level proxying, invalid or inappropriate commands on protocols such as HTTP are not blocked.

Recommendations

The following are recommended for consideration:

- Consider the creation of a true DMZ and place all externally available servers there.
- Install proxies to act as an inbound and outbound gateways.

Finding 5: Anomalous Network Events

During Your Company's test of the network, two anomalous events occurred. The first was a series of SYN floods that were detected by the IDS system Your Company uses to verify its findings during the network scans. These SYN floods came from various IP addresses on the Internet. Detailed capture files are included on the CD-ROM for CLIENT review. The second event involved a SYN flood followed by a port scan from inside the CLIENT network to various hosts. Your Company determined that it could be one of the custom

CLIENT applications, but the capture files from that event as well as a light scan to determine the identity of the machine are included in the reports on the Supplemental CD.

Urgency Rating**

Risk

These events may be an indication that activity is occurring that CLIENT had no prior knowledge about.

Recommendations

Deploy an IDS and I&A services to track incidents and determine the identity of the originator if the incident originates from the internal network.

Applications and Systems Security

Finding 1: Developer Access to Production Systems

Interviews with the system administrators indicated that developers had access to the production systems and that they can still have access through other vulnerabilities discussed in this report, such as the XXX Admin account and the NFS vulnerabilities.

Urgency Rating*****

Risk

Developers should not have access to production systems or data. This is one of the underlying principles of information security codified in the concept of "separation of duties." The concerns are due to the fact that because developers produce the applications that run on systems, they should not have access to production systems so that any malicious code included in the applications can be detected by the system operator. If developers have access to the production system, they may be able to alter the system in such a way as to hide their malicious activities.

Recommendations

Install an intrusion detection system (IDS) and an Identification and Authentication (I&A) service to monitor the actions of users, including developers. Additionally, an "authenticity" product such as Tripwire to ensure that files have not been modified should also be installed.

Finding 2: Sun Development Cluster

Several critical problems were found with the Sun Development Cluster. Many of these problems individually would not be critical, but combined they allow for compromises of the Sun Development Cluster. If these same vulnerabilities exist on the Production Sun Cluster, then that cluster is also at risk.

The vulnerabilities found included:

- *CDE rpc.ttdbserver (ToolTalk).* The ToolTalk server is vulnerable to a series of buffer overflow exploits that can allow a user to elevate their privilege level to root.
- *FingerBomb.* The FingerBomb is a denial-of-service (DoS) attack against the Finger daemon, which can result in a reboot, restart of network services, or a crash of the protocol stack.
- *NFS issues.* NFS shares are mountable, writeable, and exportable outside their domain. The test machine was able to mount shares used by all users to store code and other files, thereby allowing a Trojan horse to be installed.
- *RPCstatd remote file access.* The RPCstatd exploit allows a remote user to remotely add, list, or delete files. This process can be used to replace telnetd with a trojaned file and then, through FingerBomb, cause the new telnetd to be run. This exploit was recently used successfully to hijack machines to cause the DDoS attacks on the Internet
- *Rsh allowed from scanning machine.* The Sun cluster allowed the scanning machine to Rsh into it. Combined with the NFS vulnerabilities, this would allow an arbitrary user to gain root access.
- *admind/sadmind.* Solaris admind and sadmind are, by default, insecure and can be exploited to gain root access to the server.
- *Trusted hosts and authentication vulnerabilities.* Several of the above vulnerabilities could be exploited to then allow an attacker to gain control over any host that trusted the compromised machine. Likewise, several NIS vulnerabilities were found that, combined with the NFS exportable beyond domain vulnerability, would allow an attacker, once root was gained, to redefine NIS relationships.
- *Information gathering.* Several services were running on the Development Sun Cluster that revealed all usernames on the box and all home directories, as well as disk space and usage and operating system patch levels and installed packages.
- *RHOST log-in.* Several DBA accounts allow log-ins through rhosts from any system, without specifying a password.

Urgency Rating*****

Risk

The combination of these risks would allow an attacker to gain root access on the Development Cluster. Scripts exist on the Internet to exploit several vulnerabilities.

Recommendations

Update all patch levels, examine all services running and justify their existence, install an IDS and I&A service to verify all access to the servers, and consider the addition of a firewall to separate the Sun Clusters from the rest of the network.

Finding 3: Mail Server

Several problems were found with the mail server that would allow an attacker to gain administrator access to the system by sending binary data to either IIS or Exchange.

These vulnerabilities were:

- Using IIS to run arbitrary code
- Using IIS to gain ODBC access with RDS
- Using IIS to create remote files
- Using IIS to view the directory server
- SMTP allows remote commands execution through the recipient and bounce filters

Urgency Rating*****

Risk

All of the above vulnerabilities would allow an attacker to gain domain administrator privileges on the mail server and grant them complete control of the machine.

Recommendations

Update the mail server to the proper patch levels and remove all sample IIS applications from the server.

Finding 4: Production Web Server ISAPI Vulnerability

Your Company discovered during its external scans across the PIX firewall that the production IIS servers could be shut down by sending repeated ISAPI calls for services that did not exist, such as Cold Fusion. The cause of this is in the way IIS handles ISAPI calls. IIS receives the binary and attempts to execute it; if it cannot, it then sends the binary data to the ISAPI handler. It is the job of this handler to communicate to the various ISAPI services running, or activate the appropriate one if it is not running. In this case, the service does not exist, so the handle returns an error and the data is dropped. The effect of multiple requests was to cause the handler to crash into an uncontrollable state where the operating system could not remove the process. This caused IIS to lock up, which then locked up or, in several cases, crashed the Web server.

Urgency Rating*****

Risk

The risk is that someone on the Internet could flood the CLIENT network with bogus ISAPI calls and shut down the Web servers.

Recommendations

Proxy servers are designed to handle this type of a situation. By placing a proxy server in front of the Web server and instructing it as to what type of ISAPI calls are acceptable to the Web server, the buffer overflow condition should not occur. Additionally, a DMZ can be set up with either the Web server or the proxy server on the DMZ to provide further isolation.

Finding 5: Development Web Server

The development Web server has several vulnerabilities in it that would allow an attacker to gain administrator privileges. Assuming that the production servers are configured the same, they would also suffer these vulnerabilities.

The vulnerabilities are:

- *Netscape enterprise buffer overflow.* Several buffer overflow exploits exist for Netscape Enterprise. Most of them allow an elevated privilege level.
- *FTPD arguments DoS/FTP PASV DoS.* The server is vulnerable to a denial-of-service (DoS) attack from the FTP server that it is running.
- *RPCstatd.* Although the server is running Windows NT, RPCstatd has been added to the machine, either as a stand-alone or through Netscape Enterprise Server. The machine is now vulnerable to the RPCstatd exploit mentioned with the Development Sun Cluster.
- *LDAP Access.* LDAP is installed on the server, and anonymous access is granted to view and modify data in the directory.

Urgency Rating*****

Risk

These vulnerabilities would allow an attacker to gain full administrative rights to the server. Assuming that the production devices are configured the same, this would also imply that the production devices are similarly vulnerable.

Recommendations

Update all software to the current patch levels and examine all services running on the system. Any services not justified should be removed.

Finding 6: WINS/DHCP Server XXX_ntadmin

The server XXX_NTADMIN is used as both the WINS and DHCP server. Additionally, it runs FPNW to allow connection to Novell NetWare. The machine was tested both from the network and in a configuration audit. The system had numerous instances of Novell passwords that were blank or easily guessed, shares that were unprotected, and configuration problems within the setup of the system. The problems appear to be the result of the FPNW service and how it presents the Novell accounts to NT.

Urgency Rating*****

Risk

Because of the vulnerabilities associated with this system, it is highly susceptible to being compromised. Compromising the naming system of the network would render many services inoperable. Additionally, compromising this system would result in a loss of functionality for the Novell users who require the FPNW gateway.

Recommendations

Because of the design of the FPNW service, this system cannot be secured until FPNW has been removed from the machine. FPNW should not be on a machine that is critical to the internal name resolution of the network. A review of all services and shares running on the system needs to be conducted and any extraneous services should be removed.

Finding 7: Null Sessions

Null sessions are connections to a machine that do not require a username or password. Typically, they are the initial connection to the machine, which then presents the request for log-in credentials. Your Company found numerous systems that allowed null sessions to connect and request information without ever identifying themselves. This is a standard trait of Windows NT and it also happens to be an excellent source of information that is useful for attacking a system. Your Company was able to enumerate the shares, users, and groups of all NT machines that were tested.

Urgency Rating***

Risk

Systems that allow null sessions to gather information critical to the system expose themselves to attack. They become targets of opportunity and are usually the first systems that an intruder will attempt to compromise.

Recommendations

Install the appropriate service patches and make the necessary configuration changes to prevent Windows NT systems from revealing information about users, groups, and shares.

Finding 8: Visual Basic Scripting

End users have the ability to perform Visual Basic scripting using Visual Basic for Applications.

Urgency Rating***

Risk

The use of VBA allows users to create custom applications running on their desktops. These applications could end up impacting network performance, or possibly be used to exploit weaknesses in various operating systems to gain root-equivalent access.

Recommendations

Either remove VBA from all user desktops or monitor user network activity for unusual or inappropriate application activity.

Finding 9: Default Workstation Install

Your Company tested the default installation for all CLIENT workstations. The major issues discovered were as follows:

- Operating system revision level and patches are not up-to-date.
- Security event auditing is not enabled.
- User profiles are not defined.
- Anonymous network access to the registry is allowed.
- Registry permissions are not set securely.
- Blank passwords are allowed.
- There is no account lockout.
- Account management policies are not in place.

Urgency Rating***

Risk

Where problems with servers generally affect one or two machines, problems with the default workstation install, labeled A1 in the test documents, affects a far greater number of people.

Recommendations

Perform a risk analysis and develop standards for the base install; then implement the standards.

Finding 10: Configuration Audit and Change Control Findings

Several configuration audit and change control issues were found. Change control is the process by which changes are made to a system. Ideally, it is a formalized process that insures constancy across similar resources with identical risk levels. Your Company observed the following configuration audit findings, which indicate that an uneven implementation of the change control process has been occurring.

The following specific items are of concern:

- *Operating system patches.* Systems do not have consistent revision levels of operating system patches.
- *System auditing.* Auditing is not active on most systems; and when it is active, it is not reviewed.
- *Registry settings.* Registries on NT systems are unsecured.
- *Queue settings.* Crontabs on Solaris allow other users to modify Crontabs.
- *Remote user log-ins.* Accounts on Solaris systems allow rhost log-ins from any system.
- *NFS exportable to any host.* Portions of the file system may be exported to any host.

Additionally, statements by many employees indicated that the change management process could be bypassed and that there was no configuration management of local workstations.

Urgency Rating***

Risk

Most of these specific risks are discussed elsewhere. The primary concern here is that a configuration change control must be enforced and must cover all platforms and systems. Any change that affects multiple people must go through the change management review process.

Recommendations

Correct configuration errors, update the change management process, and then enforce the process to make sure systems are maintained properly and correctly.

5.0 Vulnerability Assessment Test Protocol

Your Company used a variety of testing tools during our vulnerability assessments. While conducting attacks against target systems and devices, Your Company placed an intrusion detection monitor on the distant side of protective devices (e.g., firewall and router) to attempt to detect any leakage of the attack through those devices. The tests began with a "zero-information-based (ZIB) attack" in which no information regarding the target was known except for the name of the client. We then performed scans of known address space to expose potential backdoors into the internal network. Finally, we tested each device and subsystem from several source points (outside, inside the internal network, and on the DMZ) and performed host/server configuration audits.

Your Company used its proprietary Redundant Test Environment (RTE) to ensure that findings were accurate and complete. The RTE requires that all findings produced by a scanner be confirmed, either with a different scanner or manually. This eliminates false positives. Your Company also ran two separate scanners to ensure that potential security holes were not missed.

The basic vulnerability assessment test protocol is as follows.

Zero-Information-Based (ZIB) Footprint Analysis

This preliminary analysis was intended to determine how much of the target's network was visible from the public Internet given no information beyond the name of the company. ZIB analysis used publicly available information to learn as much about the target as possible. Information sources included the Internet, data available through NSLookup, WHOIS, Dig, DNS zone transfers, postings to Usenet newsgroups, etc. It culminated with an effort to map the target network segment.

Address Space Scan

This was a broad scan of the target's assigned address space to reveal basic vulnerabilities and potential backdoors. A commercial scanner/attack simulator was the tool. The client was advised at this point of any critical vulnerabilities that should be corrected before continuing, especially those that might permit a successful denial-of-service attack.

Point Scan

This was a focused vulnerability scan/attack simulation of selected critical/sensitive devices on the target network segment. The tool was a commercial scanner/attack simulator different from the one used in the step above. This step includes denial-of-service attacks.

Document Examination

Your Company examined policies, standards, and practices that relate to the target network subsystem. The focus was on access control policies, including authentication and authorization, network architecture, disaster recovery, configuration control, as well as other issues described in BS 7799.

Platform Configuration Assessment

All affected platforms, including servers, routers, and firewalls, were tested thoroughly to ensure that secure configuration practices are being followed. The assessment tools were commercial tools supported by Your Company proprietary manual techniques.

Network Scan/Attack Simulation from within the Target Network Segment

This testing focused on network vulnerabilities that may not have been detected from the Internet due to packet filtering at the Internet router. During this testing, a commercial intrusion detection system was placed such that data leakage through firewalls and packet filters could be detected. Access controls such as VPNs were tested at this time, as was the susceptibility of individual platforms to denial-of-service and penetration attempts from within the protected network.

Verification

This final test step included the use of manual techniques to verify questionable results of the prior scans and examination of appropriate logs to ensure that the system was logging as well as could be expected.

Analysis and Reporting

Following the completion of the testing, a security analyst examined the raw logs and reports produced by the scanners, the test notes of the testing engineer, and the logs of critical systems in the target network segment. The analyst prepared this report that describes the test methodology, results, significance of the individual findings, and recommendations for corrective actions. Copies of source logs and scanner reports will be included as a supplemental CD to the report. Optionally, this assessment may be repeated after corrective action has been taken to ensure that all security holes have been plugged.

The following procedure is generally used when testing. The testing Your Company conducted was typical of this process:

1. Analysis of policies, standards, and practices
2. Zero-information-based (ZIB) tests using public information to identify information assets exposed to the public Internet
3. Top-level analysis from the Internet using a security scanner to identify exposed information assets more completely, search for backdoors into the protected network, and expose major vulnerabilities that can be attacked from the public Internet
4. Use of publicly available cracking tools to obtain a "cracker's view" of the exposed devices
5. Focus on individual high-risk devices using a detailed point scanner
6. Analysis of actual system maps and the results of efforts to map the network from the public Internet
7. Repeat of tests using redundant scanners from within the DMZ (testing of DMZ devices) and from the protected network looking out to the DMZ and the public Internet
8. Configuration audit of individual devices using various configuration audit tools
9. Denial-of-service attacks against all devices using a scanner capable of denial-of-service attacks
10. Examination of system logs for the test period(s)
11. Examination of application code
12. Examination of intrusion detection monitor data
13. Examination of data collected during sniffer tests of application behavior (attempting to identify critical data that could be captured on the network wire)
14. Examination of physical security measures and operational procedures
15. Use of social engineering techniques
16. Review of policies and procedures as well as administrative controls
17. Dialing of all phone numbers to check for unauthorized or exposed modems
18. Final data analysis and report production

The detailed list of tests can be found in Appendix C-1.

While Your Company can never be 100 percent certain that all possible vulnerabilities have been addressed — new vulnerabilities are discovered frequently — Your Company believes that correcting the vulnerabilities listed in this report and monitoring for new vulnerabilities will make the target application or system acceptably secure.

The objectives in all tests were:

1. Test for vulnerabilities in the following areas:
   - Interface to the public Internet
   - Interface to the DMZ
   - Interface to the internal network
   - Specific system platforms (i.e., Web servers, authentication servers, etc.)
   - Applications
2. Validate applicable security policies
3. Validate physical and operational security measures
4. Validate administration procedures for the affected system and subsystems

6.0 Exceptions to the Vulnerability Assessment Test Protocol

The following exceptions to the standard Vulnerability Assessment Test Protocol occurred during our examination CLIENT:

- CLIENT does not have a true DMZ — a network separate from the internal network protected by their firewall; therefore, DMZ tests could not be performed.
- CLIENT did not contract Your Company to perform social engineering or application-level reviews.
- CLIENT requested Your Company to perform tests on development environments instead of production environments.
- CLIENT requested Your Company not to examine certain sections of the network beyond specified demarcation points (see exhibit in Appendix C-3).

Vulnerabilities that exist beyond these exceptions will not have been discovered by the Your Company test procedures.

7.0 Standards Applied

Testing and analysis is performed at all identified interface/vulnerability points, except as noted above. Your Company applies the following criteria in the testing and analysis process:

1. The CLIENT corporate policies, standards, and practices
2. Common Criteria and Common Methodology, where applicable
3. Testing against six functional areas of vulnerability
4. ISO 17799, where applicable

Common Criteria

The Common Criteria is an ISO standard that specifies the creation of protection profiles and targets of evaluation. If the client's model for information protection includes their resources evaluated to a certain evaluation level of a protection profile, this will be noted and testing will be done to see if the systems to be tested do indeed meet that evaluation level.

Common Methodology

The Common Methodology used is a model of information security based on that which is common within the information security industry and that which is codified as domains of the Common Body of Knowledge (CBK) maintained by the (ISC)² (International Information Systems Security Certification Consortium). The (ISC)² is the organization that certifies information security professionals and maintains a standardized reference list of those domains that are common to the profession. Those domains are:

1. *Security Management:* the use of policy and procedures in managing the protection of information resources as well as looking at risk analysis and best practices for information protection.
2. *Security Architecture:* the architecture employed for securing information assets from the enterprise level to the individual data component.
3. *Access Control Methodologies:* controls and methodologies used to control and monitor access to information resources.
4. *Physical and Operational Security:* physical protection measures of the site and operational practices to provide controls to protect information resources.
5. *Disaster Recovery and Business Continuity Planning:* planning and procedures used to resume normal business operations in the event of a disruption of those operations, and to protect information resources during a disruption while also providing alternate resources to meet information processing needs.
6. *Cryptography:* the use of encryption to maintain the confidentiality and integrity of information.
7. *Telecommunications and Network Security:* the security of the telecommunications and information processing networks.
8. *Application and Systems Development:* practices and procedures in the development, selection, and deployment of information processing resources.

Additionally, Your Company used evaluation criteria that were originally developed for the government and financial services industries. These criteria make users individually accountable for their actions through log-in procedures, auditing of security-relevant events, and resource isolation.

1. *Security Policy: Discretionary Access Control.* The system defines and controls access between named users and named objects.
2. *Security Policy: Object Reuse.* All authorizations to a storage object must be revoked prior to initial assignment, allocation, or reallocation.
3. *Accountability: Identification and Authentication.* All users must identify themselves before performing any other actions that the system is expected to mediate.
4. *Accountability: Audit.* The system must be able to create, maintain, and protect from modification or unauthorized access or destruction an audit trail of access to the objects it protects.
5. *Operational Assurance: System Architecture.* The system must maintain a domain for its own execution that protects it from external interference or tampering such as modification of its code or data structures.
6. *Operational Assurance: System Integrity.* Hardware and software features must be provided to validate the correct operation of the system resources.
7. *Life-Cycle Assurance: Security Testing.* The security mechanisms of the system must be tested and found to work as presented in system documentation.
8. *Documentation: Security Features Users' Guide.* The protection mechanisms provided by the system, their use, and how they interact with each other must be provided.

9. *Documentation: Trusted Facility Manual.* A manual addressed to the system administrator must present cautions about functions and privileges that should be controlled when running a secure facility.
10. *Documentation: Test Documentation.* The system developer must provide a document that describes the test plan and procedures that show how the security mechanisms were tested and the results of the testing.
11. *Documentation: Design Documentation.* A document must be provided that describes the developer's philosophy of protection and how the philosophy was implemented in the system.

Functional Areas of Vulnerability

The success with which these vulnerabilities are addressed determines the security of the system. The six functional areas are:

1. *Identification and authentication (I&A):* functions intended to establish and verify the identity of the user or using process.
2. *Access control:* functions intended to control the flow of data between, and the use of resources by, users, processes, and objects. This includes administration and verification of access rights.
3. *Accountability:* functions intended to record exercising of rights to perform security-relevant actions.
4. *Object reuse:* functions intended to control reuse or scavenging of data objects.
5. *Accuracy:* functions intended to ensure the correctness and consistency of security-relevant information.
6. *Reliability of service:* functions intended to ensure the security of data over communication links.

ISO 17799

Although U.S. organizations are not expected to comply with ISO 17799, this standard has become a guideline for many large U.S. companies due to its comprehensive approach to risk and vulnerability assessment requirements. The key areas of ISO 17799 define the important administrative security issues within the organization that require testing/validation. These areas are:

1. *Information security policy document.* A written policy document should be available to all employees responsible for information security.
2. *Allocation of information security responsibilities.* Responsibilities for the protection of individual assets and for carrying out specific security processes should be explicitly defined.
3. *Information security education and training.* Users should be given adequate security education and technical training.
4. *Reporting of security incidents.* Security incidents should be reported through management channels as quickly as possible.
5. *Virus controls.* Virus detection and prevention measures and appropriate user awareness procedures should be implemented.

6. *Business continuity planning process.* There should be a managed process in place for developing and maintaining business continuity plans across the organization.
7. *Control of proprietary software copying.* Attention is drawn to the legal restrictions on the use of copyright material.
8. *Safeguarding of organizational records.* Important records of an organization should be protected from loss, destruction, and falsification.
9. *Data protection.* Applications that handle personal data on individuals should comply with data protection legislation and principles.
10. *Compliance with security policy.* All areas within the organization should be considered for regular review to ensure compliance with security policies and standards.

8.0 Reference Model

Reference models relate information security practices to the business rules or standards of an organization. They also help provide a model upon which one can refer to when discussing information protection issues.

The Standard Information Protection Model

Your Company's Information Protection Model is an advanced four-layer model that effectively maps the needs for confidentiality; integrity, and availability into product and service layers designed to help a client achieve maximum protection of their data. Those four layers, and how the vulnerability assessment maps into them, are:

1. *Prevention:* all measures taken to protect information assets. These are the system and control measures that the vulnerability assessment is designed to test and analyze.
2. *Detection:* all measures taken for the purpose of detecting an attempt to access, modify, create, or delete an information asset. Detection measures may be used as an additional control beyond the prevention measures, or may be used in cases where prevention measures are not used. The vulnerability assessment will also analyze data from these controls to further review the prevention measures. The vulnerability assessment can also analyze the detection measures themselves to provide a level of assurance about their functioning.
3. *Containment:* all measures taken to contain a problem, should one occur. The vulnerability assessment is an assurance process; it is designed to assure the client that the client control measures are functioning as designed.
4. *Recovery:* all measures taken to return to normal functioning after an incident has occurred; this may include an investigative component as well. The vulnerability assessment may also provide a level of assurance regarding the procedures and methodologies in place to facilitate the recovery process.

Client Trust Model

CLIENT has as its basic trust model the underlying premise that all internal traffic can be trusted. In an effort to balance the business needs of their users, they have decided to have an almost completely open internal environment with almost no centralized internal controls in place. The model is one in which each resource provides its own protection controls in accordance with the risk associated with that resource while the outer perimeter is protected by network-based control measures. The model also assumes that all trusted external links, such as links to corporate headquarters, are a part of the internal network.

Appendix C-1: List of Tests Performed

This appendix lists the tests that were performed. Detailed information as well as the original data files on each test are provided on the supplemental CD included with this report.

Network-Based Tests

Scanner Location	IP Address	Monitor Location	IP Address	Test Description
External to firewall	XXX.XXX.96.88	Internal to firewall	XXX.XXX.42.88	Phase 1 tests, NetRecon, and ISS
Internal of firewall	XXX.XXX.42.88	Internal on VLAN of target	Varied, based on target host	NetRecon and ISS on specific targets
Internal of firewall	XXX.XXX.42.88	Internal to firewall	XXX.XXX.42.89	NetRecon and ISS general scan on entire network

List of IP Addresses Tested

XXX.XXX.96.0 to XXX.XXX.97.255
XXX.XXX.247.248 to XXX.XXX.247.255
XXX.XXX.42.0 to XXX.XXX.42.255
XXX.XXX.113.0 to XXX.XXX.113.255

XXX.XXX.118.0 to XXX.XXX.118.255
XXX.XXX.125.0 to XXX.XXX.125.255
XXX.XXX.128.0 to XXX.XXX.128.255
XXX.XXX.0.0 to XXX.XXX.255.255
XXX.XXX.0.0 to XXX.XXX.255.255
XXX.XXX.83.102
XXX.XXX.83.86
XXX.XXX.129.245

Specific IP Address Targeted for Point Scans by ISS and NetRecon

XXX.XXX.94.10   XXX.XXX.95.10
XXX.XXX.148.31   XXX.XXX.148.32
XXX.XXX.64.10   XXX.XXX.239.3
XXX.XXX.32.15   XXX.XXX.84.185

Specific IP Addresses Used for the ESM Configuration Audit

XXX.XXX.94.10   XXX.XXX.16.57
XXX.XXX.226.2   XXX.XXX.148.31
XXX.XXX.148.32   XXX.XXX.84.160
XXX.XXX.32.15   XXX.XXX.32.3

Specific ISS Tests Conducted during Point Scans

ISS performs several hundred tests. The configurations that tell ISS which tests to run are known as ISS Policies. Your Company ran a full range of policies, including a policy that tested for all vulnerabilities in the ISS database and a policy that tested for all denials of service in the ISS database. All ISS Policies used by Your Company are located on the Supplemental CD at <CD ROM>\ ISS Reports\Policies.

Specific NetRecon Tests Conducted during Point Scans

NetRecon collects data from the target machine by sending it queries. Given the responses that NetRecon gets back, it then looks into its database to determine which vulnerabilities would be present. The process by which NetRecon does this is known as a path analysis. All NetRecon tests and the resulting path analysis are included in the NetRecon data files located on the Supplemental CD at <CD Rom>\Data Files\Axent NetRecon.zip.

Specific ESM Policy Tests Conducted

ESM runs configuration audit tests against the data it collects from agents installed on machines to audit. These tests are known as ESM Policies. All

ESM Policies are located on the Supplemental CD as.html files at <CD ROM>\
ESM Reports\Policy.

Remote Access Phone Dialing Tests

Number Range Dialed
Duplicate numbers were removed during dialing.

    XXX4480 to XXX4499
    XXX7160 to XXX7179
    XXX7100 to XXX7299
    XXX7300 to XXX7499
    XXX2360 to XXX2399
    XXX6000 to XXX6499
    XXX1400 to XXX1999
    XXX2000 to XXX2019
    XXX2100 to XXX2119
    XXX5500 to XXX5599
    XXX3753 to XXX3852
    XXX1400 to XXX3999
    XXX6000 to XXX6999
    XXX7300 to XXX7999
    XXX6500 to XXX6999

Numbers Captured (responses received)

XXX4489	XXX4496	XXX7126	XXX7191	XXX7200
XXX7201	XXX7203	XXX7204	XXX7205	XXX7207
XXX7284	XXX7291	XXX3761	XXX3810	XXX3839
XXX1411	XXX1412	XXX1414	XXX1425	XXX1427
XXX1430	XXX1434	XXX1437	XXX1438	XXX1441
XXX1447	XXX1448	XXX1487	XXX1541	XXX1544
XXX1545	XXX1546	XXX1559	XXX1586	XXX1594
XXX1625	XXX1628	XXX1642	XXX1655	XXX1659
XXX1677	XXX1698	XXX1708	XXX1752	XXX1765
XXX1769	XXX1799	XXX1821	XXX1835	XXX1836
XXX1845	XXX1856	XXX1881	XXX1907	XXX1908
XXX1917	XXX1918	XXX1930	XXX1944	XXX1983
XXX2106	XXX2109	XXX2392	XXX2500	XXX2511
XXX2512	XXX2513	XXX2514	XXX2515	XXX2517
XXX2520	XXX2522	XXX2523	XXX2526	XXX2535
XXX2536	XXX2537	XXX2538	XXX2552	XXX2564
XXX2565	XXX3761	XXX3810	XXX3839	XXX3988
XXX6019	XXX6097	XXX6100	XXX6101	XXX6155
XXX6208	XXX6227	XXX6228	XXX6245	XXX6300
XXX6322	XXX6324	XXX6351	XXX6363	XXX6400

XXX6413	XXX6420	XXX6424	XXX6550	XXX6557
XXX6588	XXX6589	XXX6594	XXX6631	XXX6632
XXX6633	XXX6635	XXX6648	XXX6649	XXX6669
XXX6687	XXX6727	XXX6772	XXX6774	XXX6800
XXX6806	XXX6807	XXX6811	XXX6851	XXX6926
XXX6989	XXX6550	XXX6557	XXX6588	XXX6589
XXX6594	XXX6631	XXX6632	XXX6633	XXX6635
XXX6648	XXX6669	XXX6687	XXX6727	XXX6772
XXX6774	XXX6800	XXX6806	XXX6807	XXX6810
XXX6811	XXX6851	XXX6926	XXX6989	

Numbers Responding with a Log-In Prompt

XXX-2500	XXX-2535
XXX-2512	XXX-2536
XXX-2513	XXX-2538
XXX-2514	XXX-2556
XXX-2515	XXX-2564
XXX-2517	XXX-2565
XXX-2522	XXX-6811
XXX-2523	XXX-6810
XXX-2526	XXX-6811

Physical Security Tests

A survey of the physical site was conducted along with interviews of the CLIENT guard force. Additional findings were discovered through the course of normal observation. Your Company specifically looked for places or times where an intruder could gain access to critical or sensitive areas or systems.

Social Engineering Tests

Social engineering tests were not performed.

Appendix C-2: Summary Information

This appendix contains a summarization of the primary test phases performed and the results of those tests that did not result in findings. Also, any additional information that the tests produced that would provide value to CLIENT, but did not necessarily indicate vulnerabilities, is included here.

Zero-Information-Based (ZIB) Summary

The ZIB was conducted with the assistance of the Sam Spade tool. Sam Spade is a collection of tools designed to retrieve information from various public

Internet sources and provide them in a user-friendly interface. Logs of these tests are included on the CD in the \Additional Data\ZIB Data directory. The test resulted in no significant information being made available to the testers. The firewall and other external devices did not yield their identities without direct probing, and that probing was detected by the PIX firewalls. The results of this test did not yield any findings for this report.

Administrative Controls Summary

The administrative controls testing involved several components. Your Company examined the policies and procedures provided to us by CLIENT as one component. Physical and operational controls were tested as another component and, finally, interviews were conducted with system and network administrators as the final step in these tests.

Interviews Summary

Interviews with various IT employees revealed three common themes:

1. A desire to do good work
2. A belief that the word "no" was not in the vocabulary of IT when it came to the business users
3. A belief that developers were evil and that business users were almost as bad

   The people within the IT group at CLIENT are good people who wish to succeed; they are, however, tired of being in a reactionary mode and wish to move to a proactive mode. Their primary concerns and complaints have made it into this document as parts of findings, but all of them also expressed pleasure in their work and want to see their environment be successful.

Appendix C-3: Figures and Diagrams

This appendix contains any drawings, figures, or diagrams referenced in the report or included for explanatory value. Additionally, a network diagram is also included as a reference for the location and scope of the tests performed by PA.

Information Security Concept Flow

Exhibit C-3.1 describes how information security concepts flow into and relate to each other. Of particular concern to this document are the relationships to vulnerabilities. The goal of this report is to make the owners of assets aware of the vulnerabilities that lead to risks to the assets that the owners are responsible for and value.

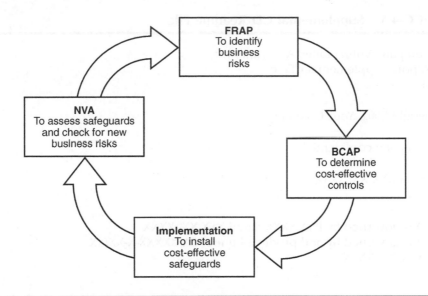

Exhibit C-3.1   Information Security Concept Flow

CLIENT Network Diagram

Following is a diagram of the CLIENT network. [Diagram removed to sanitize this document]

<Name> provided the previous diagram to Your Company as a hand drawing on a whiteboard in the Your Company Workspace at CLIENT. Your Company then transcribed the drawing to its present format. The Visio file of this drawing is located on the Supplemental CD; the file is <CD>\Additonal Data\CLIENT.vsd.

Appendix C-4: Supplementary Information

This appendix contains any supplementary information that does not have a specific category elsewhere within the report. All of the information referenced in this appendix can be found on the Supplemental CD that accompanies this report.

Supplemental CD Readme File

Exhibit C-4.1 lists the text of the readme file from the Supplemental CD provided with this report.

Exhibit C-4.1　Supplemental CD Readme File

Your Company Vulnerability Assessment
Final Report Supplemental CD for
CLIENT

© Copyright 2002, Your Company

Your Company confidential

Version 1.3 XXX XX, XXXX

This CD is governed by PSA XXXX dated XXX XX, XXXX
This CD is governed by and produced under EA XXXXX-X-XX/XX
Dated XXX XX, XXXX

This CD contains information that is supplemental to the VULNERABILITY
ASSESSMENT Final Report
Referenced above.

All reports are available in HTML, Text, or Microsoft Word 97 format.

Contents of this CD are as follows:

\readme.txt　　　　　　— This readme document

\VULNERABILITY ASSESSMENT Supplemental Reports TOC.xls
　　　　　　　　　　— A Microsoft Excel 97 spreadsheet listing the name and
　　　　　　　　　　characteristics of all ISS, NetRecon, and ESM reports on the
　　　　　　　　　　Supplemental CD.

\index.html　　　　　　— HTML file containing links to the ISS, NetRecon, and ESM
　　　　　　　　　　reports on the Supplemental CD.

\Additional Data　　— Contains data from the Zero-Information-Based Scan, password
　　　　　　　　　　crackers, and other miscellaneous tools and tests designed to
　　　　　　　　　　verify what PA found in other tests.

\Data Files　　　　　— Contains the original ISS Scanner 6, Axent NetRecon, and Axent
　　　　　　　　　　ESM Data Files.

\ESM Reports　　　　— Contains the reports produced by ESM as a part of the
　　　　　　　　　　configuration audit.

\ISS Reports　　　　— Contains the reports produced by ISS as a part of the directed
　　　　　　　　　　vulnerability scans. ISS performs tests that attempt to directly
　　　　　　　　　　test for vulnerabilities.

Exhibit C-4.1   Supplemental CD Readme File

\NetRecon Reports — Contains the reports produced by NetRecon as a part of the inferred vulnerability scans. NetRecon collects basic information and then uses a database of known vulnerabilities as its test procedure.

\NetProwler Data — Contains the data and capture files from NetProwler used to look for data leakage that the scanners may not have detected.

\PhoneTag Data — Includes the PhoneTag captured files and the Dial-List used for the War Dialing test.

\VULNERABILITY ASSESSMENT Final Report
— Contains a copy of the VULNERABILITY ASSESSMENT Executive Summary and The VULNERABILITY ASSESSMENT Final Report. Both documents are in Microsoft Word 97 and HTML format.

= = = END OF FILE = = =

Appendix D

NIST Special Publications

The following National Institute of Standards and Technology (NIST) documents can be obtained by accessing the NIST Web site at csrc.nist.gov/publications/nistpubs.

NIST Special Publication Number	Title	Date
SP 800-2	Public-Key Cryptography	April 1991
SP 800-3	Establishing a Computer Security Incident Response Capability (CSIRC)	November 1991
SP 800-4	Computer Security Considerations in Federal Procurements: A Guide for Procurement Initiators, Contracting Officers, and Computer Security Officials	March 1992
SP 800-5	A Guide to the Selection of Anti-Virus Tools and Techniques	December 1992
SP 800-6	Automated Tools for Testing Computer System Vulnerability	December 1992
SP 800-7	Security in Open Systems	July 1994
SP 800-8	Security Issues in the Database Language SQL	August 1993
SP 800-9	Good Security Practices for Electronic Commerce, Including Electronic Data Interchange	December 1993
SP 800-10	Keeping Your Site Comfortably Secure: An Introduction to Internet Firewalls	December 1994

NIST Special Publication Number	Title	Date
SP 800-11	The Impact of the FCC's Open Network Architecture on NS/EP Telecommunications Security	February 1995
SP 800-12	An Introduction to Computer Security: The NIST Handbook	October 1995
SP 800-13	Telecommunications Security Guidelines for Telecommunications Management Network	October 1995
SP 800-14	Generally Accepted Principles and Practices for Securing Information Technology Systems	September 1996
SP 800-15	Minimum Interoperability Specification for PKI Components (MISPC), Version 1	January 1998
SP 800-16	Information Technology Security Training Requirements: A Role- and Performance-Based Model (supersedes NIST Spec. Pub. 500–172)	April 1998
SP 800-17	Modes of Operation Validation System (MOVS): Requirements and Procedures	February 1998
SP 800-18	Guide for Developing Security Plans for Information Technology Systems	December 1998
SP 800-19	Mobile Agent Security	October 1999
SP 800-20	Modes of Operation Validation System for the Triple Data Encryption Algorithm (TMOVS): Requirements and Procedures	Revised: April 2000
SP 800-21	Guideline for Implementing Cryptography in the Federal Government	November 1999
SP 800-22	A Statistical Test Suite for Random and Pseudorandom Number Generators for Cryptographic Applications	October 2000 Revised: May 15, 2001
SP 800-23	Guideline to Federal Organizations on Security Assurance and Acquisition/Use of Tested/ Evaluated Products	August 2000
SP 800-24	PBX Vulnerability Analysis: Finding Holes in Your PBX Before Someone Else Does	August 2000
SP 800-25	Federal Agency Use of Public Key Technology for Digital Signatures and Authentication	October 2000
SP 800-26	Security Self-Assessment Guide for Information Technology Systems	November 2001
SP 800-27	Engineering Principles for Information Technology Security (A Baseline for Achieving Security)	June 2001
SP 800-28	Guidelines on Active Content and Mobile Code	October 2001

NIST Special Publication Number	Title	Date
SP 800-29	A Comparison of the Security Requirements for Cryptographic Modules in FIPS 140-1 and FIPS 140-2	June 2001
SP 800-30	Risk Management Guide for Information Technology Systems	January 2002
SP 800-31	Intrusion Detection Systems (IDS)	November 2001
SP 800-32	Introduction to Public Key Technology and the Federal PKI Infrastructure	February 2001
SP 800-33	Underlying Technical Models for Information Technology Security	December 2001
SP 800-32	Introduction to Public Key Technology and the Federal PKI Infrastructure	February 2001
SP 800-33	Underlying Technical Models for Information Technology Security	December 2001
SP 800-34	Contingency Planning Guide for Information Technology Systems	June 2002
SP 800-38A	Recommendation for Block Cipher Modes of Operation — Methods and Techniques	December 2001
SP 800-40	Procedures for Handling Security Patches	September 2002
SP 800-41	Guidelines on Firewalls and Firewall Policy	January 2002
SP 800-44	Guidelines on Securing Public Web Servers	September 2002
SP 800-45	Guidelines on Electronic Mail Security	September 2002
SP 800-46	Security for Telecommuting and Broadband Communications	September 2002
SP 800-47	Security Guide for Interconnecting Information Technology Systems	September 2002
SP 800-51	Use of the Common Vulnerabilities and Exposures (CVE) Vulnerability Naming Scheme	September 2002

Appendix E

Glossary of Terms

AAL:	ATM Adaptation Layer
AARP:	AppleTalk Address Resolution Protocol
ABR:	Area border router
AC:	Access Control (Token Ring)
ACK:	Acknowledgment
ACL:	Access Control List
ADSL:	Asymmetric Digital Subscriber Line
ADSP:	AppleTalk Data Stream Protocol
AFP:	AppleTalk File Protocol
AH:	Authentication Header
ALE:	Annual loss expectancy
AM:	Amplitude modulation
AMI:	Alternate Mark Inversion (T1/E1)
ANSI:	American National Standards Institute
API:	Application programming interface
APPN:	Advanced peer-to-peer networking
ARP:	Address Resolution Protocol
ARPA:	Advanced Research Projects Agency
AS:	Autonomous system
ASBR:	Autonomous system boundary router
ASCII:	American Standard Code for Information Interchange
ASIC:	Application-specific integrated circuit
ASIS:	American Society Industrial Security
ASK:	Amplitude shift keying
ASP:	AppleTalk Session Protocol
ATM:	Asynchronous Transfer Mode
ATP:	AppleTalk Transaction Protocol
AUI:	Attachment unit interface
AURP:	AppleTalk Update-Based Routing Protocol
BCP:	Business continuity plan

BDR:	Backup designated router
BECN:	Backward Explicit Congestion Notification (Frame Relay)
BER:	Bit error rate
BGP:	Border Gateway Protocol
BIA (1):	Business impact analysis
BIA (2):	Burned-in address
B-ISDN:	Broadband ISDN
bit:	Binary digit
BOOTP:	Bootstrap Protocol
BPDU:	Bridge Protocol Data Unit
BLP:	Bypass Label Processing
bps:	Bits per second
BRI:	Basic rate interface (ISDN)
CBR:	Constant bit rate
CCITT:	Consultative Committee for International Telegraph and Telephone
CCO:	Cisco Connection Online
CCP:	Compression Control Protocol
CCS:	Common channel signaling
CCTV:	Closed-circuit television
CD:	CARRIER DETECT
CDDI:	Copper Distributed Data Interface
CDP:	Cisco Discovery Protocol
CER:	Crossover error rate
CHAP:	Challenge Handshake Authentication Protocol
CIDR:	Classless interdomain routing
CIR:	Committed information rate
CLP:	Cell loss priority
CLNP:	Connectionless Network Protocol
CLNS:	Connectionless Network Services
CMI:	Coded mark inversion
CO:	Central office
CO$_2$:	Carbon dioxide
COTS:	Common off-the-shelf software
CPE:	Customer premise equipment
CPU:	Central processing unit
CRC:	Cyclical redundancy check
CSMA/CD:	Carrier Sense Multiple Access/Collision Detect
CSNP:	Complete Sequence Number PDU
CSPDN:	Circuit-switched public data network
CSU/DSU:	Channel service unit/digital service unit
CTS:	Clear to send
CUD:	Caller user data (X.25)
DA:	Destination address
DAC:	Dual attached concentrator
DARPA:	Defense Advanced Research Projects Agency
DAS:	Dual Attachment Station (FDDI, CDDI)
DBMS:	Database management system
DCE:	Data circuit-terminating equipment
DDP:	Datagram Delivery Protocol (AppleTalk)

DDR (1):	Dial-on-demand routing
DDR (2):	Dual data rate RAM
DES:	Data Encryption Standard
DHCP:	Dynamic Host Configuration Protocol
DIMM:	Dual Inline Memory Module
DIX:	Digital-Intel-Xerox
DLC:	Data Link Control
DLCI:	Data Link Connection Identifier (Frame Relay)
DMT:	Discrete multi-tone
DMZ:	Demilitarized zone
DNA SCP:	Digital Network Architecture Session Control Protocol (DECnet)
DNIC:	Data Network Identification Code (X.25)
DNS:	Domain Name Server
DQDB:	Distributed Queue Dual Bus (SMDS)
DR:	Designated router
DRAM:	Dynamic random access memory
DRP:	Disaster recovery plan
DS-0:	Digital Signal Level 0 (64 kb)
DS-1:	Digital Signal Level 1 (1.544 Mb)
DS-3:	Digital Signal Level 3 (45 Mb)
DSA:	Digital Signature Algorithm
DSAP:	Destination Service Access Point (LLC)
DSE:	Data switching equipment
DSL:	Digital Subscriber Line
DSR:	Data set ready
DSS (1):	Digital Subscriber Signaling System 1
DSS (2):	Digital Signature Standard
DSU:	Data service unit
DTE:	Data terminal equipment
DTR:	Data terminal ready
DUAL:	Diffused update algorithm (EIGRP)
EBCDIC:	Extended Binary Encoded Decimal Interchange Code
EBGP:	Exterior Border Gateway Protocol
ECC:	Elliptic curve cryptography
EDI:	Electronic data interchange
EEPROM:	Electrically erasable programmable read-only memory
EGP:	Exterior Gateway Protocol
EIA:	Electronic Industries Association
EIGRP:	Enhanced Interior Gateway Routing Protocol
EMF:	Electromagnetic field
EMI:	Electromagnetic interference
EMP:	Electromagnetic pulse
EOT:	End of transmission
EPROM:	Erasable programmable read-only memory
ERP:	Emergency response plan
ESF:	Extended Super Framing (T1/E1)
ESP:	Encapsulated Secure Payload
ET:	Exchange termination
ETSI:	European Telecommunication Standards Institute

FBI:	Federal Bureau of Investigation
FC:	Frame Control (Token Ring)
FCC:	Federal Communications Commission
FCPA:	Foreign Corrupt Practices Act
FCS:	Frame check sequence
FD:	Feasible Distance (EIGRP)
FDDI:	Fiber Distributed Data Interface
FDM:	Frequency division multiplexing
FECN:	Forward explicit congestion notification
FEP:	Front-end processor
FFIEC:	Federal Financial Institutions Examination Council
FIC:	Federal Interest Computer
FIFO:	First in, first out
FIPS:	Federal Information Processing Standard
FMBS:	Frame-Mode Bearer Service
FPA:	Federal Privacy Act
FRAD:	Frame Relay Access Device
FSIP:	Fast serial interface processor
FSK:	Frequency shift keying
FTP:	File Transfer Protocol
GIF:	Graphics Interchange Format
GIGO:	Garbage in, garbage out
GLB:	Graham–Leech–Bliley Act
GNS:	Get Nearest Server (Novell)
GOSIP:	Government OSI Profile (U.S.)
GRE:	Generic Routing Encapsulation
GZL:	Get Zone List (AppleTalk)
HDLC:	High-Level Data-Link Control
HIDS:	Host-based intrusion detection system
HERF:	High-energy radio frequency
HIPAA:	Healthcare Information Protection and Accountability Act
HSRP:	Hot Standby Routing Protocol
HSSI:	High-speed serial interface
HTML:	Hypertext Markup Language
HTTP:	Hypertext Transfer Protocol
HVAC:	Heating ventilation air conditioning
IA:	Intra-area (OSPF)
IAP:	Information Awareness Program
IBGP:	Interior Border Gateway Protocol
ICMP:	Internet Control Message Protocol
ICZ:	Intensive Control Zone
IDN:	Integrated digital network
IDS:	Intrusion detection system
IEEE:	Institute of Electrical and Electronics Engineers
IETF:	Internet Engineering Task Force
IGP:	Interior Gateway Protocol
IGRP:	Interior Gateway Routing Protocol
IOS:	Internetwork Operating System
IP:	Internet Protocol

IPC:	Inter-process Communications (Vines)
IPL:	Initial program load
IPSec:	Internet Protocol Security
IPX:	Internet packet exchange
IRB:	Integrated routing and bridging
IS:	Intermediate system
(ISC)²:	International Information Systems Security Certification Consortium
ISDN BRI:	Integrated Services Digital Network — Basic Rate Interface
ISDN PRI:	Integrated Services Digital Network — Primary Rate Interface
ISIS:	Intermediate System Intermediate System (OSI standard routing protocol)
ISO:	International Organization for Standardization
ISP:	Internet service provider
ISSA:	Information Systems Security Association
ITL:	Information Technology Laboratory
ITSEC:	Information Technology Security Evaluation Criteria
ITU:	International Telecommunications Union
ITU-T:	ITU Telecommunication Standardization Sector
JPEG:	Joint Photographic Experts Group
LAN:	Local area network
LAPB:	Link Access Procedure — Balanced
LAPD:	Link Access Procedure on the D Channel
LAPF:	Link Access Procedure for Frame-Mode Bearer Services
LAT:	Local area transport
LCN:	Logical Channel Number (X.25)
LCP:	Link Control Protocol (X.25)
LDN:	Local dial number (ISDN)
LLC:	Logical Link Control
LMI:	Local Management Interface (Frame Relay)
LSA:	Link-state advertisement
LSP:	Link state packet
LT:	Local termination
MAC (1):	Mandatory Access Control
MAC (2):	Message Authentication Code
MAC (3):	Media Access Control
MAN:	Metropolitan area network
MAP:	Manufacturing Automation Protocol
MAU:	Media Attachment Unit
MDx:	Message Digest (e.g., MD5)
MIB:	Management information base
MIDI:	Musical instrument digital interface
MW:	Multi-channel interface proccessor
MLP:	Multi-link PPP
MMP:	Multi-chassis Multi-link PPP
MOP:	Maintenance Operation Protocol
MP:	Multi-link Protocol
MPEG:	Motion Picture Experts Group
MPR:	Multi-protocol PC-based routing

MRRU:	Maximum Received Reconstructed Unit (PPP)
MSAU:	Multi-station Access Units (Token Ring)
MTU:	Maximum transmission unit
NAT:	Network address translation
NAUN:	Nearest active upstream neighbor
NBMA:	Nonbroadcast multi access
NBP:	Name Binding Protocol (AppleTalk)
NCP:	NetWare Core Protocol
NCP:	Network Control Protocol (PPP)
NDIS:	Network Driver Interface Specification
NetBIOS:	Network Basic I/O System
NFS:	Network file system
NIDS:	Network intrusion detection system
NIC:	Network Interface Card
NLPID:	Network Level Protocol Identifier
NLSP:	NetWare Link Service Protocol
NNI:	Network to Network Interface (ATM, Frame Relay)
NOS:	Network operating system
NT-1:	Network Termination 1
NTN:	Network Terminal Number (X.25)
NTP:	Network Time Protocol
NVA:	Network vulnerability assessment
NVE:	Network-visible entity
NVRAM:	Nonvolatile random access memory
OC:	Optical circuit
ODI:	Open datalink interface
OSI:	Open system interconnection
OSPF:	Open Shortest Path First
OUI:	Organizationally unique identifier
PAD:	Packet assembler/disassembler
PAP (1):	Password Authentication Protocol
PAP (2):	Printer Access Protocol (AppleTalk)
PBX:	Private branch exchange
PCM:	Pulse code modulation
PDN:	Public data network
PDU:	Protocol data unit
PGP:	Pretty Good Privacy
PIDAS:	Perimeter Intrusion Detection Assessment System
Ping:	Packet Internet groper
PKI:	Public key infrastructure
PLP:	Packet Level Protocol (X.25)
PMD:	Physical medium dependent
POP (1):	Point-of-presence
POP (2):	Post Office Protocol
POTS:	Plain old telephone service
PPP:	Point-to-Point Protocol
PRI:	Primary Rate Interface (ISDN)
PROM:	Programmable read-only memory
PSDN:	Packet-Switched Data Network

PSK:	Phase shift keying
PSN:	Packet-switched network
PSNP:	Partial Sequence Number PDU
PSPDN:	Packet-switched public data network
PSTN:	Public switched telephone network
PTT:	Post, telephone, and telegraph
PVC:	Permanent virtual circuit
QA:	Quality assurance
QC:	Quality control
QAM:	Quadrature Amplitude Modulation
QoS:	Quality of service
RADIUS:	Remote Authentication Dial-In User Service
RAM:	Random access memory
RARP:	Reverse Address Resolution Protocol
RBOCs:	Regional Bell operating companies
RCP:	Remote Copy Protocol
RFC:	Request for Comments
RIP:	Routing Information Protocol
RISC:	Reduced Instruction Set Computer
RJE:	Remote job entry
RLP:	Remote Location Protocol
RMON:	Remote monitoring
ROI:	Return on investment
ROM:	Read-only memory
RPC:	Remote procedure call
RSA:	Rivest, Shamir, Adleman (public key encryption)
RTFM:	Read the fine manual
RTMP:	Routing Table Maintenance Protocol (AppleTalk)
RTP:	Real-Time Transport Protocol
SA (1):	Source address
SA (2):	Security Association
SABM:	Set asynchronous balanced mode
SABME:	Set asynchronous balanced mode extended
SAP (1):	Service access point
SAP(2):	Service Advertisement Protocol (Novell)
SAS:	Single attached station
SDH:	Synchronous digital hierarchy
SLDC (1):	Systems development life cycle
SLDC (2):	Synchronous Data Link Control
SDU:	Service data unit
SHA:	Secure Hash algorithm
SF:	Super Framing (T1/E1)
SIMM:	Single inline memory module
SIP:	SMDS Interface Protocol
SLARP:	Serial Link Address Resolution Protocol
SLIP:	Serial Line Interface Protocol
SMDS:	Switched Multi-megabit Data Service
SMTP:	Simple Mail Transfer Protocol
SNA:	Systems Network Architecture

SNAP:	Subnetwork Access Protocol
SNMP:	Simple Network Management Protocol
SOP:	Standard operating procedure
SOF:	Start of frame
SONET:	Synchronous Optical Network
SPF:	Shortest Path First
SPID:	Service Provider Identifier (ISDN)
SPP:	Sequenced Packet Protocol (Vines)
SPX:	Sequenced Packet Exchange (Novell)
SQL:	Standard Query Language
SRAM:	Static RAM
SRB:	Source route bridging
SRTB:	Source route transparent bridging
SRTP:	Sequenced Routing Update Protocol (Vines)
SS7:	Signaling System 7
SSAP:	Source Service Access Point (LLC)
SSH:	Secure Shell
SSL:	Secure Sockets Layer
SSN:	Social Security number
SVC:	Switched virtual circuit
TA:	Terminal adapter
TACACS:	Terminal Access Controller Access Control System
TA/NT1TCB:	Terminal Adapter/Network Termination 1 (ISDN) Trusted Computing Base
TCP:	Transmission Control Protocol
TCP/IP:	Transmission Control Protocol/Internet Protocol
TCSEC:	Trusted Computer Systems Evaluation Criteria
TDM:	Time division multiplexing
TE:	Terminal equipment
TE1 and TE2:	Terminal endpoints
TFTP:	Trivial File Transfer Protocol
TIFF:	Tagged Image Format
TTL:	Time-to-live
UART:	Universal Asynchronous Receiver/Transmitter
UDP:	User Datagram Protocol
UNI:	User network interface
UTP:	Unshielded twisted pair
VBR:	Variable bit rate
VC:	Virtual circuit
VCI:	Virtual channel identifier (X.25)
VCN:	Virtual circuit number (X.25)
VLAN:	Virtual local area network
VLSM:	Variable-length subnet mask
VPN:	Virtual private network
VTAM:	Virtual Terminal Access Method
WAIS:	Wind Area Information Server
WAN:	Wide area network
WDM:	Wavelength-division multiplexing
WFQ:	Weighted Fair Queuing

WWW:	World Wide Web
X.509:	Digital Certificate Standard
X.25:	WAN Protocol
X.400:	E-mail ITU standard
XNS:	Xerox Network Systems
XOT:	X.25 over TCP
ZIP:	Zone Information Protocol (AppleTalk)
ZIT:	Zone Information Table (AppleTalk)

Index

Z